As someone who doesn't buy th
peeks), I tried to put this d
couldn't!

> **Liz Sheridan**, *Actress,* Seinfeld *(Jerry*
> *and author,* Dizzy and Jimmy *(about her young*
> *life as James Dean's girlfriend in the 1950s)*

You'll see Hollywood from the inside out, and have
a great time doing it...Barbara Sternig is the Hollywood F.B.I.: *F*irst, *B*est *I*nformation.

> **Jay Bernstein**, *Legendary Hollywood*
> *Manager and Starmaker*

Left me panting for more...the author's intimate writing style instantly makes you feel part of her Hollywood adventures...love the way she builds tension
and mystery... a page turner and a great read!

> **Kathy Garver**, *Actress, always remembered in*
> A Family Affair *(Sissy); and Voice-Over Artist*

Anyone who has ever sneaked a surreptitious peek at
the *Enquirer* on the supermarket line will want to read
this zany book in its entirety...More fun than a barrel
of *Enquirers*...A really entertaining read!

> **Robert Easton**, *Actor and Dialect Coach*
> *a.k.a. "The Henry Higgins of Hollywood"*

This is one book that everyone interested in the real Hollywood scenario shouldn't miss! Secrets surround every corner. If you're famous, you'll recognize yourself somewhere in these pages! Dazzlingly dished, and I should know!

> **Mookie Rosen**, *Hollywood Socialite,*
> *Long-time Sternig Insider*

Every celebrity in Hollywood who ever tried to keep a secret out of the press ought to read this book. They'll see how futile it is, with reporters like Barbara Sternig on the job...Fascinating...Read it!

> **Ivan S. Markota, Jr., M.A.**, *Acting Coach;*
> *Founder/President, Van Mar Acting Academy,*
> *Hollywood, California*

Barbara Sternig, a supreme investigative reporter in the rarified atmosphere of Hollywood, often became an "actress" herself to gain access to exclusive parties, events and locales...a first glimpse behind the editorial walls of the *National Enquirer*...an engaging story...in fact, the kind of story that would itself make for entertaining cinema.

> **Richard V. Simon**, *Professor of Literature and*
> *Language (ret.), Orange Coast College,*
> *Costa Mesa, California*

Secrets of a Tabloid Reporter...is very well written and a lot of fun to read.

> **Alan Carl**, *St. Martin's Press*

A great inside story well told by one of Hollywood's best reporters...This gal had chutzpah and used it well! ...A fun read about madcap adventures with celebrities in Hollywood, and a revealing how-to handbook for any young journalist, tabloid or otherwise.

Doug Kriegel, *Reporter, KNBC-TV News,*
Los Angeles, California

Famous celebrities, glamorous locations, hot stories...and the inventive and outrageous ways one girl reporter used her wiles to get 'em into the pages of the *National Enquirer*... engrossing...a rollicking must-read...

Dick McInnes, *Producer, Hollywood, California;*
Author, The Other Side of the Road
(with Dorothy Lamour)

Once upon a time there was a lady named Barbara Sternig who had a Hollywood story to tell...but this is *not* just another Hollywood story book!...Passion meets Action... Read carefully so you do not miss a word...

Jean Kasem (Mrs. Casey Kasem), *Actress;*
Founder/President of Little Miss Liberty
Round Crib Company,
Beverly Hills, California 90210

"A fast-moving page-turner and really a great read...especially the Sinatra chapters...felt I got to be a voyeur...It's the first expose I've seen about how these wily reporters get their inside info."

Stan Rosenfield, *President, Stan Rosenfield*
Associates Public Relations,
Los Angeles, California

To Gorgeous Maire —

SECRETS
OF A
TABLOID
REPORTER

And it's a good thing you're right here in Hollywood — where I hope — Barbara Sternig

for helping

Barbara Sternig

Secrets of a Tabloid Reporter

10 9 8 7 6 5 4 3 2 1

ISBN: 0-9722208-0-1
Library of Congress Control Number 2002092932

Published by Front Row Publishing
P.O. Box 1125, Studio City, CA 91614-1125
Book and cover design by Casa Graphics, Inc.
Burbank, CA

Dedication

In loving memory of my mother, Tillie Sternig. Now she knows.

Table of Contents

Acknowledgments

I would like to acknowledge Margie Smith, my fifth-grade teacher, under whose encouragement, and energetic and creative tutelage I discovered that I was a journalist. Because of her, from the age of 10 onwards I knew my life was to be in the media.

I give also my everlasting nod of gratitude to all the beautiful people—famous, infamous, or not—who have participated in my crazy life before, during and after the *Enquirer*. This, of course, includes all the scintillating personages delineated within these pages, especially Frank Sinatra and Tammy Wynette, but also the many others who make it constantly amazing, amusing, light-hearted, musical, eye-popping, heart-stopping, sexy, informative and most of all, fun. You know who you are.

A very special hug to the wonderful Norm Chandler Fox, who shared his microphone with me on KMPC and KLSX Radio, Los Angeles, giving me a chance to share all the travel and dining knowledge I gained on *Enquirer* assignments and my own treks. If not also for Norm and his dynamic wife Loreen Arbus, Bam Bam wouldn't be romping at my house.

To Patty and Ernie Weckbaugh, my "book shepherds"—many thanks for being so supportive and helpful—and to the talented Ernie, for your fun and sparkling sketches.

Lastly, I acknowledge the late Joel Sebastian. Were it not for him, I would never have run off to California all by myself and ended up in the middle of this heady milieu.

"My job at the *National Enquirer* was
so <u>not</u> sitting in an office."

— Barbara Sternig

Introduction

Here is the world's first true inside look at the secret world of tabloids and the celebrities they expose. It's a world Barbara Sternig inhabited for twenty years as a Senior Reporter with the *National Enquirer*, the mightiest tabloid of them all.

In this madcap recounting of her zany Hollywood adventures, Sternig breaks her paid silence at last, to give the inside story of how *Enquirer* reporters get those blockbuster inside stories.

Sternig has been a part of tabloidism's coming of age, from its crazy flamboyant early days, up to today when it is an omnipresent genre in the lives of all, pervading news values in both the print and electronic media.

Each chapter is the true story of a memorable episode in a memorable career. You'll read how Senior Reporter Sternig got next to the world's most famous celebrities, invited or uninvited, to get it right from the horse's mouth; about her struggles and hijinx; how she prevailed against the odds; rose from the inevitable occasional stomping; found herself at times without courage; but always, always came up with the goods by using her noggin.

Readers will know all the famous people found in these pages, and hopefully, by the end, will also know from a very human viewpoint what it's like to be a tabloid reporter, and a female one in a male-run world at that—the good and the bad, the frightening and hilarious, the insulting, the rewarding, the unforgettable.

This book is a virtual candy store of inside info on Hollywood's biggest-name celebrities, an unknown view into the secret workings of the tabloid business, and a revelation of the inventiveness, adventures, and adrenalin rushes needed to overcome huge obstacles facing an Enquirer reporter on every single assignment.

Welcome to the daunting, demanding and dizzying world of tabloid celebrity journalism, as lived by "Champagne Babs."

Foreword

It was purely by chance a few years ago that I sat next to beautiful Barbara Sternig at a luncheon for previous passengers of the QE2. We connected immediately, after learning we had certain special interests in common.

Not only did we both love cruising, but also had both worked on board cruise ships. She told me she'd been a Magician's Assistant, and I told her I'd been the industry's first female Cruise Director. She told me she now wrote for the *National Enquirer*, and I told her I'd written an autobiography of my experiences at sea...called *The Love Boats*. When I told her that from my book I'd created the hit TV series *The Love Boat*, Barbara told me in astonishment that she'd written stories about the show for the *Enquirer* for years, and had interviewed nearly all the show's stars at one time or another.

The coincidences continued. The ship upon which my TV show was set, the Pacific Princess, happened to be the very ship on which she'd once worked for The Magician. She asked me how I'd come to write my book, and I explained that my eight-year job, up to 18 hours a day, seven days a week, 11 months a year, had been so unusual, rushed and crazy, so surprising and different, and things I'd witnessed were sometimes so naughty, that I just knew a behind-scenes look at life on a cruise ship would intrigue and amuse the world.

Is it any wonder that Barbara Sternig felt the same about the crazy tabloid industry in which she worked for nearly twenty years as a *National Enquirer* Senior Reporter?

She's now written this highly entertaining book full of revealing behind-scenes true glimpses into her unusual job covering the biggest stories about Hollywood's most famous stars. Here are her light-hearted and affectionate memories about the challenging and often hilarious, sometimes shocking, always zany world of celebrity journalism, tabloid-style. Jump on board for great fun. You'll love it!

Jeraldine Saunders

Author of *The Love Boats* and creator of the hit TV show *The Love Boat*

NB: The revised and expanded edition of Ms. Saunders' book is called *Love Boats—Above and Below Decks with Jeraldine Saunders*, and is available at your nearest bookstore.

1

Let's Start at the End

My mother would die a hundred times if she ever knew some of the crazy things I've done in pursuit of celebrity stories for the *National Enquirer.*

I've lied about who I was; garbed myself in disguises to avoid being hacked in the alley by thugs; driven harrowing car chases; hopped on airplanes without luggage; spied through peepholes; even stolen flowers off a table and hand-delivered them to a star's girlfriend saying they were from him. I have boldly bamboozled maids of the famous, then sat in the kitchen waiting for the star to come home. I've teased lascivious henchmen who expected a payoff I would never deliver, just to get close to their superstar bossman. And I've wandered around many a celebrity wedding, dressed to the nines, drinking champagne as if I'd actually been invited.

I've done naughty stuff that does not relate to my upbringing in any way, and it's important that you, dear reader, and you, dear Mom, understand this. Mom, it's not your fault.

I was a well-brought-up, well-behaved, well-educated Catholic girl, one of eight children of the principal of our town's grade school, which was naturally attended by myself and my seven siblings. Later, the nuns in the strict convent high school where we continued our education would agree—we were model children, just as good as Mom taught us to be, and Dad expected us to be.

The escapades I am about to share with you came out of no-where. A playful iconoclasm had apparently been lurking in the re-cesses of my personality throughout my early life—and it is to that pesky trait, and to nothing I ever learned at my mother's gentle knee, that I attribute all the adventures which follow.

Mom, please brace yourself. And dear Dad, you too. Readers, get ready for an inside look at how the mightiest tabloid of them all, the *National Enquirer*, really works.

****

After I left the *National Enquirer,* they paid me off for two years not to write what you are about to read.

It was part of my contract as a Senior Reporter. If I left the pa-per, by my choice or theirs, and agreed to keep my mouth shut for twenty-four months, I got a year's salary free, doled out over my two-year silent period.

As it turned out, it was their choice, and after nearly twenty years on staff, I was gone like the wind.

But my, my, it's a mighty righteous thing to extract a two-year paid vacation from the guys who just ditched you.

Today, all tabloid employees have to promise this confidential-ity just to get hired, and for no free money.

Not me. I had been there for too long and knew too much.

I could have gone to work somewhere else right away and col-lected twice, but instead, I took the two years with pay and spent them both well. I cruised a thousand miles up the Amazon, I trekked on safari across East Africa, and I climbed above the Norwegian fjords. I took Italian, I studied massage therapy, I attended daytime gym classes. Then I tiled some things and painted some things. I did a radio show with my good friend Norm Fox about travel and dining, (areas in which I had gained considerable expertise during my *Enquirer* tenure). I made a cactus garden, I went to the beach, I put all those photos in albums, and I took road trips. And of course, I visited Mom.

I took the money, I did stuff, and I uttered not a syllable about the paper.

And somehow, in no time at all, the two years expired.

I still remember all the details of all the stories.

And guess what? Now I'm legally at liberty to share them with you. So I believe the time has finally arrived for you to learn the untold stories behind all those Untold Stories.

****

What really drives the paper you love to hate, hate to love, and can't wait to read? Everyone wants to know. In fact, there were two questions most-asked of me during my long tenure as an *Enquirer* reporter, as well as today, any time and every time someone finds out where I worked. These questions always come hand-in-hand:

"Is any of that stuff *TRUE?*"

"How do you *GET* that stuff?"

The answer to the first question takes one word: Yes.

The answer to the second is a little more complex and will take up the rest of this book.

Everything you are about to read is true, no matter how outrageous it seems. Each celebrity named really did these things. Each reporter mentioned really did these things, though I have changed some of my colleagues' names to avoid embarrassment to themselves, or any possible retributive murder plots against myself.

That last is a joke, I hope, but the characters about whom I write are not. They really exist.

Read on to find out what really goes on behind the closed doors of the *National Enquirer.*

2

Angie Dickinson
Packs a Wallop

That first morning as I poked my head into the *Enquirer's* spacious ninth-floor Wilshire Boulevard offices, I figured I'd spent nearly a year avoiding coming on staff. And I still wasn't so sure on that first day whether I wanted to be there or not.

For months here in Los Angeles, three thousand miles from its Florida home office, the notorious tabloid had been running ads in the *Hollywood Reporter* and *Variety,* our two local daily show biz trade bibles.

The ads were small and businesslike: the paper was starting a Los Angeles bureau, and they were looking for experienced reporters who knew how to cover Hollywood. It was 1975 and they were offering starting pay of twenty-two thousand dollars a year. At that time in journalism, it was a *great* deal more money than anyone else was paying.

Everyone I knew had called me to tell me about the ads, just in case I hadn't seen them for myself. Of course I'd seen them. But my application was not forthcoming.

I had just concluded four years as writer/producer/leg woman/ assistant to brassy blond Hollywood TV gossipist Rona Barrett, and I knew everyone in Hollywood. I obviously fit the *Enquirer's* job description. It's just that they didn't fit *my* job description.

I was spoiled, and even though Rona was off the air and I was now scrambling hard to survive as a free-lance, I didn't feel comfortable about applying for work at what I perceived as a hardly credible tabloid, and going backwards in my career. The fact they were offering a big salary made it seem even less legitimate, kind of like blood money.

Yes, I was spoiled. As Rona's right hand, I had gone in the front door to every big event, invited to cover these exciting happenings in exchange for a TV mention on our daily three-minute Hollywood report. I was Rona's surrogate, and as such, I was also sought out. As I built my own network of sources, I even got Christmas gifts from stars and celebrity publicity firms, at least an armful to Rona's room-full.

And why? Because a mention on Rona's report, like a mention on *Entertainment Tonight* these days, was a big deal. Most of the publicity reps wanted us at all their functions mingling with their clients, because our plugs on TV made their clients happy.

Rona Barrett played the publicity game with panache. She bargained with items as if they were poker chips. "I'll do that item for you, but then be forewarned that I'm going to spill the beans about this other little matter you're trying to squelch."

Mostly, ours was a bright, breezy, fun and positive show biz blab. People liked it and talked about it. At that time, television did not have its own tabloids, nor Hollywood minutes, nor movie star coverage swamping every mainstream newscast. What television had was Rona, a special character doing her spicy syndicated Hollywood report on some sixty stations around the country every night, dropped into the ten PM news.

I learned a lot at Rona's knee, soon discerned how to use information advantageously, and made a bookful of valuable contacts of my own. After four years of writing the TV broadcast, as well as ghost-writing her byline fan magazine column, I was totally accustomed not only to coming in the front door, but to being treated with deference once inside.

It was odd that I ended up covering show business at all, because growing up, I'd paid little attention to Hollywood, fascinated instead by pop radio. One of the few movie magazines I ever had as a kid was one with a story about Lucille Ball and Desi Arnaz inside. I can still recall feeling amazed and privileged as I gained an inside peek into the real lives of these famous figures we saw on TV each week.

The irony was that as I embarked on a writing career, I ended up describing those same kinds of details about Hollywood's current darlings for Rona Barrett's famous Hollywood gossip report, and later, for the infamous *Enquirer.* It flew in the face of my conservative Midwestern upbringing.

My excellent academic background included four years of intensive college preparation and social training in a royal-worthy convent high school, followed by four years at a quiet Catholic university. Hollywood simply did not exist in any part of this world. To this day, much of my family and many of the people I grew up with along Chicago's wealthy, well-tailored North Shore, still consider such frivolity unseemly, or at the least, irrelevant. They still wonder how I got to here from there.

But to me, it was a fascinating, light-hearted world, populated by amazing, larger-than-life figures. Writing about it was fun. Being in the middle of it was eye-popping. I was like a kid in a magic candy shop.

At Rona's office, we subscribed to the *Enquirer,* just to check it out, but we certainly didn't rate it as serious competition. As few others might, we knew just how much of it was erroneous or worse. In the early seventies, long before going mainstream, the *Enquirer* was trashy and campy, not really vicious, but (we thought) tending toward the fictitious. And it was so *tacky* with its crowded black and white newsprint pages, sporting all those ads for breast enhancement cream.

We saw no comparison to be drawn between the *Enquirer* and our legitimate Hollywood gossip report. Of course, there were those who may have disagreed.

The only person I knew at that time who actually did some work for the *Enquirer* was our own photographer, a mercenary Swiss named Peter Borsari. Peter's job with us was to accompany Rona or me to swanky events to snap color slides of the stars, for use in our TV report. Since I produced the TV report and went over all the boxes of finished slides he brought in to us, I soon realized Peter was holding back his best shots. Shots I told him to get were missing. Shots I'd watched him take were missing. A week later, he'd come in to our office, beaming, brandishing a copy of the *Enquirer,* bragging that he'd gotten five thousand dollars for that picture on the front page. "But Peter, that's Burt Reynolds at the MGM party, the party I took you to," I'd say. "You never showed me that slide. It's a lot better than the one we used on the air."

"Vell, I have to make some money. I can't live on a hundred fifty a week."

That's what we paid Borsari for his services, plus all his film and processing costs. "But Peter, you work for others besides us, and they all pay you too. And wait a minute—*we paid* for all that film you used at MGM."

"Zis doesn't matter. Zese are my pictures." His legal logic may have been suspect, but Peter had a good thing going. He got to go to every fabulous party on our invitations, hobnob with plenty of contacts, set up other shoots, view gossip happening firsthand, *and* market his pictures anywhere else he could. Not a bad deal.

The *Enquirer* was paying him thousands for pictures that technically belonged to us. Rona never pushed that point, but in behalf of our show, I complained to Peter, "The least you could do is let us have first crack at the slides, instead of plucking all the best ones out for the *Enquirer.*" I secretly thought Peter was lying about the sums he said the tabloid was giving him, but it turned out to be perfectly true.

Had I but known whom to contact, I too could have been scoring thousands under the table for some of my items which Rona rejected, for hot stories I knew about that we couldn't or wouldn't use on our show, or even for simply passing on tips.

But it never would have occurred to me. For one thing, I felt true loyalty to Rona and to our show. And I think I speak not only for myself, but for most of the young journalists I began with in this town, when I say we were all happy in those days simply to be working in our field, having an amazing time covering the most exciting events in the world, mingling and partying with all the stars, and supporting ourselves to boot.

Dare I say it? We were idealistic. None of us were too concerned about the future or accumulating money, none of us dealt with the tabloids, and certainly none of us were savvy about the selling of celebrity news. It was a process that hadn't even come into being yet. The fact is, it was largely because of the *Enquirer* that it *did* come into being.

So with all that, why was I now arriving for my first day of work at the notorious *National Enquirer*?

For starters, after Rona's show went off the air, I did a little freelance work for them and was quite happy with the results. One was a sit-down interview with George Burns when Jack Benny died, the other a photo shoot with Wayne Newton on his Vegas ranch surrounded by his Arabian horses. The *Enquirer* loved my stories, gave them a good show in the paper, paid promptly and well, and I liked the energetic young editors I'd worked with. The paper seemed a lot more legitimate behind the scenes than it did in its final form, blaring those lurid headlines from those racks in the supermarket.

They offered me a staff job. I said no, I'd rather just free-lance. That way I wouldn't have to tell anyone I worked for them.

That was before. Now, however, I was a desperate person.

****

Rona had gone off the air months ago, and in the interim, I had supplemented my free-lancing with a production job on the first *People's Choice Awards,* then had run away from Hollywood to work on a cruise ship as a magician's assistant.

A pal of mine was the magician, and he needed someone who could fill out the spangly costumes and assist him with the illusions during his nine-month contract with Princess Cruises. I was the only prospect he could think of at the moment who had nothing keeping her in L.A.—no job, no boyfriend, no real responsibilities. I'd never been on a ship. He said he'd teach me how to do the tricks. It sounded great.

So, before long, I found myself on the promenade deck of the Island Princess, waving goodbye to no one in particular, tossing colorful serpentinas over the side, and wondering if anyone in Hollywood would remember me when I came home again. A mariachi band was playing loudly, it was pouring with rain, and I felt lost, trapped, and strange, wondering what in the hell I was doing there.

As it turned out, by the next day as we drifted south into warm waters with moody pink clouds overhead, I knew I'd made the right decision. Life at sea was the life for me. I fell into it totally and soon lost all track of any cares. Off we went—L.A. to Fort Lauderdale, Fort Lauderdale to L.A., back and forth. Cruising the coast of Mexico to Acapulco, through the Panama Canal, hitting a few South American ports, up through the Caribbean to Florida—then back again, hitting different ports of call on the way home. That summer, we did Alaska. For me, this was a real life *Love Boat,* complete with handsome officers, dressy soirees, languid days on decks watching romantic islands drift by, non-stop crew parties every night after all the passengers were tucked safely in their beds, and of course, our performances every couple of days. I was living it all, the year before Aaron Spelling and his actors ever came on board Princess Cruises to tell the whole world about it.

But then, the magician's contract ended. We disembarked one last time and stood on the quay watching sadly as our ship sailed without us.

I was devastated. I sat in my apartment looking out the window and crying for three days, shocked at how harsh it felt to re-enter a mundane world.

It quickly occurred to me that I needed a real job to go to, to get my feet back on dry land, to put focus back into my days.

So I wiped my tears, blew my nose, and called the *Enquirer* to see if their job offer was still on.

* * * *

"We're looking for only one more reporter, so if you want the tryout, say it now," chided young bureau chief Alan Markfield, almost adding, "or forever hold your peace." Before, I'd turned him down in my snobbery, but right now I couldn't afford to be a snob.

"Alan, I'd really like to give it a whirl," and I meant it.

"Be here on Monday morning, and show us your stuff."

So there I was, poking my head into a busy office filled with attractive young people bustling around, talking in pairs, hunched over their desks clicking away on well-worn portable typewriters, with two secretaries in the middle of the room, and Alan in a glass-enclosed corner office, overlooking L.A. from two directions.

"Sternig, there you are!" he called out enthusiastically, standing, and coming out of the private enclosure to greet me. "About time you realized what a good thing we are."

I laughed as he showed me to my new desk. Alan was about thirty, cute with a playful air, heavyset, ruddy, with thick black hair and a strong masculine walk. "Meet Glenn Lovell. New reporters get partnered, and Glenn will show you the ropes."

Glenn was handsome, late twenties, immaculately groomed and preppyish, with a gentle manner.

After Alan walked away, Glenn confided, "You know, I only came on staff a month ago myself, but if you have any questions at all, here I am. Maybe we can figure them out together."

As I looked up and down the parallel rows of desks, I saw eight or nine casually dressed reporters at their typewriters, some busily working on files, some schmoozing, one or two on the phone, various ages. It turns out the group included a few faces I recognized from my years on the Hollywood beat.

There was a pleasant feeling in the *Enquirer's* office, without the frantic stress I associated with a busy newsroom or even with our TV newsroom at channel 11. I liked it.

One by one I met my new colleagues. Nick Longhurst was thirty-five-ish, bearded, quick-paced, a Brit who'd got his training on Fleet Street.

Ken Potter was a burly and congenial Australian from our Florida headquarters, working in the Hollywood office that week. His big white smile and unabashed friendliness would have melted anyone. He knew of my background and seemed to admire it. We immediately hit it off.

Eirik Knutzen was a sardonic, negatively humorous transplanted Norwegian. He was a brain, a wonderful writer. Eirik viewed Hollywood from its downside, and was certainly not impressed. I got the feeling he wasn't too happy about working for the *Enquirer,* nor about anything, for that matter, but there was something dear about him.

Editorial assistant Barbara Merlin was probably the most qualified person in the room. She and her husband Milton were Hollywood veterans who had had a fabulous career writing early TV shows, including the Ronald Colman show, *The Halls of Ivy.* She'd been in the middle of show business for decades, was lifelong friends with many stars and insiders, and she was meticulously efficient to boot. I later learned that Barbara was a recovering alcoholic, an ex-heavy smoker, and one hell of a humble woman.

Next I recognized longtime Hollywood writer Jim Gregory, with whom I'd had a few free-lance dealings after the Rona show folded. The fact is, it was Jim who'd suggested me to Alan Markfield in the first place, and I shook his hand to express my very genuine gratitude to him. He said, "I wasn't sure if we'd reel you in, but I'm glad you decided to join. We could use about three people with your contacts, and don't worry, I made a few points finding you." Jim was such a nervous and sensitive person that I wondered how he handled working under the tabloid cloud.

Yes, I liked it so far, and was beginning to feel a connection with these new coworkers.

In the corner I spied yet another familiar face—Eddie Sanderson, the paper's staff photographer. I knew Eddie, but had totally forgotten he worked there. I'd met him a few months before, at a party given by my friend Monica Mancini at her parents' Malibu beach house. Monica was head over heels for ladies' man Eddie, and had bubbled to me that he was a cool guy even though he worked for this crazy tabloid rag.

When I saw him, I suddenly put it together that, yeah, he was an

Enquirer guy, that's *right*. I waved happily. He waved back, brought his coffee over, and slung a leg across a corner of my desk. "I heard you'd be in today," he smiled, making me feel instantly that I was in the "in" crowd.

"Seen Monica lately?" came his query. Apparently, they'd broken up.

"Yeah, last weekend. You two lovelorn?"

"I'm gone so much, it finally got to her. Just got back from India. That's what did it. And they're sending me to Japan next week." Eddie took out a sheaf of airline tickets from his back pocket. "Just look at all this. I won't be back home for about a month."

I suddenly related Eddie's well-discussed travels with my own brand new job potentials. With feet still twitching from my peripatetic life at sea, I wondered how soon, and where, *I'd* be sent to cover a story.

Settling into my desk, I took out my priceless contact book, containing the home phone numbers of most of the biggest stars, or at the least, numbers of their publicists, agents, managers, assistants, bodyguards. I noticed several people eyeing my book, but I didn't really stop to think why. At Rona's I was the only staff reporter, and I always left my book right on top of my desk, even when I went home at night.

When it was time to go to lunch, Glenn tugged at my arm. "You're not going to leave that there, are you?"

"Leave what where?" I responded.

"Leave your contact book on your desk."

"Why? Is that a problem?"

"Well, you might find it in the xerox machine when you get back, that's all," said Glenn. "That happened to Nick not so long ago."

I picked it up, stuffed it into my large leather handbag, and took it to lunch with me, a habit I kept from that day onward.

That afternoon, I sat on the phones contacting everyone I could think of to break the news that I was doing an *Enquirer* tryout and would rely on their help. Almost everyone owed me a favor for items of theirs which I'd gotten into Rona's broadcasts or columns. It was payback time.

A few contacts I called were also social friends and were cordial, but the reactions of other publicity pals weren't that encouraging. Though all immediately took my calls and were uniformly polite, it became clear after a few hours on the phones that certain important offices would not be so happy to hear from me in the future.

Even though it's what I'd expected, it still made me feel uneasy and a little down. I was sitting at my desk reflecting on these things when Alan came barreling out of his glass enclosure clutching a yellow lead sheet.

"Sternig, let's get you started. You're going out to the Busch Brewery this afternoon to interview Angie Dickinson."

Dickinson was a TV hit at that moment, playing Pepper Anderson, a sort of busty crimebuster in *Police Woman.* She'd been a sexy starlet in the fifties and sixties, and now, after years in the shadow of her composer husband Burt Bacharach, she was hot again, hotter than she'd ever been as a starlet, in fact. The series was kicking off its third highly-rated season.

Though women's groups went apoplectic about the skimpy costumes Pepper wore while fighting street crime, her fans loved the show. Looking back, it seems Angie was a prime time pioneer— playing a working woman who could maintain her career, her independence *and* her sex appeal.

Alan continued, "They're filming her show out there on location, and you'll meet with her between shots, to talk about her being a role model for women. When you get to the gate, just tell them you're there to do an interview with her."

This was definitely easier than free-lancing. It seemed that Alan had set the whole thing up and all I'd have to do was materialize and do the sit-down interview. I was a bit surprised that Angie Dickinson had actually said yes to the *Enquirer.* I knew her publicist was a curmudgeonly and contentious old Hollywood gay with a haughty superiority complex about himself and his clients. I hadn't called him yet, and dreaded doing so.

But maybe the idea of reaching six million readers and their families had persuaded him. Maybe I was judging the paper too harshly. Maybe the stars really liked it.

"Gee," I thought, "that Alan really gets things done."

I gathered up my tape recorder and my reporter's notebook, and headed for the underground garage, reviewing what I knew of the star I was about to interview.

Angie Dickinson had great legs. One of the publicity gimmicks her people came up with during the early sixties was to insure them for a million dollars. These gams were her calling card, and on her two-seasons-old show, she usually showed them off with flair, in slit skirts and minis. Even though she was in her mid-forties, Angie was still known as a sassy sexpot. She'd once been Frank Sinatra's steady, and was always linked with sexy men—including Johnny Carson and David Janssen.

Further embellishing her image were persistent rumors that during the Camelot era, she had had a torrid affair with President Kennedy. Angie furiously denied it throughout the seventies, although about ten years later, her home curiously sprouted large framed pictures and small photos of the slain President, coffee table books about him, and lots of JFK memorabilia.

But in 1975, "no" was her story and she was sticking to it. Just a few months earlier, Angie threatened to sue *Ladies Home Journal* when they published a piece alleging the affair.

Alan told me as I left, "Work a question about the JFK stuff into your interview. We'd love nothing better than a hostile, anti-*Ladies Home Journal* quote."

As I headed out toward the Valley and Busch Gardens, I continued my mental review of Angie facts. She had been married for ten years or so to composer Burt Bacharach and they were considered one of Hollywood's golden couples. When they married in1965 (second marriage for both), he was a struggling composer and she was far better known than he was.

All that changed when Burt teamed with lyricist Hal David and went to the top with a non-stop string of hits that included "Alfie," "The Look of Love," "What the World Needs Now," Broadway's "Promises, Promises," and the Academy Award-winning "Raindrops Keep Fallin' on My Head."

As Burt's fortunes rose, Angie stayed home with their frail daughter Nikki and told everyone she'd hate it if she were a bigger star than her husband.

But now, things were changing again. Her career had taken off with *Police Woman,* even as Bacharach's career went on the wane. Could this be causing trouble in Paradise? I heard she had a clause in her contract that she got to go home at six o'clock every night so she could cook dinner for her husband. I also heard she was getting the reputation for being a bitch on the set. Was she angry about her work/home dilemma?

The Busch Brewery was in the far end of the San Fernando Valley, a good hour from my Hollywood stomping ground, but I finally arrived at the gate. As Alan had suggested, I told the guard I was here to interview Angie Dickinson, and he pointed and said, "Just follow those trucks. They're on their way to the location site, and you'll find Ms. Dickinson's trailer right there. Just ask anyone."

As I wound around the grounds, I could smell the hops in the air, and wondered what the *Police Woman* episode was about, and why they were shooting at a brewery. I felt like a real pro—first day on the job and already doing an interview with a major star. I knew I could deliver many others, but it was wonderful how the editors evidently sometimes set things up for their reporters. Maybe my fears about working for the *Enquirer* were unfounded. Maybe it was going to be okay after all.

As I rounded a bend, somewhere in the very middle of the brewery grounds, I saw a cluster of studio trucks, a catering tent, people milling around, cameramen checking their equipment, a dolly.

"Bingo—this is it."

I parked my Toyota and headed toward a couple of sound guys to ask where I'd find the star of *Police Woman*.

"Excuse me, would you be able to tell me where Miss Dickinson's trailer is?" I inquired, flashing my whitest.

"Sure, it's over there," the cute one answered, his face breaking into a big flirtatious smile. He gestured with his arm, checking me out approvingly. Fortified by this unsolicited compliment, I walked in the direction they'd pointed me, straight toward a mobile dressing room on the outside of which hung a star-shaped placard with Angie's name on it. "Boy, this is really going well," I congratulated myself, thinking of the questions I'd organized, and the score I'd make coming back to the office with my first interview.

The trailer's door was open, and right there, standing on the steps that led up and inside, was Angie Dickinson. She was garbed in jeans and a plaid shirt, her mid-length, tawny hair swept back in a somewhat disheveled hairdo, with a big plastic clip holding it. She had on little makeup, but still looked every inch the star.

There it was—the familiar thrill of standing face to face with a Hollywood star, and I smiled happily as I approached the steps. I looked up at her, extending my hand, and said, "Good afternoon, Miss Dickinson. I'm Barbara Sternig from the *National Enquirer.* I'm here for our interview."

All of a sudden, my day started going not so well.

The look on her face slowly changed from the pleasant smile we all knew and loved, to a contorted, fierce, aggressively screaming mask. I stepped backwards involuntarily, dumbfounded and horrified. Angie Dickinson was coming at me like a banshee.

I suddenly gathered that this woman was NOT expecting me.

"What in the FUCK do you think you're doing here? How DARE you come to my set! How DARE you come to my dressing room! The *ENQUIRER?*"

I whimpered, "But Alan Markfield sent me. He told me our interview was all set up..."

"All set *UP*," she shrieked. "Who the fuck is Alan Markfield? Are you out of your fucking *MIND*?"

The shock of having Angie Dickinson—beautiful Angie Dickinson—Burt Bacharach's wife, right? beautiful, classy Burt Bacharach, right?—waving her arms, looking so ugly, screaming obscenities, threatening me this way—well, it was too much to take in. I just stood there. "Wait a second," I wanted to say. "I'm *good*, I'm one of the *good* people."

To Angie at that moment, I was a long way from one of the good people.

She raged, arms flying, hands wagging, "You've been following me for months, talking to everyone I know. You've been harassing my family and everyone in my home town. Now you've actually come here to hound me in person??? Get the hell *OUT OF HERE!*" A vivid red color was rising in Angie's face and the veins on her pretty forehead were sticking out.

I was having trouble synthesizing what she was talking about. She must have me confused with someone else. Following her for months? Everyone she knew? What does that mean? My mind raced. Obviously, somebody else must have been trying to get a story about her. Was it someone at the *Enquirer*? I was completely in the dark, and bereft. My heart sank, my face fell, and I just stood there. There was nothing I could say.

Suddenly, almost in a flying leap, Angie was in my face. She hauled off, and before I knew what was happening, she shoved me, causing me to reel back in surprise.

"Get the fuck *OUT OF HERE* before I have you **arrested**," she shrieked again.

I was now in a state of pure shock and panic. I backed away, still disbelieving, stunned that anyone, much less a television celebrity, would behave like this, or that such an outburst could be directed at me. And just to make things really awful, as I looked around, the whole crew was staring.

How could this have happened, and on my very first day? How to keep a modicum of dignity while walking toward my car? I fished inside my huge bag for my keys, praying my hand would find them so I could disappear quickly. Why did I have to have all that *junk* in there? Notebooks, spare cassette tapes, batteries, who needed them anyway? At the car, I pulled out my tape recorder, put it on the ground in frustration, then dug around in my purse until at last I felt the ring of keys. Looking back at Angie and her cohorts ruefully, I opened the car door and got in. As I threw the car into reverse and backed up, I could see Angie in the rear view mirror, still yelling about me to anyone near her who would listen.

The two crew guys who had pointed me in the right direction were standing by the side of the road as I went past, and the cute one said, "Don't worry, gorgeous, it's not you. She's been in a mood at everyone today."

I smiled weakly, and drove on, sinking lower and lower in my seat all the way to the exit. Mood Schmood, this was a full-on disaster. As I drove down the freeway toward Hollywood, the tears started, and I wailed in privacy all the way back to the office.

My tear-streaked face said it all as I walked back into the office and headed at a determined pace for Alan's glass enclosure. He looked up as I stomped in and stood before him. "Sternig!" There was a half-grin on his face. "So how'd you fare with Angie?"

"Alan, you didn't tell me this was a doorstep deal. I thought it was all set up. She not only threw me out, but she shoved me and screamed bloody murder at me in front of her entire cast and crew. I've never been so embarrassed and humiliated in my entire career. That was *so lousy* of you not to tell me I was showing up without an appointment." My lips began to quiver and my face to scrunch anew into a mask of tearful misery.

"Sternig! I'm sorry. I thought you knew. Ohmigod, please, don't cry."

"How would I know if you didn't tell me? And what in the heck was she talking about—that I'd been following her for months and bugging her and her family and her hometown and...and..."

"*Geez*, you know, Sternig, I never even thought of it." Alan bared his teeth, drew in a breath and tweaked his head to the side. "Shit! We've had two or three reporters working on her 'Childhood' for months. We do this feature in the *Enquirer*—about the childhoods of celebrities. Shit, I forgot all about that. Man, I really sent you into the lion's den. I *am* sorry. She really did all that?"

That funny little half-grin returned to Alan's face. He seemed genuinely pleased to hear I'd gotten such an intense reaction.

"Yes, Alan, *she really did all that,*" I stated, symbolically rubbing my shoulder and feeling extremely wronged and sorry for myself. "I can't believe a major star would act like that. How could she do that to a journalist, or *anyone*?"

How indeed. I hadn't stopped to think that fiery, temperamental stars have expressed themselves emotionally ever since Hollywood began.

"You're something, Sternig," said my new boss. He was looking at me as if I were a hero. "Don't hold this against the paper, *PLEASE*. It's only your first day, and it's not always like this. Really and truly. But, kid, you did so great, let me make it up to you. Come on, let me take you for a drink. Get your stuff. I'm taking you to Pip's."

I sniffed, "Pip's? Alan, taking me to Pip's isn't going to fix what happened today. I can't do this j........."

"Sternig, get your purse. I want to have a big talk with you and buy you a big dinner." He seemed so unruffled, so confident. I looked at him and suddenly saw my protector.

Pip's was L.A.'s trendiest watering hole, disco, backgammon club and dining hangout. Celebrities, young executives on the move, rich socialites, rat and brat packers, movers and shakers—they all went there. "Come on." He grabbed my hand and nearly yanked me out the door. "We have a membership."

That evening, Alan and I shared a bottle of expensive champagne and a lavish dinner, and he spent many hours soothing my shaken nerves and giving me words of wisdom that would become my professional brief for the next two decades.

"If we want a story, we get the story. Don't you worry about what happened today. They can cooperate or they don't have to cooperate. They can be nice, or they can be nasty. We have sources everywhere, Sternig, and we *will* get the story. Don't ever doubt that. We *will* get the story. What happened today—it can only make your stock go up. You found her, you approached her, and for Chrissakes, you took a royal reaming. And you're a *broad!* Sternig, you've got what it takes. You are going to be a superstar on this paper."

It was so exciting the way Alan put it. It made me feel so confident, so affirmed, so valued—like a member of the elite corps, the Seals, or maybe the mafia. It made everything OK. It was the can-do enthusiasm and support of Alan Markfield that did it for me that night.

I believed what he said. I believed I could do the job. Despite the tears I had shed, I was hooked.

3

Meet the Boss

Ａs the weeks went by, I felt better and better about my new job. But, true to public perception, The *National Enquirer* could also be a pretty nasty place.

There were power- and money-mad managers at the top. There was intense and determined vying for stories and glories. There was vicious competitiveness between colleagues, and there were managers who encouraged this for their own amusement, if not for profit. There was sexual discrimination, (as has been litigated by several former female employees, myself not included, though I also experienced it). There was editorial impropriety of every description, stretching of the truth, manipulation of quotes and reporters, wasteful spending, gleeful stealing, ignoring of promises to sources, commandeering by editors of reporters' bylines, crushing of the weak, off-handed firings, pettiness, romantic shenanigans, greed, and jealous rivalry.

So why did I have such a great time working there? Well, minefield though it was, the *Enquirer* was exciting, interesting, fast-moving and very, very exhilarating. The challenge was to do the work at hand but stay clean as a journalist, and most of all, not to lose your credibility back in Hollywood.

If you kept your nose out of the politics and the rest of your body out of the home office as much as possible, if you were a pro at your job and gave it your all, then you could have a good time, earn a six-figure salary, and not be sucked into the dark side which always lurked south and east at headquarters in Florida.

Some reporters figured that out, and luckily for me, I was one of them.

Really, in looking back, it's the crazy, fun times that stand out, and not some of the nastier moments. Call me a Pollyanna.

When I left the *National Enquirer* in 1995, the adventure as I'd known it was tapped out. I had had the best of times, the golden days, at the multi-million selling tabloid, and now things were different.

But once upon a time, July of 1975 to be exact, it was all happening.

That's when I first walked through the *Enquirer's* front door. The paper was a shiny new toy, the first Hollywood tabloid, the successor to the fan magazines, owing nothing to anyone, and owned one hundred percent by a megalomaniac eccentric who believed his reporters should be flamboyant and daring, stop at nothing to get their story, invade any inner sanctum no matter how private, and put their very safety on the line for him.

Generoso Pope, Jr. wanted his top reporters to have their own adoring minions, sources who knew everything, in every nook and corner of Hollywood. He was willing to pay unthinkable sums to buy up these sources. And because he paid us equally unthinkable salaries, we did what he wanted.

At the home office in Lantana, Generoso "Gene" Pope, Jr. was known as "The Boss." Everyone called him The Boss. He *was* The Boss. Whatever way he wanted was the way we did things. The Boss was the first one into the *Enquirer's* sprawling office in the morning, and The Boss was the last one to leave at night, driving his low-profile white Chevrolet Caprice Classic four-door sedan the short distance to and from his spectacular mansion on the ocean at Manalapan Island.

The Boss, then in his late forties, was a contradiction on many levels. And he expected his highly paid staff to take their every cue from him. All of his well-rewarded higher-ups didn't dare drive Jaguars or Cadillacs to work, even though they could afford them.

Mr. Pope set a peculiar middle-class tone for all to follow. Executive editors making six figure salaries showed up to work in invisible Honda Accords or battered Toyotas, and wore khakis and K-Mart polo shirts to the office. Mr. Pope himself was always attired in a white short-sleeve dress shirt, collar open, no tie, and navy blue trousers. The color of the trousers might stray to gray, but somehow The Boss always looked exactly the same. Appearances, as the unwary sometimes discovered, could be deceiving at the *Enquirer.*

In a world that was all his, Mr. Pope's word was law. This extended even to the setting of the office thermostat.

Being a new recruit, I'd only heard the stories. But this soon changed when it became my turn to spend a month working out of the home office in Lantana, Florida. The Boss ordained that all Los Angeles reporters appear in Lantana yearly for re-orientation (or brain rinse, as we called it) under his watchful eye. His thinking was, to keep keen, the L.A. staff needed to report on a full range of news, not just Hollywood stories; and we needed to work with other editors, not just our own Hollywood guys.

Far from complaining about going south for a month, I welcomed the idea. Hey, I loved Florida, and I knew I'd enjoy getting immersed in this strange new *Enquirer* world I'd entered. It was all so quirky. It amused and intrigued me.

So that fall of 1975, I duly moved myself and my work out of L.A. and down to Lantana. During this first command performance, I wasn't the only new hire in the office. A week after I got there, a reporter from a small paper in the Midwest arrived, pasty white and a little bewildered.

On this morning, it was very hot outside, but Mr. Pope found the air in the office too cold for his liking, and came out to change the thermostat. Everyone knew, of course, that no one but Mr. Pope touched the sacred knobs controlling his office air conditioning system. It's one taboo even I had been warned about.

The Boss walked from his office, as always without looking at anyone, without saying anything. His gaze was firmly fixed on the air conditioning controls for which he was heading. Undaunted by a new desk which had been moved directly in front of the gauge, The Boss simply climbed up on top of it and proceeded to fiddle with the temperature dial. Hunched over, glasses on the end of his nose, he began adjusting.

The reporter from the Midwest had been sitting there all morning, making phone calls, slightly nervous, trying to look busy, trying to appear professional amidst a sea of confident staff reporters. He was using vacation time from his twelve-thousand dollar a year job back home to try out for the *Enquirer.* He badly wanted the at-that-time unheard-of starting salary of twenty-two grand a year plus expense account, (later, top-rung reporting salaries hit six figures) and he was just beginning the *Enquirer's* standard on-the-job test to see if he could cut it. No one had met with him yet to explain about The Boss, or even to point out who he was.

So when a tall, ordinary-looking man in white shirtsleeves, navy blue trousers, and spectacles climbed onto his worktop, the would-be employee indignantly pushed his chair back. Mouth gaping, eyes wide, he snapped, "Do you *mind*, pal?"

The Boss completed his adjustments, oblivious to the intrusion as only the truly powerful can be, then stepped off the desk top without a word and walked back to his private office suite, disappearing around the corner.

Reporters in the immediate area looked nervously at each other and raised their eyebrows. One wry Britisher tapped on his watch face and nodded toward the new guy, and the reporter sitting next to him slowly shook his head up and down with a knowing purse of the lip.

Within ten minutes, the hapless tryout had been pulled aside, given the news that his gig was over, had packed up his notes and contact book, hurried out the door in shock, and had presumably used his return air ticket to fly home immediately to the Midwest, his shot at the big time gone with a wisp of cool air.

Mr. Pope's concern with air conditioning did not stop at the *Enquirer's* office door. For his palatial oceanfront home in nearby Manalapan, the great man not only designed, but oversaw installation of his own vision of the perfect air conditioning system.

Workers welded, pounded, ducted, vented and in-taked, and at last, the plant was ready. Mr. Pope personally threw the switch and his new system started whirring and pushing cool air throughout the huge house. He fiddled to his heart's content with the controls until he got it just the way he liked it. His wife Lois and his kids were happy because he was happy.

He was happy, that is, until the first night.

Then there was a noise. It kept up and it kept Mr. Pope awake. Lois told him, "Gene, it's the new air conditioning."

"That's impossible."

"What else could it be?" she pleaded.

"The new air conditioning wouldn't make a noise like that," he insisted.

"I tell you, it's the air conditioning," she insisted.

"That's impossible. Not this system."

Next morning, Mr. Pope had the chief custodian from the office come over. Knowing of The Boss' pride in his design and fearful of being handed his head on a plate if he gave the wrong answer, the man pleaded bafflement at the cause of the untoward noise.

Mr. Pope took stronger measures. He called ace reporter John

South and gave him a special assignment—find and personally deliver the top air conditioning expert in America. A couple of days later, John arrived at the Manalapan mansion with the most respected technician from the most respected air conditioning firm in America, flown in at great expense and urgency.

The expert examined and prodded, tested and checked. After several hours of intensive work, the man said, "The noise is coming from the air conditioning."

"Thank you very much," said The Boss as he ushered the expert and John South to the door.

He never said another word to anyone about the noise. He just wanted the diagnosis from the lips of the nation's top expert. He could afford it and when he got it, he was satisfied.

Another not-apocryphal tale was about a woman named Barbara who worked for one of the editors. She was efficient, late thirties, and a single mom supporting a couple of kids. She came in one day wearing a certain perfume that apparently disagreed with the Boss' delicate olfactory sense.

As he strode through the newsroom, he sniffed it on the air, and intoned to his secretary, "That perfume gives me a headache. It's *awful.* Where's it coming from? Are you wearing it?"

The secretary said no.

In his nasal monotone, Mr. Pope sharply demanded, "Well, find out who *is,* and tell her to wash it off."

Quickly following orders, the secretary roamed out into the newsroom, sniffing behind the ears of puzzled women at each desk. Finally, she came to Barbara.

"It's you. Your perfume. The Boss can't stand your perfume. He wants you to go in the bathroom and wash it off."

The woman had apparently spent a lot of money on this scent and thought it made her sexy and alluring. Insulted, she responded, "Wash it off? No. I won't wash it off. Mr. Pope is in his office; what does he care how I smell?"

The secretary replied, "Trust me, he can smell it. He says he can't stand it. It gives him a headache. You'd better go wash it off."

"No, that's too much. I'm busy at my desk, I'm not washing it off, and that's final."

The secretary shrugged and toddled back around the corner into Mr. Pope's office to deliver the unwanted news. The Boss' headache suddenly became Barbara's headache.

"Get Bill Dick in here," Mr. Pope ordered.

Big Bill had been with Mr. Pope since the beginning of the

Enquirer back in New Jersey. A huge bear of a man, Bill was an excellent British tabloid journalist of the old school who had earned Mr. Pope's trust. He was an Old Boy. He was also as kindly as the day is long, an alcoholic Scotsman who wouldn't hurt a fly.

"Fire her," commanded the Boss.

Kindly though he was, Bill also understood where his bread was buttered. He headed back into the newsroom straight to Barbara's desk.

Within minutes, toting her few personal belongings, Barbara was tearfully exiting the *Enquirer* with the scent of her perfume trailing strongly behind her, out of work, and never to be seen, heard or smelled again.

That's the way it was with Mr. Pope. That's the way it was at the *Enquirer.*

Nobody crossed Mr. Pope. Yes, Boss. No, Boss. Three Bags Full, Boss. If you could play his game by his rules and just swallow it, you could secure your future big time. The smart ones did. In fact, the really smart ones learned to think exactly like The Boss so they didn't even have to check his pulse to know the game plan.

Mr. Pope loved reporters, loved writers. He respected people who knew how to do those jobs well. And he had a rather expansive finer side. The lush tropical gardens which graced the *Enquirer's* grounds were famous throughout Florida, and they were Mr. Pope's baby. He had spent years planning and executing the landscaping and the extravagant array of exotic flora which graced the paper's manicured grounds. After a day of aggressive desk work, he'd take time walking around the grounds with his gardeners, making suggestions, examining flower beds, learning about the plants. At his insistence, each blossom, shrub, and tree was labeled with its English and Latin names.

The Boss often stepped out of his office and into the gardens even during work, tarrying amidst the greenery and the fragrant blooms, to clear his own head.

And if he noticed a reporter gazing vacantly over typewriter or computer, he knew how to solve the problem. Instantly recognizing writer's block, the Boss would insist that the employee step out and go for a walk around the grounds, enjoy the beauty of nature, take to the spongy lawns, stroll along the paths that snaked through flower beds and groves of palm trees. It was his gift to his work family.

The Boss graciously granted the timid request of many an *Enquirer* employee, to be married in the *Enquirer's* beautiful gardens. It was Mr. Pope's pleasure to oblige. He took a minute interest in each event and sometimes watched secretly from inside the office as groom kissed bride amidst the calla lilies.

When you own one hundred percent of something, you can run it any way you want. Everyone you hire is, in a sense, yours. That's the way Mr. Pope ran the *National Enquirer.*

In the early days, he had an extremely talented photo editor named Bob Young, and one week Young scored some exclusive paparazzi pictures from Europe of a much-wanted celebrity. He ran into a meeting in Mr. Pope's office to show The Boss, and Mr. Pope was duly impressed.

"They're good. But there's just one problem. How can we be sure they're exclusive? How do we know these paparazzi photographers didn't hold some of their pictures back to sell to someone else?"

Young pondered with the Great Man. "Yes, point taken. Can we trust them?" he concurred. "After all, they *are* Italian."

Bob Young didn't recall The Boss' proud Sicilian roots until it was too late.

Generoso Pope Jr. ended the meeting. Bob Young returned to his desk.

Nervously, someone else who'd been in the meeting crooked his finger to Young, and clued him in about his unwitting faux pas. Young groaned in agony, his *Enquirer* career passing before his eyes. Mr. Pope acted swiftly, and within a few weeks, Young was history and a new photo editor was sitting where he used to sit.

Mr. Pope always took great pride in the pictures he featured within the pages of his paper, and he was very clear on what he wanted them to portray.

One time I was sent to Cypress Gardens, Florida, to write a "Fantasy Fulfilled" genre story. The *Enquirer* did this feature now and then, in which we made a dearest dream come true, preferably for someone famous.

This time a young actress on some now-forgotten sitcom wished she could water-ski in the world-famous Tommy Bartlett Water Show. We were making it happen, flying her and her entourage to Cypress Gardens, giving her some lessons with the top ski artists in the water show, then photographing her as she stood on their expert shoulders, water skiing around the lagoon.

My good friend Vince Eckersley was the lenser on the assignment, and we babysat the young lady as she learned to stand on someone else's shoulders and water ski. She was athletic, an apt pupil, and after a day or two of lessons and rehearsal, she was ready. Vince and I got in the ski boat that would pull her, and he snapped away as we whooshed across the lagoon with the girl and the two expert water skiers in tow, doing their acrobatic moves in our wake. Vince got great shots of the girl as she swung up onto the men's shoulders perfectly, stood tall as the water sprayed them, and struck a beautiful and very professional-looking pose, a huge smile beaming across her face.

We rushed the pictures to Lantana, thrilled at how well the shoot and story had gone.

The next morning, the office called. "Mr. Pope doesn't like the pictures. He wants you to do them over."

"What? Why?" Vince and I were dumbfounded. The whole exercise had gone off like clockwork, the girl had performed like a pro, the shots were beautiful.

The photo editor continued, "He can't see the boat."

"The boat? What boat?" Vince puzzled.

"The boat that's pulling her. He can't tell from the pictures that she's actually being towed, that she's actually behind a boat. He says unless the readers can see the towboat, they won't know for sure that she really did it."

"But I was *in* the towboat. The pictures were taken *from* the towboat," Vince protested uselessly.

"I know that. But The Boss wants to see the boat. Figure out how, and then do the pictures over."

Vince and I and the girl and her entourage stayed an extra day and did the pictures again, from a second boat that whizzed alongside the tow boat. Now Mr. Pope had photographic proof that the little actress was skiing behind a boat, and so did the readers. Now he was happy. Heck, maybe he was right. Either way, he was Boss.

The Boss was very quirky about his pristine white 1976 Chevrolet Caprice Classic sedan, which was always parked in Space #1 in the *Enquirer's* lot. He believed so strongly that it was the finest American car ever made, that he had a standing offer of fifty thousand dollars to anyone in America who could deliver to him an un-driven, showroom-new '76 Caprice, with all zeros on the odometer, just so he'd have a spare. His offer stood until he died in 1988.

The Boss knew his car was special because he never even had to change the oil and it still ran like a top, year after year. He did not subscribe to conventional wisdom that the viscosity of engine oil breaks down in time, especially not in his Caprice, and he bragged to all his lieutenants that this car had never had an oil change. What he didn't realize was that every month or so, when gassing up the car for The Boss, one of his maintenance men made sure it got a lube job and oil change.

A little dog named Lucky was the *Enquirer* mascot. He was a Benji type pooch someone had saved from a pound death with about an hour to spare: hence, his name. And Lucky was about as cute as any dog could be. Pictures of the little fella often appeared in our pages, his fuzzy face looking appealingly out. The readers loved him and so did Mr. Pope. We even had a comic strip about him, called Life with Lucky.

Lucky's care was entrusted to a rotund Florida editor named Joe Cassidy. Lucky lived at Joe's house and Joe and his wife treated the little dog like the true prince he was in *Enquirer* Land. Whenever Lucky traveled to a photo shoot, the dog went first class. Joe would fly first class too, booking one seat for Lucky and two seats for himself, because Joe was a very big man.

One day, the Boss called Joe Cassidy into his private office and said, "Let's make Lucky into a family man. Let's find a cute little girl dog, get them together, and cover the whole thing from start to finish. The pregnancy, the birth, pictures of the puppies at every stage, and Lucky in every shot as the proud papa. It's a winner."

Joe Cassidy went white as a sheet.

"What's-a-matter, Joe," said Mr. Pope. "You look like you don't feel so good."

"Uhh, well, I, er..." Joe stammered.

"What is it?" demanded the Boss in his distinctive nasal accent.

"We won't be able to do that idea."

"Whatdya mean, won't be able?" asked the Boss.

"Well Boss, last time we took Lucky to the vet he suggested it would be better for the dog to get him..."

The pause was painful.

"....fixed? Is that what you're gonna tell me?" said the Boss, steam appearing around his head.

"Don't tell me you had Lucky fixed. I don't wanna hear that."

"I'm sorry, Boss," whispered a forlorn Joe in barely audible tones, sinking his entire three hundred pounds lower and lower into his chair.

It was a tribute to Mr. Pope's regard for Joe Cassidy that the portly editor remained not only employed, but also entrusted with the continuing care and feeding of Lucky. The only puppies Lucky ever spawned were on paper, in his weekly *Enquirer* comic strip.

I myself had a close call with Lucky one time. The adorable mutt was coming to California to appear on a TV show, in a specially arranged *Enquirer* promo, and I was tapped on the shoulder to go to the airport and collect the dog along with his human chaperone, Joe

Cassidy's look-alike son.

I headed out to LAX airport in plenty of time, and was waiting at the gate as man and dog came off the plane. It was love at first sight. Who could resist this scruffy little terrier mix, all floppy ears and wet kisses? No wonder he had such good luck. He was precious, simply precious, and had perfect manners.

Walking Lucky on a splendid rhinestone leash, we headed across to the parking garage and found my car. Joe's son piled into the front seat of my small Toyota coupe, while the well-behaved Lucky got comfortable on the passenger side in the back seat, one little front leg propped on the arm rest, his bottom resting on the seat, head up, ears perked, looking out the window, exactly like a fuzzy little kid.

I was in a row of straight spaces, not angled ones, with two-way traffic behind me, and as I shifted into reverse, I craned my neck hard to each side to make sure no cars were coming. I saw none, and began backing out. All at once, a brown Buick blazed from my right, never noticing my backup lights, not seeing my car easing out, not even slowing, and with a crumpling crush, it plowed into my rear passenger side.

Right where Lucky was sitting.

"Oh noooooo!" I screamed. "The dog! The dog!" I jerked on my emergency brake, jumped out, opened the car door and gathered the bewildered pooch into my arms.

Storming around to the offending motorist, all I could yell at her was, "Are you out of your *mind*? Don't you know who this *is*?"

Apparently, the woman didn't read the *Enquirer* and hadn't a clue what I was talking about. "Who *what* is? The *dog*?" she asked, thoroughly puzzled.

My car was badly smacked, but that was the least of my worries. All I cared about was Lucky. Or should I say, Lucky and my job.

But, true to his name, Lucky was unharmed, and so were we, apart from a few sad-looking pleats in my fender. I got the lady's insurance information and made Joe's son promise me on a stack of *Enquirers* that he'd never mention the accident to Mr. Pope. Not wanting, any more than I did, to put himself in the line of fire with The Boss, he kept the smashup our little secret and never said a word.

They said Mr. Pope had mafia connections. I'd heard it long before I joined the staff.

What may have started such rumors was that Generoso Pope, Jr.'s godfather was Joe Profaci, the head of New York's Gambino Family.

Profaci took a great interest in his godson. Generoso was an extraordinary student to whom academic success came naturally, and his mental agility was well noted in his godfather's circles. Young Gene was reputed to have a near-genius IQ, which could account for the eccentric streak which showed up later in his life. In a bizarre twist, the CIA also noticed Pope's intellectual prowess and college success, and in hopes of getting such a man on their side, recruited him. Open-minded young Gene took the job.

Many years later, he told the *Washington Post*, "I wanted to see what it was like. I was in a section called psychological warfare. I would sit there and read newspapers...and nobody would let me do anything."

Before long, he tired of the experience and left. "It was pretty bad," he succinctly explained.

The youthful Mr. Pope did not lack career choices, and considered joining his brothers Anthony and Fortune in the family concrete business, or in the operation of *Il Progresso*, the Italian-language newspaper founded by their father. However, as happens in families, the brothers didn't see eye-to-eye on business matters. Gene figured, "I'm not going to get anywhere in this deal. It's two to one."

So in 1952, with five thousand dollars of his own, and another twenty thousand borrowed from friends, the twenty-five-year-old entrepreneur purchased an unseemly blood and guts weekly tabloid newspaper out of Fort Lee, New Jersey. It was called the *Enquirer*, sported headlines like "Boy Born With Dog's Head" and "Nude Rings Doorbells," and had the distinction of being the only paper in New York to be published on Sunday afternoon. It had a circulation of 17,000.

By 1962, with what Pope called the "gore era" well under way, he'd renamed the paper the *National Enquirer*, raised circulation to nearly a million, and formed an ever-bigger vision for his tacky and slightly prurient little black and white rag. How he would turn that vision into reality became his crowning inspiration. Gene Pope decided to sell the *National Enquirer* in America's supermarkets.

However, the major chains balked at the paper's contents, reasoning to Pope that his stories about the removal of victim's intestines, hands, or heads might not sit well with people shopping for their dinner.

Obligingly, Mr. Pope reinvented the *Enquirer* to fill the new bill. And thus came into existence the paper's special mix of celebrity stories and "gee whiz" pieces about love, health, pets, kids, and other assorted oddities, perfect escapist reading to take home to the family.

Starting then, and almost single-handedly, Gene Pope made show biz gossip and "gee whiz" journalism a real part of real people's lives, bringing Hollywood tidbits and blockbusters and other unusual tales to America's kitchens and living rooms, not to mention bathrooms, each and every week.

And whether they believed what they were reading or not, middle class shoppers began to snap it up. By the millions, they began to snap it up.

It was a continuing home improvement, as Gene perked the *Enquirer* up, getting bigger and better stories, reducing the paper's size for easier handling, going to color, switching to a higher quality paper, initiating the rotogravure printing process for excellent photo reproduction, always keeping the price low.

And as its lively, spicy gossip format spread across America, the *Enquirer* eventually went beyond even Gene Pope's vision, actually revolutionizing the very way in which news was reported in all the media.

In a very real sense, Generoso Pope, Jr. and his new American tabloid, heavy on show biz content, began the current swamping of news values by entertainment and sensational values. The impact can be noted in all of today's printed publications, even the serious weekly news magazines, and more so on television, where myriad gossip shows like *Entertainment Tonight, Extra, Hard Copy, Access Hollywood, Real TV* and many others assault the viewer nightly with sensational tabloid tales and titillating Hollywood trivia.

Mr. Pope may have had his eccentricities, but his business intuition was flawless.

For many years, even before he owned the *Enquirer*, it was Mr. Pope's habit to fly the New Jersey coop every winter to vacation in the luxurious warmth of South Florida. He loved the swaying palm trees, the idyllic turquoise waters off the Florida reef, the balmy temperatures. And something innately appealed to him about Palm Beach's swanky lifestyle juxtaposed with the sandy neighboring middle-class communities full of retiree snowbirds and unassuming Florida natives.

As he thought about how to transform his *Enquirer*, he liked the idea that South Florida was about half-way between California and Europe, that it was the one American location best suited to convenient world travel almost anywhere .

Something else about South Florida appealed to him. It had no industry whatsoever, apart from tourism. Gene Pope reasoned that, therefore, all consumer goods had to be brought to the end of that long Florida peninsula...by what? By trucks. And since the tourist industry didn't produce anything but tans and relaxed smiles, all those trucks were leaving South Florida *empty.*

He began to compose a plan. He would buy up a big chunk of land in a flat little town nestled along the Intracoastal Waterway—just west of the water, strewn with tiny clapboard beach houses and flimsily constructed stucco bungalows. He would locate his new editorial headquarters there and let it be the biggest fish in that sunny little pond. What's more, he would locate his publishing plant nearby, in Pompano Beach, so he could supervise even the printing process, hands on.

Gene Pope's mind was ticking. All those trucks bringing the provender of life to South Florida were leaving empty. He would fill them with his *National Enquirers,* millions of *National Enquirers,* hot off the presses, bound for every corner of America, and he'd get a hell of a sweet deal from the teamsters, who'd be happy to fill those trucks with product of any kind, to make their long trip to Florida worthwhile. In 1971, he moved the paper lock, stock and barrel to Lantana, Florida, just south of Palm Beach.

But Gene Pope's mind didn't stop there. He was an ardent admirer of the British tabloid newspapers, those rip-roaring, tell-it-like-it-is rags which have always had the insidest of the inside stories, complete with thunderous quotes and more or less undeniable pictures, good taste notwithstanding.

He thought those British reporters must be the best, the most tenacious, the most flamboyant, the most of everything a tabloid reporter should be. And he wanted to hire as many as he could.

He knew the British tabloids paid fairly well and offered open-ended expense accounts. So why would the best of British reporters come to work for him? Why would they want to move across the ocean, to the colonies, to work for an unknown new tabloid? Gene Pope knew why. Because he'd offer them the same work, but much better salaries, plus even more outrageous expense accounts, *and* life in the tropics. He'd relocate them to the lush greenery and warm sparkling beaches of Florida—away from the rain, sleet, and gloom of filthy British weather. Their kids could play in the sea every day, they could all have boats on the Intracoastal Waterway, their wives could take tennis lessons, they could get loads of lifestyle because of the low cost of living and lack of state income tax, and he'd pay them the kind of money that would make them rich by Florida standards, not to mention English standards, and probably by *any* standards.

His double whammy worked like a charm. He soon had a full complement of experienced Fleet Street reporters who'd packed up, left the Mother Country, and brought with them their well-ingrained expertise at sensational writing, digging, rooting, and not taking no for an answer.

And as he transformed his seamy rag into a gentler journal more acceptable to mainstream America, there it was, in the one place Americans were sure to see it—the supermarket. In a perfectly executed deal, he got markets to display his handy tabloid-size gossip sheet right at the point of purchase, and part of the deal was that the *Enquirer* would always have the last racks before the checkout.

In later years, when other magazines jumped on the tabloid bandwagon and also got displays along the checkout aisle, the *Enquirer* still kept its prominent placement. To this day, you will always find the *National Enquirer* in the best rack, at eye level and handy as you offload your goodies onto the conveyor.

Gene Pope arranged for that back in the sixties, and his deal still stands.

So now he has the teamsters shipping his newspapers all over the United States for a sweet tariff; he has his offices in an out-of-the-way Garden of Eden that's central for travel all over the world; he has his British reporters on staff burrowing out the best stories; and he has his papers where America can't miss seeing them—right at the checkout stand when they buy their eggs and lettuce, *and* in the primo spot before they pay, thank you very much.

Yes, Mr. Pope was quite a canny fellow.

I didn't know it then, but I was to have a long and interesting career working for him.

4

Into the Spider's Web

When it came to celebrities, Frank Sinatra was the biggest, the baddest, the boldest and the best.

And for the *Enquirer* in 1975, this was especially so. I soon became aware that Mr. Pope was a voracious fan of Frankie. "The Chairman of the Board" and The Boss had both come up on the tough side of the tracks in New Jersey, they'd both made it big, there were rumors of mafia connections around both men, and Mr. Pope liked to know what Frankie was up to.

I was therefore thrilled and flattered, but also slightly horrified, to be given my first on-the-road assignment covering none other than Frank Sinatra.

Sinatra had been around forever, it seemed, and had gone from boy band singer, to teen heart-throb, washed-up has-been, Oscar winning movie star, king of saloon singers, gold record champ, chief of the Rat Pack, playboy, bad boy, cool guy.

He'd retired once and was in the midst of a comeback, labeled "The Noblest Roman of Them All Returns." Over the years, I'd gotten an inside view into the ways of the Chairman of the Board.

My ex-boss, Rona Barrett, had been an intimate of the Sinatra family, best girlfriends during her youth with Frank's older daughter, Nancy Sinatra, Jr. In fact, word was that the girlish friendship had been so close that Frank had actually fronted Rona the money for a down payment on her first Beverly Hills home. It had been the start of her real estate success story, which, incidentally, continued after she dropped off the edge of the gossip world.

But as I began to cover Hollywood, I observed that Frank always managed to cancel out the good things about himself. I discussed this with Rona one day.

"It's uncanny," she said in her nasal New Yorky accent, brushing her bulletproof blond hairdo with a perfectly manicured hand. I'd just brought in the front pages of a couple of papers. "Here it is…," I said. "Sinatra bloodied someone's face in a drunken Las Vegas hotel brawl, because the guy tried to take his picture. Look, it's on all the front pages."

What made it so ironic was that Rona had just finished telling me about how Frank flew a dying kid across country in a private jet, paid for all the kid's medical treatments, footed the family's bills, and arranged for the child to recover with a round-the-clock nurse at his side. Rona said, "That, he kept anonymous."

Now every paper in town had run the picture of Frank punching the guy, replete with obscene gestures, with his face contorted into a graphic mask of pure fury. No one even knew about his good work, but now everyone knew about his foul temper.

Frank hated the press. I'd always known that Sinatra was a genuine fast lane tough guy, that he loved women but liked them in their place, that he always had his coterie of henchmen with him, that he clashed with the press often, and that he especially hated lady reporters.

Once I joined the *Enquirer*, I was to learn that he wasn't above having his pals beat up reporters, and that even a lady reporter had better stay out of his way or be prepared for trouble.

During that era when people got away with saying what they *really* felt, Sinatra freely crowed his opinion about female columnists. Sinatra once had a huge row with D.C. celeb columnist Maxine Cheshire, and had gone on the record to describe her (and presumably all of us) as a bunch of "Two Dollar Whores" (his words).

That memory of Frankie's take on women journalists stuck in my mind in July of 1975, when my byline began appearing on celebrity stories in the *National Enquirer.*

Eirik Knutzen and I had just hit the cafeteria three floors below for a quickie lunch. We were making inane jokes as we ambled back into the *Enquirer's* spacious ninth floor office suite. We were both in the middle of writing stories, and we separated to go back to our desks. I was looking forward to spending the rest of the afternoon writing up an interview I had had the previous day with "Miss" Peggy Lee. The legendary songbird had revealed for the first time that she was kept alive only with the aid of a large mechanical breathing apparatus that she took everywhere she went. Her respiratory system was totally shot, but the unflappable star had found a way to go on singing.

I had just sat down at my typewriter and was reviewing the notes from my taped interview when our heavyset young bureau chief burst out of his glass enclosure.

Markfield headed straight for me, barking, "Sternig, *there* you are! I'm sending you out. You're going to Lake Tahoe on a Sinatra story. It's only a spec assignment, but the boss REALLY wants it. You're a broad and I know you can do this one better than anyone. Use all your wiles and tricks.

"Sinatra's appearing up at Tahoe on the same bill with that goody-goody country guy John Denver. There's a story there somewhere."

I'd covered John Denver's wildly successful career from his first Los Angeles appearance as a wide-eyed cowboy crooning heartfelt tunes at the Troubadour. I liked him, his clear Colorado pipes, his reverent nature boy songs. He was old-fashioned, pure and very sincere.

And then of course, there was Sinatra. Everyone knew all about his wee-hour antics on the town, his ribald partying, his chauvinistic bad-boy rat pack, his drinking, his dames, his fights.

"Hmm," I responded. "You mean like a contrast? Their opposite lifestyles? I'm sure we can count on Sinatra to show up around the casino. He always does." I cocked my head and stroked my chin. "Smokey barroom Sinatra and his hard-drinking womanizing pals— and fresh-air Denver with his blue-sky granola gang. That sort of thing?"

Markfield beamed with that quirky little gleam in his eye. "Yeah, yeah. I love it." I'd only been on staff a month, but I was getting used to "we can do anything" tabloid journalism.

He handed me my airline tickets and car reservation, and said, "You're leaving in two hours, and uh, by the way, all the flights into Tahoe are full, so you'll fly into Reno. And all the rooms are booked at Harrah's where they're playing, so you'll have to find a room somewhere else when you get up there."

For all my unruffled exterior, my heart was now pounding at the sheer responsibility of getting packed, rushing to make my flight, getting booked in somewhere, and most of all, going out there on company expenses all by myself to score an inside story about one of the toughest stars there ever was, and who incidentally hated female journalists.

I was confronted for the first time with that overwhelming question: "How in the hell am I going to do this?"

Of course, in front of my new boss who thought I was Miss Hot Hollywood, I did not let on, but appeared perfectly cool and collected.

I simply scooped up my tape recorder and notebooks, grabbed the tickets and papers he handed me, told him I'd call him when I got there, and started heading for the door. Suddenly, Alan added, "Wait, Sternig. I want you to take Tracy with you. She'll be at your disposal to use in any way you need her. She's the tryout and you're the staff reporter, so I want you running the story. You tell her what to do. Get the story and don't come home until you do. It's your show, Sternig."

Tracy Cabot had once worked at the notorious scandal rag *Confidential,* so I knew she'd be a capable accomplice, tryout or not, and I was relieved to know I'd have company, somebody to bounce off of, somebody to connive and scheme through the story with.

As I roared my small yellow Toyota up Crescent Heights, toward my Havenhurst Drive apartment just off the Sunset Strip, I started formulating the plan. Obviously, knowing how Sinatra hated ladies of the press, we'd need a well-crafted, believable undercover pose. The story was so natural—Vegas high-roller Frankie, and country boy Denver.

Okay, so what have we got to work with? I'm long-haired and curvy, with large brown eyes. Sinatra loves babes—so I'll be a little sex-pot fan dying to meet him. Tracy's more of a plain Jane, smart, kind of matter of fact, with glasses, pitch black hair. We'll get her into country western garb and set her adoring fan persona upon the Denver brigade.

I raced up the stairs to my apartment, threw open the door and stood in the living room collecting my thoughts. Clothes! Think of all the situations that might come up. I grabbed a suitcase, set it on the bed, and began yanking through my closet to see what would work.

I threw in a pair of tight jeans, a skinny little yellow angora sweater, cropped; a pair of slinky slacks and a fitted top; a silver pleated mini dress with matching silver shoes; a hot pink number; and most important, a sexy backless jumpsuit that left little to the imagination. In an afterthought, I also tossed in a short blond wig. As I grabbed my cosmetics, shoes, and shampoo, the phone rang. It was Tracy. I gave her the plan so she could pack her costume—and we arranged to meet at the airport.

It didn't take long before I clicked my bag closed, threw my office stuff into a duffel, and grabbed my car keys. I was about to run out the door when I suddenly realized—"Wait a minute. My sister

Marylou, her husband, and their seven-year-old are arriving in two days! Will I be back? They were already on the road from Colorado and, in those days before cell phones, unreachable. I quickly picked up the mike on my Phone Mate answering machine and programmed a new greeting with a cryptic message for them. They were to get my key from the landlady and make themselves at home in case I wasn't back yet. Then I called the landlady, described them in detail, and got her cooperation. As I locked the door and ran to the garage, I prayed Marylou would call my phone number before arriving in L.A. and get the message.

I swung my car left down La Cienega Boulevard toward L.A. Airport, and about half-way down Restaurant Row, broke out in a fit of uncertainty. Is this thing really going to happen? I'm flying into Reno. Am I going to find a hotel room, much less Sinatra, Denver, and an inside story about them? Will Sinatra and Denver be hanging out in the casino? Will we get great sources? Will we get next to the stars? Will we pull off our charade? What'll happen if Sinatra figures out I'm a reporter? What if my sister doesn't get my message?

And by the way, from now on, is this going to be my life, just leaving behind all my personal plans to jet off in pursuit of stories? That doesn't feel good. But I'm getting so much money, they have a right to expect complete devotion. They had made it very very plain from my first week that that's *exactly* what they expected. My first weekend on staff I had announced I couldn't do a Saturday night stakeout because I was giving a dinner party. Alan warned me, "Only because you're new, Sternig, will that fly *this time*. In the future, you cancel your plans and you go."

As I drove across L.A., the full impact hit me. The future Alan spoke of was here, and I was going. And I felt giddy. I was in the boys' world now. On the road. Chasing big-name celebrities in a way I never had during my ladylike front-door days with Rona. This was it. I was in charge of a tough assignment and I wasn't invited. I had my expense account, I had my cash advance, I had my airline ticket and I had my car reservation. Most of all, I had my ingenuity, and that's what I would need above anything else. I was exhilarated. I was on an adrenalin rush that was about to become a way of life. My brief was—"Follow Sinatra wherever he goes. Infiltrate his inside circle. Don't come back until you have the story."

****

Tracy and I lucked into an off-strip motel room, just about the last one in Tahoe. We felt fortunate even though we had to share. As we unpacked our costumes and roared at the idea of what we were about to do, we discussed strategy. Trying hard to be leaderly, I told my tryout helper, "We'll go straight to Harrah's and scope it out for any and all leads. We'll talk to pit bosses, ladies room attendants, dealers, restaurant hostesses, bartenders and cocktail waitresses— anyone who could be in the know. We'll try for tickets to the dinner show, or at least the midnight show. And if we get in, we'll work on meeting entourage members. You know Sinatra always has his body-guards and hangers-on, and Denver probably has his own gang of pals, too. They'll be our ticket in. You're the John Denver groupie, I'm the Sinatra groupie. We'll have to come on avidly and fawn about how we're dying to meet them. Play it as close to the edge as you dare. So will I. If either of us gets in trouble, let's not be too far apart."

We hit Harrah's immediately. On the casino floor, we split up and went our separate ways. In my skin-tight jeans that had "The End" emblazoned in nailheads across the seat, I wiggled and flirted my way up to the first pit boss I saw staring at me. He obviously thought I was kind of cute, and when I asked, he decided to be a hero and let me in on Sinatra's whereabouts.

The pit boss—whose name I gathered from his badge was Paul— informed me that if I really had the hots to see Frankie boy, he al-ways dined between shows in the Summit restaurant on the top floor of Harrah's. Paul told me Sinatra always had his entourage around, including comic Pat Henry who opened his show, and assorted "guys." These guys, he pointed out, were always wandering around the ca-sino and could be easily identified because they'd all been given sky blue satin team jackets commemorating the Sinatra/Denver pairing at Harrah's. He said, "Look over there. There's one of them now. See that jacket? Everyone in the entourage will be wearing one just like it. Oh, and they like to hang out over there in the Hideaway Bar in the afternoons and after Sinatra's midnight show. Sinatra always comes in and joins them for a round or two, so you're sure to meet him if you just go in there about two AM and sit at the bar. He'll notice you, sweetheart, he'll notice you."

I goo-goo'd and gah-gah'd over this windfall of information, and thanked Paul profusely, winking at him and tweaking his arm in gratitude. "Maybe I could talk to you again tomorrow and let you know how I did."

"You do that, sweetheart. I'll be right here." His eyes were on his tables, players, and dealers, and also on my nail-studded behind as I walked away. I wanted to make sure he'd remember me and tell me what he knew as Sinatra's game plans unfolded. I looked back over my shoulder and shamelessly blew him a pouty little air kiss.

I hurried over to the lounge where Paul told me da boys hung out, just to get the lay of the land. I did this instinctively, but learned over the next years always to scope out these locales before the celebs were actually *in situ*, so as to know where the exits, corners, ladies rooms, paths to the outside and possible safe hiding spots were, just to have the blueprint in my mind.

While I was standing there gazing around, a heavyset man suddenly loomed in the entrance. He had thick curly black hair, a babyface, and the thickest, curliest eyelashes I had ever seen on a man. He looked through me, intently scanning the room for someone, then walked back out into the casino. He had on a sky blue satin jacket with the Sinatra/Denver/Harrah's logo emblazoned on the back. I memorized his appearance.

After a thorough wander through the Hideaway, I sidled up to the bar, and with a naive inflection in my voice, asked the bartender, "Does Sinatra really come in here at night?"

He smiled and said, "He sure does—and he always sits right over there in that corner booth with his gang."

I could hardly believe my snowballing good luck. Perfect. Now I knew exactly where I hoped *I'd* also be sitting, in the company of Sinatra and Entourage, before this was all over.

I wondered how Tracy was faring and re-entered the brightly lit casino. My eyes were still adjusting from the dim of the lounge when I nearly ran into her. She was smiling broadly and very excited. "What? What? What?" I quizzed. "OK, he had a girl in his suite, she gave him a blow job, he paid her what an IBM executive would earn in a week!"

"Omigod! *John Denver*??" I gasped incredulously.

"No, not Denver! YOUR boy! Sinatra!"

"Lord, that's incredible information! Who's giving you that? How in the heck can we put it in print?" The words tumbled out of Tracy's mouth. "It was the maitre d' in the Summit restaurant." The Summit! That was the dining room on top of the hotel where I already knew we would be dining that night, in our plan to bump into Sinatra. "Tracy, did he give you any details?"

She said, "He told me this chick was standing in the cancellation line and one of Sinatra's guys noticed her, picked her up, and took her to the show. Later, they were all partying and she caught Sinatra's eye. He took a liking to her, and eventually she disappeared with him. She gave him the blow job and came away with a queen's ransom. The girl came by and showed the maitre d' the cash."

It seemed a good omen for our getting close to Sinatra, even though we had no intention of getting *that* close. Right then, I didn't worry about how I'd put such racy stuff into my copy. But Tracy and I congratulated ourselves on the day's progress.

"OK," I said, "Since you've met the maitre d', why don't you go back up and tell him your girlfriend loves Sinatra and she heard he dines up there between shows so we want to make dinner reservations for tonight. Get him to give us a table right next to Frankie's." Tracy's eyes lit up.

"Is that true? Every night?"

"Yup. I got it from a pit boss," I told her.

"Great. A great dinner, and on expenses to boot!" With that, she headed off toward an elevator, disappearing in the casino throng.

Right after she left me, another blue satin jacket went by—and this one stopped me in my tracks. I instantly recognized the man topping Sinatra's inner retinue, the man known as Sinatra's best friend. It was the tough-talking, swaggering, high-rolling Jilly Rizzo.

Jilly stood about five-feet-ten, with enormous shoulders and a rubbery broad face. His large head sat atop a bull neck. He had white-grey, slicked-back, thinning hair—and once you saw him, you didn't forget him. I'd seen him around Las Vegas many times while covering opening nights for Rona. But I also knew that face very well from seeing him in the background of every Sinatra paparazzi shot. The pair of them were inseparable.

Even indoors, he was wearing wire-rimmed sunglasses—the kind that change to darker tones as you move from shade to sunlight. The lenses in Jilly's glasses were rose-colored.

Jilly talked tough. He was motioning to an Italian-tailored gent, "Lemme take care-a ya." I pretended to be reading a stand-up sign, and moved closer. His conversation was punctuated by crude jokes and raucous lurid laughter.

Jilly had been Frank's personal bodyguard for many years until becoming his all-around companion and factotum. He rarely smiled, and as one Sinatra aide put it, "Jilly takes shit from no one. Jilly is in control and the boys all look up to him. He's the top banana."

I felt that at that moment, the better part of valor was again to be as invisible as possible, so I looked down, hiding my face, and looked away from him. I didn't think he noticed me. After listening as long as I dared, I slithered unobtrusively out of his path.

As soon as I was sure Jilly had left the area, I went over to a young security guard and began conversing. "I'm a HUGE Sinatra fan and I want to get close to him. How do I do it?"

To my amazement, he responded, "If a girl wanted to get close to the Sinatra crowd, all she'd really have to do would be to wear something low-cut, bend over a lot, and rub up against Pat Henry. He's a sucker for women. He's insatiable. He has a never-ending parade of women, some who want to be near him, and some who are going for the higher stakes of Sinatra himself." I felt myself blushing a little bit. It seemed so tawdry, so easy.

Just then, Tracy came back down with a thumbs up for our dinner reservations. We were booked between shows in the Summit Restaurant on top of Harrah's, the same as Frank Sinatra. Our reservation was for nine-fifteen PM. His was at ten o'clock.

Back in our hotel room, Tracy and I placed a call to Markfield to give him the dirt. He was elated.

I took out my little backless number, and Tracy got dressed in her country-girl getup—a long prairie skirt and a pair of cowboy boots. She had a little string tie around her neck.

I put the finishing touches on my makeup—plenty of mascara and bright red lips. I practiced my jiggle in front of the mirror. Tracy twirled in her prairie skirt. Then we got in the car and left for Harrah's.

*****

It was nearly nine-fifteen as I drew our non-descript rental car up toward the hotel's canopied entrance. We'd have time before Frankie and da boys arrived—to get settled in the restaurant, scope the layout and exits, check out the ladies room, chat up waiters, bartenders, and anyone else who could help.

I inched the car forward, as we were last in a long line of cars waiting for valet parking, then glanced nervously at my watch. "This may take a while," I said to Tracy. "Maybe you'd better go on up to the Summit and let them know we're here. I'll be right up."

Tracy popped out of the car, and a minute later when the valet got to me, I swung my legs to the pavement and stepped into the windy evening. Silently, I cursed the breeze for mussing my hair and, as I walked briskly into the casino, I used the mirrored wall on the right to adjust not only my hairdo, but also my flimsy outfit.

I had to admit, my gownless evening strap looked *grrr*eat, but I would have to check throughout the evening that the halter front was tied tightly enough around my neck so that my breasts didn't accidentally escape.

Suddenly, out of nowhere, my boarding school background popped to mind. An involuntary smile crossed my face as I envisioned my years in uniform, maintaining silence in the halls, wearing my white gloves, walking into chapel singing the traditional songs our strict nuns had taught us. "Reverend Mother would have cardiac arrest if she saw me right now," I chuckled. "She wouldn't believe this in a million years." I had been the perfect little soldier of obedience, the perfect blue-ribbon girl, the perfect pious epitome of purity. Maybe that's why this role was so much fun now.

I scurried to the bank of elevators and carefully stepped in. Somewhat breathless from my lobby sprint, I pushed PH for Penthouse, and stepped back against the railing, only to feel a pair of eyes moving across my body, and finally resting on my face.

"Hiya, doll. You are a bee-ootiful doll."

I blushed, batted my eyes, and what I saw made my heart pound. The guy was wearing a sky blue satin jacket.

He was short, wiry, Italian-looking, and had a cocky kind of swagger. I took note of his aviator sunglasses, large jewelry, forceful energy, and the barely detectable toupee that nestled amidst his graying black hair. Even the part looked very natural.

"I seen you running across the casino, so I held the elevator for you," he leered.

"Well, thanks," I drawled.

As the elevator went *ding* and the doors slid towards each other, he noted, "You're heading to the Summit, huh doll?"

"Why, yes I am. My girlfriend and I have dinner reservations, 'cause we heard Frank Sinatra comes up between shows. I'm a VERRRRY big fan."

"You are, are ya? Well, it just so happens, I'm having dinner with your idol in a little while."

My mouth dropped and I demurely clasped my hands in front of my chest. The truth was, it was more than I could have hoped for. "No. You're lying."

"I never lie about the big stuff."

I blinked with wide eyes and sighed profusely.

"I'll tell you what," said the man. "I'll find you at your table and bring you over, how'd you like that? Is your girlfriend as cute as you are?"

I tried to titter as air-headedly as possible, and said, "You'll have to judge that for yourself. She loves John Denver almost as much as I love Frank Sinatra."

"Well, dis is your lucky night," the man said, throwing another predatory leer my way.

The elevator *ding'd* again and stopped on eight. "Hey, this is my stop. I gonna grab a shower so I be sweet for ya, doll," intoned the wiry little man, talking like Dean Martin. "I'll see you up there. When you get there, you tell the maitre d' da Spider said to take good care-a-ya. On second thought, I'll find you and take good care-a-ya myself."

Da Spider stepped off, then held the door open from the outside and poked his head back in. "Hey wait—What's your name?"

"Barbara," I cooed.

"Barbara. Brown eyes. Bee-oootiful," he said in a deep growl, and the elevator doors shut.

"Yes!" I silently gloried. I couldn't believe my good fortune. I'd stepped right into the elevator with one of Sinatra's lascivious henchmen. Right into the Spider's web, I thought. And if this spider knew who I really was, I'd be dispatched as quickly as a gnat. I knew I'd have to use his web carefully, so he himself—and not me—would get stuck in it.

If Mama could see me now.

****

Up on top in the Summit Restaurant, all was soft lights and sweet music. Tuxedoed waiters scurried from table to table, fashionable diners clinked their silverware, the lights of Tahoe twinkled below, the solicitous maitre d' greeted me.

"I have a nine-fifteen reservation," I said, "joining another lady who's already here. I'm the big Sinatra fan, remember? and I do hope our table is near his. Spider said you'd take good care of us."

With a glimmer of immediate recognition when I mentioned Spider, he smiled, "I don't think you'll be disappointed," and led me right to a window table, where Tracy sat sipping a glass of white wine. Our spot was next to a long table set for eight. We both tittered and acted sappy. The maitre d' seemed to get a kick out of it.

As soon as he walked away, I spilled the news to Tracy about meeting Spider in the elevator. "Bingo, bingo, bingo," I whispered to her, sliding forward in my chair.

We both had to watch it so that our girlish glee didn't attract undue attention. The elation of success filled me as I thought of how this thing was coming together. But there was still a long way to go —and a Spider's web to get into and safely back out of.

It wasn't long before Spider arrived in a heavy cloud of Polo cologne, surrounded by the Sinatra entourage. It slightly electrified me, when among them, I saw the burly guy with the eyelashes, the one I'd seen scanning the Hideaway Bar earlier. I hadn't had time to take in his whole appearance that afternoon, but now I couldn't avoid noticing his long, wavy black hair, slicked back with hair oil and puffed into a greaser-type bouffant. This really was Sinatra's gang. And these were *all* very distinctive characters. I detected suspiciously gun-looking bulges beneath the expensively cut tuxedos of several of them.

As soon as he spotted me, Spider excused himself from his group and smarmed his way straight to my table. "Barbara, Barbara, Barbara," he crooned.

"Hello again," I smiled, looking up from under heavily mascara'd doe eyes. "So you really *are* with Frank Sinatra," I batted.

"That's his table right over there, sweetheart," said Spider, nodding his head towards the table for eight.

"By the way," I said, "Spider, this is Tracy. Tracy, this is Spider. Tracy loves John Denver."

With goo-goo eyes, Tracy played her role to the hilt. "Oooooh, do you know him?" she gushed.

"All in due time, sweetheart," promised Spider. "Right now, we're waiting to see if Frank comes up for dinner. If he doesn't, you'll come over and eat with us. And you DO look like dessert. See, he doesn't like any broads at the table between shows—just da boys."

Under the table, I felt Tracy's foot kicking mine hard. Just in case she had any doubts, it was now amply clear my encounter with da Spider had been no illusion. Spider hunched his short wiry frame over our table and smiled his cocky smile that began on one side of his face and never quite made it to the other side. He was about forty-five, and his banter was the banter of the streets.

"So goils, I want ya to meet some of da boys. I be back," he said, in that bad Dean Martin imitation.

We ordered and ate an appetizer. In a short time, true to his word, Spider slid back to our table. The message had apparently been delivered to da boys that Sinatra was having dinner in his suite between shows that night and wouldn't be up.

Spider came and ceremoniously pulled my chair out for me, leading me and Tracy toward the beseated inner circle of Ol' Blue Eyes' entourage. We were about to meet Da Boys.

At the head of the table was Pat Henry, the raunchy comic who always opened Sinatra's shows. Pat was very good-looking in a tough guy sort of way. He gave off bored, kind of antsy vibes. Next to him was the blubbery guy with the slick hair and the eyelashes. A couple of other underworldly-looking characters hunched over their salads.

"Girls, meet Pat," Spider intro'd, and Pat nodded with bored disinterest. "And this here's Frankie Eyelashes." No one could deny the nickname was apropos. Frankie showed no signs of recognizing me, thank God, but looked up through those thick eyelashes out of large bloodshot orbs and managed a wan smile.

"My roommates," said Spider with a raucous laugh. "It's happenin' in our suite, you KNOW dat." I couldn't imagine just *what* was happenin'.

We gave slight smiles at each introduction. "Funny nicknames," I ventured.

"Yeah, well, Pat gave all us old classmates our nicknames. The whole gang's not here, ya know. We got other guys with nicknames. Joe Tomatoes, Lefty da Brush, Willy da Broom.

"Anyhow, dis here's Tony Navarro—Tony, say hello to da goils."

Tony was a guy so dour-looking you'd believe he'd just lost his last friend.

"And that's Charlie."

Charlie had a very strangely-shaped head.

"Pat, we just call Pat. Boys, meet Barbara Brown Eyes. And Colorado Tracy."

These guys were experts at looking women over. Their eyes checked out our vital stats, then they all gestured and shifted and made room for us at the table. Tracy sat down next to Eyelashes, and of course, Spider scooted my chair very close to his own.

Now the men were getting their entrees, and Spider called the waiter over to get menus for us too. "Sorry we couldn't bring you over before, baby. Frank was supposed to come up for dinner with da boys, but he changed his mind."

Trying hard not to show it, I took complete mental notes, hoping for more detail. I had my tape recorder somewhere in my purse, but this wasn't the time to fish around and attempt to turn it on.

Pat Henry suddenly chimed in, "Yeah, The Old Man's eating in his dressing room with the Denver kid. I can't believe they're hitting it off. What a hayseed goofball." Did I detect a note of proprietary jealousy?

Tracy now stepped easily into her role, suddenly transforming herself into a wide-eyed little-girl type, oohing, aahing and gushing, "John Denver? He's eating with John Denver? Oh, I just *love* him. Don't you think he's *so great*?"

Pat Henry just rolled his eyes.

Spider insisted we order the most expensive things on the menu, and as we dined, sexual innuendo flowed like hair oil. Pat Henry told one dirty joke after the other, and da boys nearly creamed themselves laughing. Glances were shot in our direction with every ribald reference, already taking for granted what was supposedly to come for da Spider, and perhaps Eyelashes.

The best wines were ordered, caviar, heart of palm, filet mignon, whatever anyone wanted, and it all went on a tab. It was a private glimpse into the way things work every night when you're part of Sinatra's gang.

I noticed that Tracy was getting on famously with Eyelashes. She burbled, "Ooooh, Frankie *EYE*-lashes. What a cute name." She paused. "Why'd they name you *THAT*?"

I watched Eyelashes' face go blank, then he shot a "Can you believe this dumb broad?" look toward one of his compadres across the table, after which da boys just howled.

At one point, Pat Henry discussed with Spider Sinatra's orders for new clothes. "Okay, I just talked to the Old Man. Go to the men's shop at Caesar's when you get home. Get a forty-four suit, yellow, and a beige, and ship it to the Waldorf Astoria. He wants to buy two outfits." Spider replied, "Do we have to buy dem?" Pat shot back, "Of course you gotta buy them. You can't steal 'em, can you? Ship 'em COD to Pat Henry, Waldorf Towers, New York. I'll get 'em to Frank." Would my Boss want even this tidbit? Probably.

As we lingered over espresso and New York cheesecake (Sinatra's favorite), Pat Henry got fidgety and pushed his chair back. "Okay, I'm going down to the Racebook. I got my tips for tomorrow. You know, I won six doubles today. It bugged the shit outa me that they have a thousand dollar limit on payoffs in there. First coupla bets I laid down, I never knew about that limit. Then I won an exacta and went up to collect my thousand-fifty-five, and they'd only give me a grand. It's just a good thing I didn't lay down more than a hundred, because if I'd bet five hundred, for instance, I woulda lost thousands, not knowing about that thousand buck maximum. I woulda been steamin' cuz I woulda bet it all myself, insteada having each of da boys lay down a C-note for me, and collectin' all around."

Henry seemed to be going on and on and on and I didn't really understand what he was talking about, but da boys hung on his every word, like pearls of wisdom. He seemed to me like a schoolboy with a mean streak. He was definitely top banana amongst the minions.

"Okay, I'm gone. Got to bet, then get into my tux. We start right on time, midnight. You boys comin' to the show tonight?"

Spider spoke for them all. "Nah, we're going to cruise the casino, take our goils gambling, then head for the Hideaway. We'll catch you in dere later, Pat." Pat turned and walked toward the elevator, ultra cool, mugging and gesturing to the maitre d' and hostess as he departed.

"Oooh, Spider, would you take us to see Frank's show at midnight? Did Pat mean that? I just *know* we'd have the best seats in the house if you take us."

"Tell ya what, doll. I'll arrange with Jilly to get you ringside—and then you'll meet me in the Hideaway after, how's dat? And den when Frank comes in to shoot the breeze wid us, you'll meet him. He'll probably remember you from ringside. We'll all be sitting wid him in da booth. How's that, you little fox? But you better stick with da Spider and not go after Frank," he said, tweaking me in the ribs.

Da boys guffawed. Evidently, as I'd been told, a lot of girls used them to get close to the Old Man.

It was nearly eleven-forty when we all got up, strolled across the restaurant, and rode the lift back down to the casino. Spider went to a white phone and paged Jilly Rizzo. He'd apparently used a special code name to show it was he calling Jilly, because it only took a second for Jilly to get on the line. I could hear Spider mumbling something about a babe, and I caught, "So take care-a her for me, my man."

Spider hung up, turned to me and said, "Okay, he'll be by the showroom entrance in five minutes, to the right of the show line. You know what Jilly looks like, don't you, sweetheart? He'll take you in. I'd go wit ya, sweetheart, but I seen the show a million times and I gotta meet someone for baccarat. Don't stand me up now— the Hideaway right after da show.

"Don't you *ever* worry about that," I said, squeezing his stiffly powerful bejeweled hand. "I'll be there.

"And Spider..." I added, moving closer to him and planting a perfumed kiss on his cheek, "...thanks."

"G'wan, get outa here—go find Jilly," he said, feigning annoyance, but loving it.

We raced across the casino to the showroom, and there, as promised, stood Jilly Rizzo, he of the rose-colored glasses. Since the last time I saw him, I had miraculously become *connected*.

"I'm Barbara, the girl Spider just called you about."

Jilly didn't crack a smile. "Yeah, come on wit me." He took my arm and led me through a curtained doorway into the darkened showroom, Tracy bringing up the rear. It was packed; I didn't see even one empty seat. To boot, the aisles were filled with a slowly moving crowd, nearly shoulder to shoulder. I was amazed at how this Red

Sea of humanity just parted as Jilly led us in. Waiters stepped aside, aisles magically opened. The most famous Sinatra pal of them all led us directly to two empty front row seats right below the stage. We couldn't have been any closer unless we'd been sitting on Frank Sinatra's lap.

I turned to Jilly to say thanks, but before I could utter a word, he had grabbed the waiter, mumbled something in his ear, then walked briskly away.

Lights in the South Shore Room went dim. The table captains all went to the back of the showroom to count how many twenty, fifty and hundred dollar bills they had in their pockets. The people sitting around us, who'd pressed those bills into the captain's palms for better seats, went hushed.

A low, sexy female voice resonated through the room's speakers: "Ladies and gentlemen—welcome to the South Shore Room and the Frank Sinatra Show. And now—PAT HENRY!"

Out from stage left prowled the tough-guy comic with whom we'd just been brushing elbows in the Summit Restaurant. He grabbed the mike and started pacing around the stage in front of the still-closed curtain, delivering his rapid-fire, somewhat off-color routine.

We had a couple of water glasses on our table, and Pat came over to us, reached down and grabbed one of them, pleading, "Hey, I'm so dry I can't stand it. What's in here," he asked me. I shrugged, wondering if he recognized me and Tracy from upstairs. He continued, "You play a classy joint and whadda they give you—ice cubes with holes in them. I should know about ice cubes with holes. I was married to one for eighteen years."

Boom boom. Everyone laughed—except a heavyset, fortyish lady sitting near us, who hadn't had quite enough to drink. She clapped her hand over her mouth and murmured, "How crude! He's not even funny." Her opinion aside, *Frank Sinatra* had thought for many years that Pat Henry was funny, and that's really all that counted. Pat cleaned it up a little. "Nixon had his good points. At least he kept us out of Ireland. Now we got Ford. With Ford, at least if he gets sick, we can always get parts." The shocked lady liked that one. Pat did about twenty minutes.

I watched as Henry strode offstage, wondering what would happen the next time I saw him. Whatever it was, I figured it would be before morning. Immediately, the curtain opened and a large platform started moving forward. On it sat the orchestra, playing slow, lilting, soft jazz strains of "Where or When."

Suddenly, from amidst the musicians, up stepped none other than

Sinatra. Flicking his hand in the direction of Pat Henry's exit, he joshed, "Get him off!" Frank smiled and winked, I thought, right at me.

He went right into a swing version of "Where or When," and then segued directly to the next song.

From my front row seat, I could see that his round cufflinks were gold and enamel, that his well-cut boots were black and Italian, and that he had some kind of black goo applied to the bald spots on his head.

It was a special color-matched paint created to hide his hairlessness while he was performing. This was 1975, before he took to wearing a toupee, and I knew from a story I'd written that Sinatra had had his makeup man, Shotgun Britton, invent this trick. Shotgun was good. He'd created all the elaborate makeup for *Planet of the Apes,* and he knew what he was doing. Nobody beyond the first row would have dreamed. Unfortunately for Frank, however, the *Enquirer* was *in* the front row, and we'd be sure to tell everyone else. I knew The Boss would love that personal little grooming detail, and would want it written in somewhere.

The once-skinny matinee idol from Hoboken looked puffy. His gut stuck out and his tuxedo shirt strained against its studs. The moves were the same as I'd seen in old movies and TV shows, but now slowed down by the extra pounds.

I noticed that Sinatra's face was pitted near his ears. From my ringside seat just below the stage, I could see *EVERYTHING.* I could see his shoeshine and the rings on his fingers. I could see a special shadow makeup applied on his cheek to hide an area of puffiness. I could see that his eyes really *were* blue. I could hear his labored breath when he bent down. I could even see the hand-stitching on his expensive tux. I figured I'd better make mental notes of all these details, no matter how silly or minute, just like Pat Henry's bon mot about the yellow suit.

The show was incredible. Ol' Blue Eyes still had it, all right. The whole room was transfixed. He moved and caressed and pored over each song and got deep inside the music as if it were a woman he adored. I thought to myself, "Now I understand why he's such a legend, such a star." You just could not fault him musically. His own involvement in each song clutched and held you almost breathless.

After each number, his face just glowed. He'd comment, "That's such a pretty, pretty song." Or "That's a *great* song, isn't it?" It struck me that Frank Sinatra wasn't just a pushy Hollywood prima donna. He was a music lover. The phrasing was immaculate; he was exciting to watch. I stared and inadvertently caught his eye many times during the show. I thought, "God, I hope he'll remember my face later."

Then Frankie paused and toasted the audience with a sip of his usual—vodka rocks with a twist.

Suddenly, from the left wing, in walked John Denver. He was holding a huge glass of milk. Sinatra's audience went berserk. As the youthful Denver stood next to thick-set Frankie, Sinatra looked even heavier. Denver started kidding, "I beg your pardon for interrupting, but I wanted to tell you I got everything ready for the hike. You said you don't go out in the daylight, so I got a path all lit up."

Sinatra played along. "What do we do for refreshment?"

"I got a bar every fifty yards, Frank—and a pretty girl with not only drinks, but an oxygen tank."

"Get my hat. We'll go now," chimed Sinatra to laughs.

Denver proffered the milk. "I don't want you to drink this now, because it's pretty potent. It's got wheat germ oil in it, and honey, and protozoic protein."

Sinatra grimaced. "I just discovered. Milk ain't for *every* body."

Denver marched off, turned, and yelled, "See ya on the hike."

This would all fit great in my story of contrasts. I wondered what Sinatra was *really* thinking as he listened to the tumultuous cheers. Two women in back kept screaming, "JOHN DENVER, JOHN DENVER, JOHN DENVER," and finally Sinatra airily spat, *"Shaddap!*

"I'll make him Sicilian before I'm through widdhim," he smiled. He paused, then said, "He's cute. He looks like a butch Barbie doll. But I gotta teach him how to drink and fool around. Actually, it's dangerous being on the bill with him. I hear he's very critical of the press."

Ha ha, Frank. Truth was, of course, that Denver loved the press and vice versa—and, as everyone knew, Sinatra himself was the guy with the contentious media relations. Sinatra's little stage joke gave me a bit of a chill—here I was, front and center, a reporter, female to boot (remember Sinatra's famous "two dollar whore" line?), seated in his own house seats by his own #1 henchman Jilly, scheduled to meet up later with his other henchman and maybe even *himself,* fully intending to get the dish, the whole dish, and nothing but the dish. And right from the horse's mouth. And undercover. And all for the *National Enquirer.*

If Mom ever knew. If *Frank* ever knew.

I drank in every detail, knowing I'd soon have to write it all. Mr. Pope would love the way I was so close to the edge, not to mention the stage. Mr. Pope wouldn't care about Sinatra's performing magic. I knew I'd get the question, "Why did he come out of retirement?"

Mr. Pope would want to know if Frankie was broke, bored, a has-been, or just horny. And I'd have the answers from the star's own inner circle.

I'd already gotten some of it at dinner. Da Spider had told me, "Sinatra dried up sitting around retired. He needs all dat love he gets from the audience. See, one person, two people, a whole entourage, cannot satisfy his needs. An audience of twelve hundred people every night, dat's the only thing dat can. He gives love in his show. He aint' so good at giving it one on one. I don't think I wanna be around if he ever really has to retire. He'll be a junkie widout a fix."

Up on stage, Frank looked toward Denver's exit. "GO ON A HIKE? Me? When I got a guy carrying me to the john?" The audience howled. They loved Sinatra's surrender to dissipation.

When the show ended and the lights came up, our bill was brought to our table and the waiter whispered to me, "Just sign it. Compliments of Jilly."

****

We sat there, marveling at everything that had just happened, as twelve hundred people surged toward the exit. Why push and shove, when we had Spider and Frankie Eyelashes waiting expectantly for us outside. They weren't going anywhere this evening without us babes.

Finally, we strolled out and into the casino. It was full and bright and noisy with the clank of dropping coins, as we headed in the direction of the Hideaway Bar to meet Da Boys.

But first, I detoured into the ladies room, that bastion of total privacy. I went into an end stall, securely bolted the door, and opened my bag. Inside was my small portable cassette recorder. It was my prize new acquisition, one of the first hand-held Walkman-size tape recorders on the market. I'd ordered it from a catalog, and since joining the *Enquirer*, I went nowhere without it. It had a condenser mike on top, and was little bigger than the cassette it held.

I piled all the stuff in my purse under it, so that the recorder sat right at the top of the bag, just below where the zipper opened. I made sure it was solidly perched there, then zipped the bag just enough to hide the recorder but secretly expose the mike.

Voila! Ready to roll tape, I came back out and rejoined Tracy. Just before we got to the Hideaway entry, I reached into my bag and pushed the "record" button. I was rolling tape as we came in and spotted Da Boys. My heart was pounding so hard I thought it must show, and I just hoped I could keep my act together.

I had thirty minutes on side one of the tape, so I'd have to keep an eye on my watch and leave to turn the tape over in half an hour.

They sat, tux jackets unbuttoned, bow ties loosened, drinks lined up on the table, checking out the doorway every time a woman entered. In we strode, past several life-sized trees hung with shiny metal leaves, and headed for the darkly mirrored corner booth—exactly the one where I'd been told they always sat.

I discreetly scanned the group for Jilly, but he wasn't there. I'd hoped to fawn over him with a sexy thank you for the show. Instead, I spied Pat Henry, and of course, Spider. I swooned to my unctuous arachnid, "Ooooh, it was so exciting. We were in the *front row*. Ooh, Pat, you were very funny. Did you see it was us in the front row? So, will Frank be joining us? Ooooh, I'd love to tell him how I loved the show."

"Glad you enjoyed it, sweetheart." cooed Spider. "It's my pleasure to decorate the room for my man. But you's *my* woman, so don't you go thanking him *too* much."

I giggled and snuggled and silently cheered. Yes! I was *in!*

As we sat there, it was again apparent that Pat Henry was the leader of the pack. These lesser minions could only wish they were as close to Sinatra as Pat was. He held court with Da Boys, and he had a beautiful woman by his side. When he started talking, everyone else stopped. Of course, I understood that when Sinatra was around, Pat shifted gears and became a boss-pleasing gofer just like the others. He knew his place in the pecking order. But here with his group of Boys, he was the top pecker.

I remembered what the security guard had told me about women getting close to Sinatra through the insatiable comic. That night at the table, Henry kept referring to the degree of his manly endowment. It didn't seem to occur to him that this might offend the lady fair locked under his armpit.

Just then, Frankie Eyelashes plodded in and dumped his blubber-bound form into the booth. He was over six feet tall and garbed in an ill-fitting tux. He shifted sideways into the booth and ran his hand over his long wavy hair, slicked back and greasier than ever.

"This tux don't fit good," he complained. He preferred casual clothes, probably because they fit looser and gave his billowing frame more freedom. He certainly did have long eyelashes, and as he repeatedly blinked, they nearly caused a breeze. "And I can't get no sleep. I dunno what it is. I was up all last night. I just been up to da suite and tried lyin' down for a nap. I close my eyes, but nuttin' happens. Den it was time to come down. Frank been in yet?"

"Nah, he'll be here," said Pat Henry.

I looked at my watch to see how many minutes had elapsed since I'd turned on the tape. Thirteen down, seventeen minutes to go.

Frankie Eyelashes rubbed the rolls of fat on his jiggly stomach, scratched his greasy head, yawned cavernously, and eased a little closer to Tracy. I noticed again that very defined bulge under his coat as he strained to move. It was definitely in the shape of a gun. "I'm gonna go play da tables," he announced. "Ya wanna go, Colorado?" Tracy sputtered, caught in a dilemma. "Okay, but don't forget I want to meet Frank." "Yeah, yeah, we'll be back in time." And they were gone.

I coyly asked who gave Frankie Eyelashes his moniker, and Pat Henry gave the real lowdown. "He's got those girly lashes ever since he's a kid, and he needed a special name 'cause he takes good care-a me. He's got like a sacred trust from the Godfather in New Yawk, to watch out for me, see? Anyone tries to lay a hand on me, anyone tries to hurt me in any way, Frankie Eyelashes rubs him out."

"You mean—*kills* him?" I ventured.

"I mean kills him. Shoots him. This is da word from the Godfather in New Yawk, and you better believe Eyelashes follows it to the letter. He'd never let anyone hurt me. He deserves a standout name."

I'd ask Eyelashes at a more convenient time how many guys he'd bumped off in the interest of saving Pat Henry's bacon.

Tony Navarro was in the booth, slouched down next to a high-priced lady companion named Cheryl. She was in a long, low-cut red gown, sewn all over with silver sequins. She had long pitch-black hair, sparkling teeth, a pretty face. She laughed at everything anyone near her said. I figured that to get on in this group, maybe I should pay attention and learn something from her.

Tony reminded me of Winnie the Pooh's pessimistic pal Eeyore, the depressed donkey with the tail tacked on. He couldn't seem to find anything on earth to be happy about. It turns out Tony was an ex-comic now living in Houston, and an old buddy of Pat Henry.

"See that?" Tony said, nodding toward Cheryl. "I'm gonna get in trouble tonight. See that? That's trouble." Cheryl was flirting with the guy on the other side of her.

His name was Charlie, nickname Charlie da Head. Yes, that head was unusual—kind of like a distended egg. He wore sensitized sunglasses like Jilly's, and an expensively tailored Italian tux. He was exchanging numbers with Cheryl as he stared down her cleavage. "I won't forget you, honey. Honest, I wanna see you."

Next to Charlie was an enormous-chested, tittering blonde, falling out of her thin, all-revealing green dress, and drunkenly celebrating her twenty-first birthday. She wore no bra, and everything imaginable and unimaginable was showing. She was Lori, daughter of a big Vegas bookie, and she was known to all. She'd come up from Vegas where she hung out with Da Boys any time Sinatra played the Strip.

She whispered conspiratorially in my direction, "I've never been with Sinatra, but I know he wanted me one night. I went to his show and sat ringside, and I wore a *verrry* low-cut dress. All through the show, he kept staring at my chest, and afterwards, I got to meet him in a restaurant. His girlfriend—whatzername—Barbara Marx—was with him. But she left for the ladies room just when I got there. So Frank sez to me, 'Cheez, I'd give anything if I wasn't with my girl-friend tonight. I really wanna screw you.' Well," Lori huffed, "you can't have everything.

"I don't know if he'd remember me now. I heard that that Barbara thing isn't with him this time. She's a golddigger, you know—she used to be a showgirl and she married that ugly little toad Marx brother, Zippo or Blippo or something, just to get next to somebody famous." This was funny. Marx's soon to be ex-husband was actually Zeppo Marx, the business brother, and it's true, they were an odd couple—the statuesque blond Barbara towering over Zeppo's small clownish person.

Lori continued, "Anyhow, I hang out with the guys in Vegas. We get drunk, laugh, have a good time, fool around. I like to gamble. I like to play big stakes, like five hundred a hand."

Lori had apparently just learned about the contents of her mother's will. Turning to Charlie da Head, she waved her hand around the table and announced to all, "I think we oughta get rid of my mother, guys, and then I'll get lots and lots of money." Lori was slurring her words and her eyes were rolling. She giggled seductively and sidled up to Charlie. Tony crossed his arms and moaned.

As Lori kept busy with Charlie, plotting her mother's undoing, Spider put his arm around me and said in a low voice, "Dat broad never got next to Sinatra. We drink wit' her, but she's dinghy. She's empty upstairs. We humor her along 'cause she's nice. Beautiful too. And she's a few laughs when she gets drunk. But she comes on to everybody. She'd take us all on. She came on to me just last night. She's dinghy.

"Sinatra never wanted her. When Da Man wants somebody, he gets 'em. The other night, I spotted a great-looking dame in the cancellation line and took her to the show. Later on, when we were all partying, she caught Frank's eye too. He took a liking to her. She disappeared with Frank and gave him a blow job for two hours. He gave her a bundle. Ten times more than her normal fee.

"What am I gonna say?! Dames!! But you, honey, you like da Spider now, don't ya?" he oozed at me. Spider pushed his face into my hair as he whispered in my ear, and I hunched my shoulders and giggled, trying not to get unnerved. "Da Spider likes you. You got class. You got more dan air in your head. You wouldn't dump out on da Spider now, would ya honey?"

Oh Spider, if you only knew how dumped out upon you're going to be, once I have all the info I need!

I glanced down at the top of my bag, casually placed right next to me in the booth. From my vantage point, I could see the condenser mike peeking out, perfectly positioned to catch the flow of conversation. It was my insurance that I'd have the story word-for-word for Mr. Pope.

Next in the booth was George Paulson, a clean-cut young law school graduate who looked like he could be Wayne Newton's kid brother. George had a career making commercials. He'd never met this crowd until today, and the only reason he was along was to chaperone his extravagantly gorgeous red-haired sister Georgette.

On this evening, Georgette certainly appeared to be Pat Henry's woman—but I knew from covering the Hollywood beat that she was the wife of an ultra-millionaire L.A. businessman who had built and named after himself a medical center near the end of Hollywood Boulevard. From seeing them at Hollywood parties, and from all accounts in the papers, Georgette and her wealthy husband had always seemed a happily married couple. And I had always thought of her as a refined society lady.

But on this night, you wouldn't have guessed either of the above from her attire or her companion. She was poured into a cinch-waisted, calf-length black sequin dress, cut to the navel, and with a slash in the skirt that ran from the hem to eight inches above the knee. Her flaming red hair was puffed out big, and she looked exactly like Rita Hayworth in her prime. Only more so.

She sidled up to Pat, cooed, stared at his lips as he talked, and oohed and aahed at his every remark. None of this was lost on me. It was like I was trying to be, with Spider. Only more so.

Despite his blasé tough-guy act, Henry was riveted on her. Georgette purred, "I'm cold." Pat gave her his jacket. Georgette purred, "I want something sweet." Pat had the waiters running for a dessert menu.

When she left for the ladies room, all I could think was, "Good, she left first. I'll have to do the same thing any minute now when my tape runs out."

When she didn't come back for a while, Pat turned to one of the boys and said, "I wonder where Georgette is. I wonder if she's okay." He really cared, I observed. How sweet.

When she finally reappeared, he said to the group, "Hey, I'm glad she's back in one piece. I forgot I had five grand in the pocket of my jacket. I got worried."

Georgette cooed, "Oh Pat, I should have tipped the bathroom lady more." Everybody laughed raucously.

I giggled too, grabbing the diversion as a chance to look down at my handbag and check that the tape recorder was still positioned properly with its microphone peeking out.

Suddenly, my heart stopped. The tape recorder began making a high-pitched squeaking noise. I knew exactly what it was. Side One was used up and the machine must be signaling to turn the tape over. Did they notice that my eyes got as big as saucers and a cold sweat instantly appeared on my brow?

I cursed my luck that the first time I'd ever recorded a tape to the very end had to be now. I had had no idea an electronic signal would be emitted: a great feature if you're in a sit-down interview, but *not good* if you're secretly recording a bunch of Sinatra henchmen with your tape recorder hidden in your handbag.

I acted instinctively, grabbing my purse and dragging it down under the table, then pushing it with my foot to try and get the sound as far away from myself as possible. I squeezed Spider's arm hard and said, "Ooooh, my turn. I really have to *go...NOW!*" I meant it.

The savvy and ever-vigilant Spider perked his ears. "What's dat noise? You got a watch goin' off?" Thank God I didn't answer, for his question was directed to Tony Navarro, who was looking at his wrist and frowning. Under the table, I let out some of the shoulder strap and, with my foot, softly kicked the purse in Tony's direction.

I hoped I didn't sound nervous as I said, "Excuse me, girl for the john here." Purposely, I brushed my breast against Spider's arm to distract him from the shrill beep tone.

The others were still laughing and fawning over Georgette. I breathed a silent prayer of thanks that Frankie Eyelashes wasn't there with his gun, and I kept pushing against Spider toward the edge of the booth.

"Now wait a minute, baby girl—where are you heading to? You want da Spider to come along and help you?"

That's the last thing I wanted.

Panic was setting in as the piercing tone continued under the table. *"Beeeeeeeeeeeeeeeeep."* I clutched one end of my bag's shoulder strap under the table, pouted my lips and scrunched my face into a look of bathroom desperation. My anguish was real. "Spider, I mean it, I gotta *go*!"

"Oh all right, sweetheart. Tony turn that damn watch off, will ya?" Navarro was alternately scratching his head and tapping at his watch.

I slid out of the booth as Spider stood on the end giving me a courtly gesture with his arm, and as I rose, I pulled my bag after me from underneath. Tony was just starting to say, "Spider, dat ain't my watch. I got de alarm off. What iz dat?"

The last couple of sentences got fainter as I walked away at a smart pace, as calmly as I could, swinging my bag out in front of me, and then clutching it tightly to my chest. "Please God, don't let them call me back. Please God, don't let them come after me. Please God, don't let them put it together, and please God, don't let me feel Spider's iron hand grabbing me. Please, please, please." My whole upper body was virtually clenched as I rounded the corner out of the Hideaway Bar. My temples were pounding.

In the clear, I walked fast toward the ladies room, letting the beep continue amidst the noise of the casino. In the quiet of the ladies room, the attendant gave me a funny look as I shot past her, giving off a high electronic pitch. I ducked into the first stall, unzipped my purse, and reached inside to turn off my tape recorder. Then I put the top of the seat down and just sat there breathing heavily and trying to compose myself. It took several minutes before my heart rate slowed down.

It had been a close call.

When I came back to the booth, with Side Two rolling, everyone was in a great mood. This time, I knew I had exactly twenty-nine minutes, not thirty. I was synchronized. I felt positively high, knowing I could pull this off in dangerous company, even if things went wrong. Spider put his arm around my shoulder, but when I turned my head, I noticed the hand at the end of it was caressing the shoulder of Lori, the drunken twenty-one year old. This guy was a real operator, and I'd gotten away with a biggie.

****

About two-thirty AM, Pat Henry grabbed Georgette's wrist, looked at her watch, and began to move. "Gotta go," he said. "We're doing the employee show and I gotta open. Come on, Georgette."

As they walked out, I asked Spider, "Employee show? Could we go too?" Nothing ventured, nothing gained. We'd seen the Sinatra half, now we could check out the Denver stage show, too.

"Ya wanna go again? Yeah, we can go, but we may have to stand. Dis is just for the hotel personnel and they get first seating priority."

Later, I got the whole scoop on this employee show. It was a first for Harrah's Tahoe, or any big hotel for that matter. And it was *not* Sinatra's idea. A security chief told me later that John Denver decided to do it for the young people who work in the hotel and who were not allowed to attend, or even to purchase a ticket, to the Sinatra/ Denver pairing. Denver heard that people like busmen, cocktail waitresses, hotel clerks, security guards, table waiters, room service personnel, cleanup men, kitchen help couldn't even pay to see the show, and he was upset about this. My insider told me the next day, "Denver was also pissed off because all Sinatra's pals were getting in to see his, Denver's, show—but none of Denver's pals could crack the lines to get into Sinatra's or even Denver's own show. Sinatra wields a lot of weight with the pit bosses, and so his friends were all taken care of. A lot of the less aggressive Denver crowd got left out. So John went ahead and planned this show. He told Frank about it, and Frank agreed to come on and do a few numbers too, to open it. It was really Denver's show."

So now, my toupeed boyfriend and I stood in a side aisle amidst the frenzied, screaming showroomful of young hotel worker fans, and I silently took note of every detail of this behind-scenes extra event. Pat Henry came out, told a joke or two, but basically just introduced Frank. Then Sinatra did five numbers. He didn't banter much, just the songs, and then goodnight. It was only when John Denver came out that the crowd went loony. They screamed, they jumped up and down, they whistled, they danced in their places. they hollered Denver's trademark "Far Out!"

Denver did his entire night club show, plus two big encores. At first Spider had fidgeted, but then he actually got into the spirit and clapped.

I craned my neck to check out the room, and my eyes lighted on one booth at the very back of the showroom, where a heavy, balding man in a sky blue jacket kept jumping up and screaming out, "Denver's better than Sinatra. Sinatra's garbage compared to Denver."

"Far OUT!" screamed the man, time after time after time. "Denver's better than Sinatra."

In the booth with him I could see birthday girl Lori, who must have left after we did, plus a couple of hotel press agents, plus the guy who became my insider. The man jumping up and down and yelling "Far OUT!" was none other than...Jilly Rizzo.

At exactly five AM, as thunderous screams, applause, whistles and calls of "FAR OUT!" rang around him, Denver stepped up to the mike, raised his guitar above his head, and yelled, "Good Morning, my friends!" Then he and his sidemen rushed off and split for home. Spider grabbed my hand and we rushed too, up the aisle and out of the showroom, ahead of the masses.

Our places in the Hideaway booth were waiting for us. Pat Henry and Georgette were cuddled up as before, Tracy and Eyelashes had returned and Charlie da Head sat sipping a martini. A couple more guys had joined the group. "He's comin'," said Henry.

****

Sinatra showed at five-ten AM, in night owl mode. He cruised in with Jilly and Joey DiCarlo, the popular Italian who ran Pip's in L.A., and headed for his far corner booth where we all waited. By this time, everyone except Tracy and me was pretty well sloshed. A waiter had tucked two extra chairs along the outside edge of the booth's banquette table, and it was a crowd scene.

When Pat Henry saw Sinatra's form looming into the room, he began to push his way out of the booth, and to push Charlie out as well to make room for the Boss. But as he approached, Ol' Blue Eyes spotted the seating arrangement and put his hand up like a traffic cop. The Man looked at Henry and half kiddingly, half seriously said, "You rotten wop bastard. Why didn't you stay to watch my whole show?" Pat Henry and Georgette had apparently come back to the booth a while ago.

"You didn't see the whole thing," complained Sinatra.

Sinatra turned to Jilly and said, "Never trust a wop."

Pat Henry hemmed and hawed and said, "Hey, I saw it, Frank. I was right there in the wings. I saw you. You were great. They loved you. Those kids knew all your songs. They knew everything, the words, everything. It was great."

Sinatra sized up the scrumptious-looking Georgette clinging to Henry's arm and understood, perhaps, why Henry chose not to stay for the whole thing.

As the entourage shifted to make room, Frank waved his hand absently and said to Pat, "Don' move around, I'm not staying. We're meeting Agnew and Berle up in the private dining room for some espresso and a Sambucca. Looks like you got better things to do anyway," he added.

"Looks like you do too, Spider," Sinatra commented, while checking out the contents of my jumpsuit with a well-practiced eye.

"Hey Boss," Spider quickly offered, "Barbara here loved the show. Both shows. She's in love wid you."

"Love's a wonderful thing," said Sinatra, with a hint of a smile and a nod my way. I batted my eyes for all I was worth, saying nothing. Frankie boy took note of each woman in the booth, including a new entry, Monique, who'd been taking big sips of Charlie's martini. Her eyes wide, she tittered, held her little fingers up next to her mouth and waved, an inadvertent hiccup escaping at precisely the same moment.

Jilly just looked around the room in bodyguard fashion, hands clasped in front of him. He wasn't letting on if he recognized me and Tracy from earlier or not, and was apparently calmed down from his amazing showroom outburst only moments before.

Pat Henry turned to Georgette and said, "Hey, we stayed almost 'til the end, didn't we?" Georgette nodded.

From Sinatra, as from a General, came the command. "Okay, let's go."

With that, the tuxedoed legend, his imposing protector, and his L.A. club pal turned on their heels and moved fast through the Hideaway, heading back out into the casino, bound for Harrah's private dining room up above.

Spider leapt out of the booth and ran after them, clearly agitated that the Man had split and not sat down. Just a few moments later, Spider reappeared and announced to the group, "If we'd had the table arranged with enough room and the Old Man's place all cleared for him in the booth, he would have sat down and had a few drinks wid us. It pissed him off. You know he doesn't like to wait. You know he likes everything right."

Then, to me, "Well Schweet-heart, at least now you saw da Man, now you met da Man." Spider had turned his concentration totally to me and was wrapping his arm around my waist.

"No I didn't meet him. Not really. He left," I replied petulantly. "Ooh Spider, you've just *got* to put me next to him. I mean, *really* next to him, so I can talk to him."

I had nothing to lose by this demand.

Spider loved it. "You's a hard, hard woman, you is," he intoned. It made him feel like a big man, because he knew he had the power to do what I asked. "Tomorrow night, okay, baby? After he closes. You'll be wid me, and we'll go into his dressing room suite for a leetle bash, and den you can talk to him up close-like. Head to head-like. But remember, you's my woman. No hanky panky wid your idol, you gotta promise me."

"Oh Spider, of course not. I'm not that kind of girl anyway. I'm Catholic. We don't do things like that." I figured it wouldn't hurt to point this out to Spider, as an excuse for getting out of *his* clutches as well. Not that he'd actually honor such a premise, but it might just buy me a bit of time to escape, at the moment of truth.

Spider continued, "Tomorrow's his closing night, ya know, and dere'll be all his big time pals dere. Guaranteed to knock your sox off. Maybe some udder items too," he chuckled through his teeth, with a large grain of truth in the joke.

By this time, Eyelashes was leaning his entire weight against poor Tracy, who appeared squished into the booth's U-turn. She signaled to me with her eyes, "Let's get outa here," and I said to Spider, "Hey, let's go gambling. Will you teach me? Tracy wants to learn too."

"Well goils, it's late. But if you want to gamble, you come to da right place," said Spider in his best Dean Martin baritone. With that, we excused ourselves from the others, and headed out of the Hideaway straight for the nearest crap table.

As Da Boys rolled their dice, roving waitresses kept the complimentary drinks coming, and Da Boys didn't miss a round. Tracy and I ordered diet cokes. Not only were we nearly sober, we were at least two decades younger than Da Boys, and we figured we could easily outlast them.

We were right. About six AM, Eyelashes turned to Spider and said, "I can't go no more. I'm turnin' in." He grabbed Tracy by the arm, gesturing for her to come with him. She said, "I'm not ready to go. I wanna gamble some more. Come on Frankie, I wanna gamble some more." Eyelashes rolled his bloodshot eyes, shook his head wearily from side to side, and said, "Dat's it. You can gamble, I'm goin' to da suite to sleep."

Spider nuzzled his cologned head against my ear, and said, "Barbie babee, it's time for you to come on into da Spider's web. Let's go—I got a whole room all to myself in da suite." He kept pushing his head against my ear, and I thought any second his toupee would catch on my long dangly earring. I pulled away, saying, "I want to gamble some more too. Tracy and I are just getting good at this. Come on and teach us some more. Let's stay up all night."

Spider was too bombed and too exhausted and too broke by this time, so his protestations were not extreme.

"Naw honey, it's quittin' time for da Spider too. You wanna play, stay and play. We're going out on da boat tomorrow—so call us by noon and den come wid us." He meant Bill Harrah's private yacht. Spider figured his payoff would be tomorrow, so he would let me escape his web for tonight.

When da boys had safely boarded the nearest elevator, Tracy and I high-fived, then headed for our hotel and the sleep we too would need for the coming day.

****

We called Da Boys about twelve-thirty, never thinking they'd be up and around. Amazingly, they had already gone. Of course, they'd had no way to get in touch with us, since, with purposeful caution, we'd never given them the name or number of our hotel. So how could we complain at being left behind?

Still, we'd missed our chance to check out the yacht, which Harrah had also made available to Denver and his crew, as well as to Sinatra himself, earlier in the week. It was a big thing to have missed, and I was mad at myself. Now it was even more important to me to spend the afternoon productively, so I said to Tracy, "Let's head to Harrah's and go for the Sinatra suite."

Spider had told me that the "Old Man" was ensconced in the hotel's spectacular Star Suite, on the sixteenth floor. By hook or by crook, I was going to get in.

Since we didn't know how long we had before Da Boys returned and started buzzing around, I decided we'd split up. Tracy would spend the time checking out Bill Harrah's private dining room, where Sinatra had been the night before, and where he'd put on a couple of special dinners with his pals. I would do the suite.

When I emerged from the elevator on the sixteenth floor and stepped into the wide, quiet, pastel-colored hallway, the first thing I saw was a hotel maid's cart, with no maid in view.

I walked tentatively along the hall, wondering where she was, looking in every niche, finally opening a door at the end of the hall to discover a cleaning closet. Inside were piles of towels, cleaning supplies, brooms and cloths, stacks of Kleenex boxes, containers full of fancy soaps, some neatly folded uniforms, another loaded cart. I walked out again, back past the cart in the hallway, and casually up to the double doors marked "Star Suite." Incredibly, the right hand door was cracked open.

Like a cat burglar, I glanced both ways, then glanced both ways again—and then I pushed the door open a little wider and poked my head inside.

What I saw took my breath away. It was white, very white. Thick carpeting, elegant white furniture, richly pleated white drapes, lots of gold, a mirrored wet bar with gold and white barstools, high ceilings, a winding stairway. My heart was pounding very fast, not knowing if Frank Sinatra would suddenly appear around a corner and bust me, or if the maid was in there and would call security on me.

All at once, the tension was too much for me and I lost my nerve. I stepped back into the hallway, moving fast away from the door, in case anyone at all was around. But no one was. I was breathing hard. I needed to think. I walked back over to the cleaners closet and stepped inside.

Trying to calm my nerves, I stood under the dim overhead light and looked around again, my mind racing. Piles of towels, boxes of Kleenex, soaps, a few neatly folded uniforms. Wait a minute! *Uniforms!* I grabbed the top one and shook it out. It didn't even matter what size it was, it'd do. I stripped off my jeans and my sweater, threw them behind the door, and pulled the uniform over my head. I buttoned the sash as tightly as it would go, but I still swam in the large garment. It reached nearly down to my ankles. "All to the good," I thought. "It actually qualifies as a disguise." I reached into my purse for a hair-tie, pulled my hair back into a tight ponytail, and popped my hoop earrings off. I wiped the lipstick from my mouth, and got behind the loaded cart that was in the closet with me, pushing it gingerly into the doorway.

Craning my body above the cart, I peered into the hallway, looked in both directions, then shoved the heavy cart right into the hall, making for the open door of the suite. I passed the cart that was already there, shoved mine into the entry foyer and parked it, my heart pounding, my whole body tensed like a wound spring.

"Maid service," I called out loudly, grabbing a spray bottle and a couple of cloths off the cart and stepping forward into the living room. My feet literally sank into the expensive carpeting, as I listened for a reply of any kind.

Again I called out, "Maid service!"

Nothing. Was Sinatra deeply asleep somewhere in the suite—maybe up the winding stairway on the second floor? Did he not hear me? I'd heard he didn't rise until four-thirty PM. It was now only one-thirty. Would he awake and go into a rage at being disturbed? Then again, the door *had* been open. Was he out? Did he like the maids to clean up while he slept? Was someone else in the suite visiting him? Was the maid in the john? Just what was going on here??

I didn't linger too long over these puzzling questions, but walked quickly from room to room in the suite, spray bottle in hand, etching every detail into my brain. I peeked behind the heavy drapes out the picture windows, at a stunning view of the mountains and Lake Tahoe. I marveled at the richness of the furnishings and appointments, and could see why this suite was even more popular with VIP's than the Presidential Suite, which had been built especially for Bill Harrah and his favored guests.

I spotted a sky blue satin jacket thrown over a chair, with the words "Chairman of the Board" emblazoned over the left breast. Some golfing accessories were on the huge coffee table—a glove, some tees, and a couple boxes of golf balls. The grand piano was shiny, white, huge. Did I dare go up the winding stairway and into the vertically adjoining seventeenth floor suite above? *Of course I dared!* I was a maid. It was my job to clean, clean, clean.

Up the stairs I ascended, paying attention to my facial expression even though there was, presumably, no one there. In case I was caught in the act, I didn't want to look interested, overly observant, snoopy, sneaky, wide-eyed or just plain scared. I kept my face blank, all the while categorizing everything in every room. There were cigar ends in the ashtrays, there was an empty bottle of Rothschild Mouton Cadet, surrounded by a few cut crystal wine glasses with red dregs at the bottom. I picked up the bottle to see the label. 1964, a very good year. Nothing but the best for Frank Sinatra. That was an affirmative.

I tiptoed around the upper suite, full of dread and determination, a truly heart-stopping and irresistible combination. The door to the master suite was open. I held my breath and peered in, fully expecting to see the sleeping form of Frank Sinatra.

Empty. Bed unmade. Room service table with coffee hottle and big pile of half-eaten Danish. Towels and a few clothes strewn across a chair.

Again I called out, this time with my voice quavering, "Maid service."

No response.

My God! Sinatra wasn't here at all. What luck, what redoubtable luck. I scurried around, quickly checking out the bathroom and the walk-in closet which was hung with formal clothing and golf clothing, with lots of shoes lined up on the floor, There was also a door which led out of the suite, into the seventeenth floor hall. Frank could walk in on the sixteenth floor, and if need be, exit on the seventeenth, a convenient feature for him should he be dogged by some pusillanimous polecat of a reporter.

Not wishing to push my luck too far, I hurried back down the stairs, went to the foyer, and was just pushing my cart out the front, when I ran it smack into something. An involuntary cry escaped my lips. I'd collided with the other maid's, the *real* maid's, cart. The uniformed woman gasped and clutched at her own throat, startled to find someone else in her station. "What're you doing? What's going on? This is my area. Have you cleaned in there? Did Maurice tell you to come up here?"

"Uh, yes, ...uh...*yes,* Maurice told me. But I think I'm on the wrong floor. This isn't fifteen, is it. I thought I was on fifteen."

"No, this isn't fifteen. This is sixteen."

"Gosh, I'm sorry. I'm new and I guess I got confused. I wondered why there was a cart already in the hall. Yeah, I'm sorry."

The older woman had frowsy gray hair, weathered hands, a crisp uniform that fit, and a suspicious look on her face. "Well, you'd better get back down to fifteen. This here's Frank Sinatra's suite, and no newcomers clean in here."

"This is where Frank Sinatra stays?" I marveled in a hushed whisper.

"Yes, dearie. This is where Frank Sinatra himself stays."

"Oh, I admire him so much. He's such a great man. I knew he was appearing here, but I had no idea...."

"Yeah, well, someday you can tell your grandchildren you accidentally stepped into Frank Sinatra's suite."

"You don't think I could come in and help you for just a few minutes, do you? I'm a very good cleaner and I'll do whatever you tell me. It would be so wonderful to just see inside, you know what I mean? to see where the great man stays?"

It *never* hurts to ask.

Behind her gruffness, the woman was an old sweetie. "Well, okay. I know how excitin' it is. But just for a minute, then you'd better go to your own station, or Maurice will have both our hides." Obviously, Maurice was the King of All Cleaners.

Under the protective tutelage of my new benefactor, I stepped inside again, and checked everything out for a second time, getting a golden, calmer chance to refine my mental notes and add several new things I hadn't noticed while panicking the first time around.

The maid offered, "You know I usually never come up this early. Mr. Sinatra doesn't get up until late afternoon as a rule. Four-four thirty. But today, he went out to play golf early with Mr. Agnew and Mr. Berle and Mr. Ken Venturi, that big golfer guy. I heard it from the concierge. Then, sure enough, Maurice sent me up here early.

You're lucky. If Mr. Sinatra was here, you could never come in with me. He's very particular about having the same maid every day at the same time. He doesn't like surprises and he doesn't like extra people. He likes his privacy because in the afternoons, his friends come in and they like to order food, fool around, tell jokes, play the piano, and hang around together."

"Does he tip you?" I asked with wide eyes.

"Tip me? Honey, just pray that someday you get to clean for someone like Mr. Sinatra. The other day when I came in and did everything real special for him, real quiet-like, he tipped me what I make in a week. I'm sure when he leaves, he'll tip me again. He's real generous with everyone. My daughter's a cigarette girl downstairs and last night he gave her what she usually gets from the whole room all night. That's just for her, on top of the cigarettes, ya know. He's known all around the hotel for tipping big, real big. And he doesn't leave anyone out, not even the security guys. He gives hundred dollar bills to all the boys before he leaves."

I oohed and aahed and acted astounded, though I was aware of Sinatra's longtime reputation as a lavish tipper to the little guys in hotels where he worked.

"Awright, now go on with ya," said my friend. "And don't you dare tell anyone I let you come in here, or Maurice will hear about it *for sure*, and we'll both be in hot water up to our eyeballs. Now get down to fifteen."

I thanked her profusely while pulling the second cart out of the suite. Out in the hall, I dragged it back to the closet, then grabbed my clothes and beat it. I shoved open the door to the hotel stairway, hoiking my long maid's dress above my knees to avoid tripping over it, and then I flew on foot to the floor below. Just for good measure, I ran down one more floor, to fourteen, and quickly ducked into the maids' closet on that floor. Breathlessly, I shed my getup, undid my ponytail, and put my own clothes back on. The naughty impersonation and intrusion had been a thrill, it cannot be denied. Getting away with it had been even better.

I headed straight for the coffee shop where I found Tracy waiting for me in a booth. We ordered club sandwiches and compared notes. She'd scored in the private dining room too and had found a restaurant captain who let her in and told her all about it. Bill Harrah had spent what it would cost at that time for a whole mansion, $125,000, decorating the room, which seated just twelve. It was all in earth tones with expensive artwork, plus a special wall that featured electronically-opening etched bronze panels which contained surprises like a big-screen TV, Bill Harrah's private wine cache, buttons you pushed to summon various personnel, a state of the art music setup. Sinatra had hosted all his celebrity pals up there earlier in the week. Berle, Peck, Agnew, Rosalind Russell, a few other glamorous types. The source had even given Tracy the menu—pork tenderloin glazed with honey, and topped by a peach/pineapple/curry sauce.

Maybe we'd missed the *boat* this afternoon, but we hadn't missed the boat.

We were just finishing lunch about four o'clock when they found us in the coffee shop and sidled into our booth. Da Boys. They looked sunburned and a little wind-tousled. "What a groovy little boat dat was," crooned Spider. "We had a ball, got some rays, got a little color. They even let the speedboat down and Pat water-skied. On one ski yet. We woulda liked to take our goils, but they didn't call us."

"I'm *soooo* sorry, Spider," I apologized. "We stayed up all night after you left, and we were so tired that we overslept. We didn't even hear our wakeup call, can you believe that? We called you at twelve-thirty but you'd already left."

"Well, it was a good time. But this is a good time too—a good time to get with our goils. We's headin' up to da suite to do a little partyin', so come on wid us and we'll have ourselves a bawl, whadya say?"

Safety in numbers, Tracy and I both silently reasoned. "Sure, Spider, sure. We'd love to."

Ever the prince, Spider picked up our check, and held my arm at the elbow, leading me to the elevator and I knew not what. "I can handle myself. I'm cool. I'm Catholic, I'll just keep reminding him," I told myself, gathering resolution. This would just *have* to appeal to the Italian in him.

Once inside the suite, Da Boys sprawled over plush sofas, turned on the TV, broke out the beers and the champagne, and ordered a load of snacks from room service. "Yeah, the Old Man's out golfing today, udderwise we'd be hangin' in his suite up on sixteen," said Spider, adjusting his cream colored leisure suit, and smoothing his toupee in back.

"That must be some suite," I said, loving my little secret.

Pat Henry removed his trousers and lay on the sofa in his white jockey shorts, apparently uncaring that there were ladies present. Eyelashes stuffed his face with snacks and kept urging Tracy to do the same. Spider grabbed me by the hand and proceeded to lead me into one of the suite's bedrooms, hoping obviously to entrap me at last in the Spider's web. Of course, this was not about to happen, then or later. For now, I went totally shy on him, pulling away and heading back for the door in a befuddled fuss. Spider hadn't encountered this kind of reaction in his normal rounds and he really didn't know what to do except let me escape.

As we emerged from the room, Pat Henry revealed the depth of his crudeness. "Well, didja hump her?"

"No," replied Spider somewhat defensively, "but we gonna take care of that after while, later tonight, right honey? Right, honey? If she wants to be a Spiderette, that is. That's how she gonna earn her T-shirt. I figure she's a definite for later."

They were talking about me and my virtue as if I weren't even there. It suddenly struck me so funny that I nearly burst out laughing, but knew I'd better not. There were still arrangements to be made for our presence at the closing night cocktail party in Frank Sinatra's dressing room. Now utterly determined to nail me, Spider told us exactly where to be at exactly one AM, and warned me, "You's gonna owe da Spider for dat one, and no excuses."

It gave me the creeps to consider this ultimatum, but I had to have faith that my luck would continue, and that I could outsmart Da Spider.

On our way out of the hotel, I stopped over to my pit boss pal Paul, told him I'd met Spider and Jilly and been to the show, and that I was invited to the closing night cocktail party. "What's gonna happen at the party? Does Sinatra really sit around with everyone?"

"Yeah, he does. But he's set to leave Tahoe at two-thirty tonight. He's got a helicopter coming in to pick him and Jilly and a few others up and take them to their plane. But he always gives that party when he closes and he always has all the bigwigs and pals, so don't worry, you'll meet him. Just that he won't be staying for the whole party. He'll probably leave in the middle and just let everyone else stay and enjoy themselves."

"Wow, a helicopter. Where does it land? On the roof?"

"Nah, over on a parking lot outside. There's a tunnel that leads right from his dressing room to the helicopter pad, so he just strolls out whenever he's ready and leaves."

Back in our room, I schemed with Tracy. "When Sinatra leaves, I just *know* Da Boys will walk with him to the chopper. You don't actually think they'd stand around drinking in his dressing room, then just let him and Jilly leave all by themselves? No way! I'm going to bank that they'll all trot out with him to see him off, then come back for us." Tracy agreed. "So Tracy, as soon as they all leave the room, you'll play sick, and I'll say I have to help you to the ladies room—then we'll haul out of here before the boys get back from the helicopter.

"You'll double over and say you're going to throw up. That'll stop anyone from following us." Tracy loved it. "It won't be that tough to play sick around Eyelashes. I've been bilious ever since I met him."

As the hour grew near, we kitted up. I wore the slinky long silk jersey gown in hot pink. Tracy gave up her cowboy gear for a smart black cocktail dress. This was the moment of truth.

I bugged my handbag as before, and we left for the party.

Spider greeted me lavishly at the bottom of the stairway deep within the underground complex beneath the showroom. "He's here, baby. He just got offstage." Security guys crawled everywhere, but when Spider became our escort, we magically became OK. We were in like Flynn. Spider's hand on my arm was tight and hard. His banter exuded an edge of sexual expectation. He had no intention of letting me get away again tonight. Not after putting me in the same room with Sinatra, as promised. It made me nervous and I prayed a silent prayer that my pit boss pal was right—that Sinatra would leave mid-way through the party. I then prayed that my gut was right, and that when he left, his minions would scurry after him. We would then escape the room, escape the dreaded payoff, and make a very quick getaway out of the hotel and out of Tahoe.

These thoughts filled my mind as we approached the door to the dressing room, but the sight of Jilly Rizzo right by the door snapped me back. He was laughing it up with Sinatra's press agent, and he didn't interrupt himself just because we were there. Said Jilly, "Can't you see it now, if anyone ever got a-holt of what I said last night. Can't you see it up in quotes in the paper—JILLY SAYS SINATRA IS GARBAGE COMPARED TO DENVER."

The entire group nearly gagged themselves thinking of the scenario. "I can see it in the columns," convulsed Jilly. The press agent laughed louder and louder the more Jilly referred to what would happen if the press ever found out about his comments. "JILLY SAYS DENVER'S BETTER THAN SINATRA," Jilly called out, loud enough, in fact, for Sinatra to hear. The guffaws continued. I cringed. I *was* the press. I *had* found out. If my cover got blown tonight, I was definitely dead meat.

Led by Spider, we entered the dressing room—and there, in a brown upholstered leather chair sat the Man himself. He was wearing a light blue denim leisure suit and a red, white and blue shirt of that slinky synthetic seventies fabric, open at the neck, with a choker of beads and shells around his neck. He wore the same black boots I'd seen from the front row and the same gold pinky ring I recognized. He was joking with golf pro Venturi, saying, "I need more help, Venturi. You gotta help me."

I looked around the room and recognized a lot of famous faces— Sinatra's attorney Mickey Rudin; his musical arranger Don Costa and his missus; Roz Russell in a flame red Galanos gown, floor length; and a beautiful older lady whom someone pointed out as Irene Dunne. Roz Russell didn't look good. I knew she had been suffering for a long time with arthritis and had to take cortisone shots. They caused her to look puffy and pasty. But even so, she still had that fabulous aura, that Auntie Mame jaunt, that class. She was a true star. Sinatra must be very dichotomized, I thought, to attract this great lady one moment, and his crude pals the next. Roz Russell came over to Frank and gave him a huge hug before leaving early. He responded to her with enormous warmth, and kissed Irene Dunne too.

A Palm Springs restaurateur pal of Frank's was there with his wife, a caricature of seventies desert resort fashion. She dripped with heavy, hunky, flashy jewelry, contrasted against her wrinkled tan. Around her neck was a huge gold and turquoise creation reminiscent of an Indian squash flower. On every finger was a ring—turquoise, red coral, and an outsize marquis-cut diamond on her wedding finger. Her husband had black, slicked-down, wavy hair and wore a dark suit and a white shirt with a high Edwardian collar. They hovered around Sinatra.

Just then, John Denver and his wife Annie swept in, in a rush of fresh air. In his high-pitched western accent, Denver said, "I've been thinkin' Frank, we oughta keep workin' together. We gotta rent ourselves a *train* and just move across the country with our friends and families aboard, playin' everywhere we stop."

Sinatra said, "Yeah, kid, we'll have to think about that. Great idea. Maybe in the spring we oughta talk about it. But right now I'm booked until next Easter."

Aside, Sinatra said, "This kid has never sung in a saloon before, but he sure had the best teacher."

"Far out," grinned Denver.

They schmoozed, each in apparent awe of the other's drawing power. Sinatra embraced Denver and warmly bussed his country wife as they left, and Spider whispered in my ear, "I tell ya, he loves this kid and he loves this kid's wife. They really got ta him."

That night in Lake Tahoe, as John Denver and his Annie swept past me out of Frank Sinatra's dressing room, who could have guessed their destiny? They were blissful together that night, arm in arm, as John began his headlong hurtle into superstardom. No one could ever have guessed that in the early eighties this idyllic marriage would crumble, and that worse, in 1997, John Denver would plunge out of the sky in a small plane and crash to his death in the sea? Poof! Gone just like that at age fifty-three, gone before the brash and worldly saloon singer, thirty years his senior, who admired him so much. No one would have guessed in a million years.

"Yeah," said Spider. "Dose two kids really got ta Frank."

That night in Tahoe, Spider's next project was to get to *me*.

"Come on wit da Spider," he said, pulling me by the arm into the center of the room. I had reached into my bag and activated my tape recorder just a moment before. I was about to meet Frank Sinatra. I was going to get it on tape.

"Hey boss, dis here's my best goil Barbara. I got a Barbara too." Sinatra held out his hand, took mine, and raised it to his lips to kiss my fingertips. "There are beautiful Barbaras in this world," he said. His own Barbara, Mrs. Marx, wasn't with him, of course.

"Has Spider been behaving himself?"

"Not really," I replied, "but pretty close. He brought me here to meet you, so that's a big plus," I said breathily. Sinatra smiled and cased me, still holding onto my hand. Spider's grip tightened around my arm.

Just then, Jilly burst into the room wearing a battered Borsalino hat, brim pulled down over one ear and turned up on the other side.

"Hey Frank, how'dya like my lid?"

Sinatra smiled broadly as Jilly posed, hitched up his pants, looked both ways, and checked himself out in the mirror. "You look just like Al Capone, ya mug," said the Chairman. "If you walked into New York with that hat and those beads around your neck, you'd get shot at."

Jilly and the whole room dissolved into laughs, and Jilly said, "Hey Spider, gimme a scotch." Spider left me in the small group surrounding Sinatra.

I just listened and taped.

Sinatra would be working next in New Jersey. He said to Mickey Rudin, his lawyer. "I got a problem with the crime commission back there, but they got nothing on me. The prosecutor back there's an asshole and I'm gonna take care of him. I can't understand why they're giving me such a rough time. So I'm gonna nail this guy. It just pisses me off, that's all. I'll take care of it."

Someone brought up Sinatra's favorite topic—the press. Spider was back by now and chimed in, "You read that review they gave Paul Anka in L.A.?"

Sinatra steamed, "They panned the guy, can you imagine? They panned *Anka*. The only reason these asses in the press do something like that is to get attention. They get off on putting someone big down. Like this kid with the *L.A. Times*, Robert Hilburn. He's a real loser, that guy. He pans Anka and people notice him. He just wants to be controversial."

Spider reassured, "They all do it, all dose writers. They just do it to build demselves up. When they cut down somebody big, it makes dem feel big. It's just an ego thing for dem." There was a chorus of "yeahs" and one "Fuckin' A."

Beads of sweat began forming on my upper forehead. Would they notice my uneasy blush?

"Yeah, and don't even get me *started* on broads of the press," spat Frank. He nodded my way, "No offense to ladies like you, darling, but I just can't stand those sniveling press broads."

I could feel the top of my head sweating. It was just too bizarre.

For no apparent reason, Sinatra suddenly turned the conversation to other things. He said, "Anyhow, forget all that. We'll be in Palm Springs tomorrow. Do you know it snowed down there last June. Nobody knew how to handle it. We were sitting in Ruby Dunes when it started and the roof started leaking. Just started leaking, and Jilly was sitting there, and on both sides of him, the roof was leaking and he just sat there like this."

Sinatra put his two legs together and started imitating Jilly, dining and daintily dodging drips down both sides of him. Everyone roared.

Said Jilly, "Hey, we got a snowmobile and everything. It was June, for Chrissakes."

Sinatra's secretary Dorothy came in with Frankie Eyelashes following behind her, and Jilly told her to order more sky blue jackets, which had become real collector's items, but this time, to have them embroidered with obscene names. Eyelashes convulsed himself over the name Jilly said would appear on his new jacket: "One Ball." Jilly said to Dorothy, "Just tell them...the number One...and Ball...B-A-L-L. No, not bowel. BALL!"

Charlie Da Head described in lurid detail how Frankie Eyelashes could correct his problem of having but one testicle. Said Charlie, "All ya gotta do is take a trumpet mouthpiece, and you put it right in the top and blow hard and make two outa the other one. You gotta double time. Only a trumpet player could do dat."

The whole crowd howled hysterically. Eyelashes collapsed on a sofa, holding his ample stomach, the fat jiggling until he gasped for air, his face turning purple.

The anecdotes and the yocks went on. But all eyes were always riveted on Sinatra, including my own. Especially my own. All chairs were turned toward him, all coming through the door paid their respects to him immediately. The jokesters seemed to get some kind of silent permission from him to go on, as if he were an orchestra leader. Sinatra did not speak loudly and no conversation occurred around the edges of the room. All comments played to him. When he spoke, all ears craned to hear, and all heads bent inward, hanging on his every word.

Pat Henry got up, grabbed Spider by the neck, took a huge wheezing sniff of his hair and said, "I could get high like this." It sent Sinatra and pals into uproarious laughter, this imagery of Spider spreading airplane glue on his head to keep his hairpiece attached. I muffled my own laughter with my hand, but it escaped out the side of my mouth. Even Spider himself was breaking up.

The henchmen were a lot of fun and I could see why Sinatra loved traveling with them. Like a bunch of clowning, slightly prurient teenagers.

About fifteen or eighteen people were inside the dressing room, with another twenty-five laughing and talking in the hallway outside. Finally, Sinatra started checking out his watch. Jilly got up and said, "Hey Frank, the plane leaves at two-thirty, you know. We gotta be there at two-thirty." I sneaked a look at my own watch....two-fourteen AM. He'd be taking that walk through that tunnel any second, to board the waiting chopper, and I prayed hard that my instincts about his herd were correct—that they'd all walk him out. Jilly *had* said "we."

Frank rose and disappeared for a moment, then re-emerged with a leather flight bag slung over his shoulder. One by one, the guests, male and female, stood and kissed Sinatra goodbye. His salutations were personal and warm. "So long Ken, my pleasure," he said to Venturi. "See you here in October. I want those lessons." "Goodbye Russ." "Dorothy, see you tomorrow in Palm Springs." "Spider, stay loose. See you when you come to New York next month."

My blood chilled. Sinatra was saying goodbye to Spider *in the dressing room.* Did this mean Spider wouldn't go with him to the chopper? Did this mean I was nailed? I suddenly realized I was next in the farewell lineup and shook my head imperceptibly to get out of this horrible thought and back to the moment. Sinatra was standing right in front of me, leaning over to kiss me. I grabbed both of his hands, which were warm and fleshy. "Hey, doll, you're a pleasure. Watch out for that Spider's web now. Will I see you next time?"

As he bussed me on the cheek, I said, "I hope so. I'd like that."

Sinatra was nearly out the door now and Da Boys were lining up. He moved into the hall and so did Da Boys. I could still feel Spider's iron hand on my elbow, as he remained parked in the dressing room. Sinatra took off with Jilly at his side, and Da Boys started walking away. Still Spider clutched my arm.

Then he leaned over and planted a sloppy kiss on my cheek. "Wait here for da Spider, Doll. I'll be back as soon as the Old Man takes off, and we'll party. Dis is our night."

The relief almost made me faint. "I'll be right here, waiting," I lied in a near-whisper.

I stepped out into the hallway to see the entourage move like a seething wave behind Sinatra, all of them. It was just like I thought. It was just what an entourage is supposed to do.

Sinatra was gone. And now, so would we be.

I ran back into the dressing room and found Tracy. I whispered, "Okay, Tracy, they all went with him. Act sick and make it good."

She doubled over with a little groan, holding her hand over her mouth. "Aaargh. I don't feel so good. I think I drank too much," she said in hearing range of most of the room. "Oooh, I don't feel so good."

I put my arm around her and said, "Are you going to throw up?"

"Ohhh, I think I am..." and she gave some disgusting gulps. There was concern on a few faces, revulsion on others.

"Where's the ladies?" I asked loudly. "I've got to get her to a ladies room." Someone pointed out the door, loathe to have us use Sinatra's private bathroom inside the suite. "There's one down the hall out there." We moved into the hallway and I pretended to be looking around for a ladies room, all the while leading Tracy straight for the stairway that I knew led up into the casino.

I opened this door without a backward glance and led Tracy inside. Then we hoiked up our skirts and ran for dear life up the stairs, bursting breathlessly forth at the top, into the casino. Dodging players and cocktail waitresses, we raced across the entire length of the casino—glancing sideways at the showroom, and passing the Hideaway Bar in a blur.

Outside, beneath the entry canopy, I grabbed a large bill from my purse, along with my car's claim check, and threw them at the valet parker. My voice was shrill as I pleaded, "I need this car *NOW!*"

"Yes MA'AM!" he snapped, stuffing the bill into his pocket. Within a few moments he roared up with our rental car.

I careened out of the hotel's entry drive and sped back to our nearby motel, where we flew into our room, peeled our evening clothes off, threw on jeans and sweaters, and tossed everything into our bags. For good measure, I plopped my short blond wig on my head and Tracy donned a slouch hippie hat, just in case. Just in case "what" we didn't know, but by now adrenalin and paranoia had taken hold of us.

I checked out with cash, to leave no incriminating credit slips, and we jumped back into the car. As we drove up Tahoe's main drag, I couldn't shake the feeling we were being followed.

"We're going back to Reno. We're flying out of Reno. Who knows who's still at Tahoe airport." On the outskirts of Tahoe, we stopped at a general store/gas station and got some cokes and chips. Then we sailed the forty miles or so up to Reno, where at six AM we caught the first flight back to Los Angeles.

I wrote fifty-seven pages of copy, as my colleague Barbara Merlin transcribed my tapes, howling appreciatively with laughter for hour after hour. Markfield virtually ripped each page out of my typewriter as I finished it, cheering, "Great stuff, great stuff" with each new revelation. He urged, "Write everything, Sternig, even the bad language. Don't worry about what'll get printed. Mr. Pope wants every last detail. He wants to know every little thing Frankie did up there, whether it's fit to print or not. Mr. Pope is very, very happy with what you did."

When the story broke, in a highly cleansed version, it was a center spread—and it bore not my name, but a "house" byline. "Robert G. Smith" was an all-purpose name used on certain sensitive stories like this one, to protect reporters' identity. The last thing I wanted was my name on the story, especially because I was listed big as life in the L.A. phone directory and had no doubt Da Boys would put it together that I was the Barbara they'd met.

But even beyond protection from retribution, it turned out later that I'd need my anonymity amidst the Sinatra boys again.

At the *Enquirer,* I'd made a reputation, and in the next year or so, would be sent out undercover two more times on Sinatra stories.

I wasn't through with Spider and Da Boys, and they weren't through with me.

chapter

5

Hello Lantana

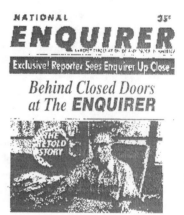

NATIONAL   35¢
ENQUIRER
Exclusive! Reporter Sees Enquirer Up Close

Behind Closed Doors
at The ENQUIRER

"Sternig, you're going to Lantana." Markfield called me into his office that morning to tell me it was time for my first command performance at the home office. "The Boss wants to meet you. He's very pleased with your work in general, but now your Sinatra story, well, he's impressed. Your stock is high, Sternig. The time is right for you to go down and let 'em see you. Trust me, it's the right thing to do."

It sounded a little mysterious and very political. But I had learned in my first two or three months with the *National Enquirer* that that's exactly the way things were at the home office.

In my mind I had only a vague and shadowy concept of *Enquirer* headquarters, of the sandy South Florida town called Lantana where it could be found, of my distant cousin colleagues who inhabited it, and of what it would be like to work there. I was going to stay for a month.

Markfield told me, "You won't be working for me for the next four weeks, but will be assigned to a team down there. You won't even be doing Hollywood stories. That's the whole idea. The Boss wants to make sure his California reporters can cover *all* the stories we do, not just Hollywood."

I'd heard editor Jan Goodwin's name a lot. She was a brain, an Easterner, and had a reputation as a real hardnose. She'd be my boss for the next four weeks. No more Alan-style coddling and tear-drying and nurturing and socializing. I was about to get thrown into the pool.

As I packed, I felt exhilarated, a condition that was becoming familiar. The prospect of a month in Florida every year had been one of the job's drawing cards for me. Turquoise waters, white sand, palm trees clacking in the warm winds, endless sunshine, and all those people wearing pastels. How bad could it be?

Deplaning at West Palm Beach airport after my red-eye flight, I felt a sultry blast of humidity engulf me as I gathered up my luggage. I'd already shed my light jacket as I got my rental car and set out for my hotel.

Dawn was just burgeoning, and the growing light cast a heavenly pinkish hue over the beautiful road along which I drove, passing lush greenery, exotic flowers, and elegant ironwork gates leading into posh unseen estates.

This was exquisite Palm Beach, oceanside haven for the rich and famous, and its dreamy beauty so struck me, that I pulled over to the side of the road, got out of my car, and leaned against it for a long time looking up at a flock of huge seabirds lazily drifting in the thermals high above me, circling around and around. It was six-fifteen AM.

When I finally found my hotel, my romantic bubble burst. To describe the inexplicably themed Hawaiian Ocean Inn, that famous Bette Davis line "What a dump!" immediately leapt to mind. There, cheek to jowl with all the gleaming high-rises of elegant Palm Beach Island stood this slightly run-down two-story motel, tacky, with only a half-hearted attempt at Hawaiian decor, comprised of an upswept Polynesian-style roof, a few unlit torches at the entrance, and a tiki mask on the sign.

It's where all out-of-town *Enquirer* reporters stayed, and tacky or no, it would be my home away from home for the next month.

I lugged my bags up the stairs, unpacked, and finally stood gratefully under a rejuvenating hot shower. Then I got dressed for my first day in Lantana.

****

One good thing about the Hawaiian: it was close to the office. I drove the few blocks, past sandy dunes topped by tufts of sawgrass, past white-haired joggers, past little wooden houses perched beside the sparkling waters. A few old men and young boys stood at the rail of a bridge over the glistening Intracoastal Waterway, absently dangling their fishing rods over the side as small boats putt-putted under the span.

I was seeing a typical and tranquil south Florida idyll, but believe me, it bore no relationship at all to what was going on just blocks away, in the private enclave that was the *National Enquirer's* home office.

I walked for the first time into this crowded, bustling newsroom, where typewriters clattered, telephones rang, buzzers buzzed, clouds of cigarette smoke rose, secretaries barked messages, editors walked hurriedly to and from meetings, and energy bristled in the air. The room was a sea of desks, lined up like phalanx, row by row, one behind the other. Editors sat amid their teams of reporters, plotting story strategy, composing leads, talking on the phone to out-of-town sources, managing problems from higher up.

Along the outside walls of the huge open room were glass enclosures reserved for certain big-shots, and in the middle of the newsroom were more glass-enclosed rooms. Into these rooms Mr. Pope would go for meetings with his top lieutenants, and here the paper's editor in chief, Iain Calder (nicknamed The Ice Pick in honor of his coldly pragmatic method of firing people), would review and criticize stories, grill quaking reporters, call his editors on the carpet, brainstorm about unfolding blockbusters, and always, always demand "more."

I stopped the first person I saw and asked where I could find Jan Goodwin.

Jan, sitting in the center of a long line of desks, was a bespectacled, short-blond-haired, kind of lumpy woman hunched over her desk. Her eyes looked beady due to her thick glasses, and her clothing was nondescript. When she greeted me, my heart sank. She seemed cold and forbidding, not fun-loving and enthusiastic like Alan. I figured she thought I must be a Hollywood poser, and probably had me on her own probation, which was fine. I intended to prove myself to her.

After the introductions and banal pleasantries had been exchanged, Jan gave me a place to work, then dumped a huge pile of newspapers on my desk. "Scan these for leads this morning and we'll go over them this afternoon." In *Enquirese*, a "lead" is a story idea, and my brief while in Florida was, "No Hollywood Leads" (short of any blockbusters called in by my L.A. insiders). Jan said, "You're looking for anything unusual, heroic, weird—anything with a sideways angle, but about real people, not celebrities."

That was an oddity of the *Enquirer.* They never thought of celebrities as real people, just as objects, or as big game on which it was always open season.

Jan then handed me a long list of non-Hollywood story genres featured in the pages of the *Enquirer:*

    *Child's Eye View,
    *Recipe for a Happy Marriage,
    *Tales of True Courage,
    *Near Death Experience,
    * Honesty in Action,
    * Odd Couples,
    *Animal Rescues,
    *UFOs,
    *Unexplained Phenomena...and more.

Compared to ferreting out Hollywood scoops, it seemed amazingly tame, straightforward, and did I dare say it? ...easy. "This may help you," she said, walking away.

As I sat there going through dozens of papers from around the country, the *Enquirer* parade streamed by me. One by one, the names I'd seen in bylines and heard about in office gossip for the past couple of months, gained faces. This was a cast of characters never to be forgotten.

There was John South, a tall, shambling, flyaway-haired Englishman, late thirties, a widower raising two young daughters, with a strong reputation for tenacity and his penchant for using certain sources others feared to touch with a ten-foot barge pole;

Harold Lewis, bon vivant, art collector, Palm Beach dweller, lover of his expense account, upper crust Englishman of infinite good taste, or at least doing a damn good imitation;

Paul Bannister, barrel-chested and burly, lively with a big laugh, English, specialist in UFO stories, devoted family guy;

Jack Grimshaw, handsome, saturnine, bad-boy blond, more going on than meets the eye, missing a thumb after reportedly blowing it off while playing with a handgun in a bar;

Charlie Parmiter, editor, smooth, predatory, the ruddy appearance of having had a boozy night before, looking up over half glasses, blond going gray, married to a Spanish woman and hankering to relocate to Spain, probably to escape some mess brewing in these parts;

Stewart Dickson, a cleft-chinned Scotsman and seasoned journalist, but apparently now in the depths of depression and dissipation, addicted to fine champagne, sick with liver complaints though only thirty-four, cynical, brooding, very expensive tastes, on his fifth month of driving a rental car he could no longer afford to return, Peter Pan in need of a mom;

John Harris, towering, slow-drawling southern reporter, reliable, scuff-shoed, thick glasses, down home affable, just back from a Mr. Pope Special, "In Search of Utopia," which had taken him clear around the world at company expense of twenty-five thousand dollars, only to conclude to The Boss, "Well sir, I can honestly tell yew there is no Utopia—it's right here in ahr back yard" (He was fired a few weeks later);

John Cathcart, John Bell, Brian Wells, Paul Levy, Mike Hoy, Alistair Gregor ... there were of course many more—editors, reporters, executives. Each had his own behind-scenes story.

I was the only female staff reporter, apart from my Tahoe cohort Tracy Cabot, who was still on tryout. Jan Goodwin was the only female editor. There were no females at all above Jan.

A young British reporter named Malcolm Boyes breezed by my desk with an impish grin that crinkled his eyes at the edges, a "Keep on Truckin' " boot walk, and nonstop flirtatious cracks. He was Jan's star reporter.

"Drink after work?" he invited. He was so cute that I accepted, thinking Lantana might turn out to be more fun than I'd envisioned.

There was apparently all sorts of hanky panky going on in the office. I learned that the secretaries, or editorial assistants as they were known, all dated the reporters. Most were local high school graduates from the surrounding small communities, who had had little hope of careers with any sophistication, future, or connection to the greater world ... that is, until the *Enquirer* arrived on their doorstep in Lantana. For them, a clerical job at the paper was a passport to the periphery of adventure, to romance (or at least playtime) with people like they'd never met before, and to advancement. If romance became part of the deal, all the better. The guys were undeniably appealing and exciting. And all had plenty of dough, particularly by local standards, from their well-paid reporting jobs.

Why not? It gave these girls a chance at a better life, and also, it was the seventies and there was no AIDS to worry about. Some of them ended up marrying their guys. Some of them were having clandestine affairs with their married bosses. Some of them were married themselves and now made more than their husbands. Some were married and made hay fooling around. A couple ended up aspiring to their boyfriends' well-paid jobs and struggling to become journalists themselves—"by injection," as the guys so crudely put it.

The truth is, Mr. Pope agreed to give more than one of these ambitious girls her true big chance in life: the famous *Enquirer* tryout. Editors and interested reporters helped and nurtured secretaries who wanted to move up and become reporters, and sometimes even did the writing for them until they got the hang of it. A few of these ladies passed, blossomed, and went on to their own successful careers in the world of tabloids.

For all his chauvinism and love of professional expertise, The Boss ironically displayed that degree of feminist paternalism. Or maybe he just liked the bald-faced pluck of people with aspirations. Or maybe he enjoyed pulling people's life-strings. Or maybe he wanted to sleep with them. All those rumors went around.

So, for all its outward appearance of pure professional tension, the *Enquirer,* like any company, had its undercurrent of personal connections holding everyone together.

And, being the new girl on the block in this milieu, I was not to be ignored. I got noticed and included.

Charlie Parmiter took me out for a gourmet Palm Beach dinner at the stylish Petite Marmite on famed Worth Avenue, and during dessert, invited me to Key West for the weekend. Only reluctantly and only when I pushed the question, did he admit that he had a wife somewhere. I declined the outing.

Ken Potter invited me to a blowout birthday bash with all the top reporters at his house on the Friday. Over the weekend, I was slated for a deep-sea fishing expedition with Jack Grimshaw and Stewart Dickson, and there were nightly after-work gatherings at popular local hangouts called the New England Oyster House and Nostalgia. My calendar was almost as busy as it was in Hollywood.

But that first evening, Malcolm Boyes took me, of all places, to the Hawaiian. Right at the beach end of the motel, fronting the sand, was the Hawaiian Bar & Grill. This instantly proved its reputation as "the" *Enquirer* watering hole. Except that water was the only drink nobody ordered. This was a hard-drinking crowd, and everyone at the bar was from the *Enquirer.* A few old folks and T-shirt clad tourists sat at tables munching on fried fish and chips or hamburgers, but mostly, it was *Enquirer* staffers, and they came here to drink.

As Malcolm and I got our brews and headed out to the pool deck overlooking the sand and the sea, I spotted a couple of other reporters in heavy confabs, one or two laughing with obviously local ladies, and an older married editor nuzzling a woman who seemed to be enjoying his attentions. It reminded me of the Golf Club, another hangout for British journalists, in Fleet Street, where many of these reporters had started their careers. Except that with the Hawaiian, you had the beach a few steps away, instead of the streets of London.

The talk was all about work, assignments, travel, The Boss, California, expenses. I noticed stares from my colleagues, and Malcolm told me, "Everyone knows who you are, Babs. You've pulled in quite the stories, and you're making quite the impression." It made me feel great, considering that many of my new colleagues were already hard-bitten tabloid reporters and nobody's fool. My advantage, and I knew it, was that I'd been covering Hollywood from the inside for several years and I had connections these good reporters simply did not have.

Malcolm added his personal admiration, which gave me a little glow. I'd heard about his romantic conquests all the way across the country, and could see from his playboy cuteness and the arm moving around my shoulder that the tales must be true. Not wishing to be added to any lists, I decided to play it cool and to aim instead for playful friendship with Malcolm. I trusted him as a professional, knew he was a good reporter, and could see he was a savvy guy.

I gave him a kiss on the cheek at my door about midnight and he left whistling. With the skinny which Malcolm had given me on my Florida reputation, Alan's words finally sunk in. My stock *was* high with The Boss.

I resolved that the next morning I would introduce myself to the famous Mr. Pope.

The first day, someone had pointed him out to me. Though I didn't know all the stories yet, I gathered he must be quite a formal sort, insisting on being called "Mr. Pope," even by his closest lieutenants.

I was a little surprised when I saw him—a tall, somehow colorless, graying guy about fifty, holding his glasses in his hand, walking from the executive offices to those central glass enclosures without making eye contact with anyone, and then back again, to disappear into his private inner sanctum. He didn't look too forbidding. In fact, he looked like he could have been from office services, checking the floor to see if anyone needed supplies. However, outward appearances notwithstanding, he *was* The Boss. And outward appearances notwithstanding, everyone did his bidding, no matter what it was.

One of the first rules of thumb I had learned in business was to make a good first impression and to let the guy in charge know who you are. I got my chance to let Mr. Pope know about ten o'clock the next morning.

He came forth from his office, walking toward the newsroom, just as I headed down the same hallway toward him. There he was. There I was. It was perfect. No one else was around. "Good morning, Mr. Pope," I chirped clearly, extending my right hand. "I'm Barbara Sternig, your new reporter from California."

Something was wrong. Mr. Pope's whole body jerked backward

away from me, shock on his face, his hands pulling back toward his shoulders. I'd done something totally wrong, it was plain. Instead of smiling and greeting me, Mr. Pope just stood there looking a little horrified. I stood in abeyance, my hand still extended toward him, my smile crumbling. Miserably, I added, "Uh, thank you for bringing me to the home office."

Taking pity on my unwanted hand, still sticking out toward him, The Boss grabbed it by the fingertips and gave it a cursory wiggle. "Yes, Barbara, glad you made it. Glad to have you."

With that, he resumed his eyes-ahead route toward the middle of the room to meet with one of his upper-echelon managers. As for me, I scurried to the ladies room and tried to recover myself.

When I related the incident to Malcolm later, he'd already heard about it. He said, "You know Babs, you'd better watch your wardrobe too, while you're here." I thought I looked pretty smart, businesslike yet ready for the sticky heat of Florida, in a darkly patterned silk trouser suit with open jacket and a matching halter top underneath.

Malcolm informed me, "Anyone wearing a halter top gets sent home."

I had blown it badly. Number one, you don't talk to The Boss until he talks to you. Number two, you dress along the same lines as The Boss. Nobody had bothered to warn me. People had been fired for less.

I'd have to learn the rest of the unspoken rules immediately, and watch it during the coming month, lest it be my last.

6

The Hunt for Burton

I'd been an *Enquirer* reporter for eight or nine months when Richard Burton, fresh out of his second marriage to Elizabeth Taylor, took up with model Susy Hunt, estranged wife of British racecar driver James Hunt.

As with every *Enquirer* assignment, I never dreamed I'd end up getting as close as I did to everyone involved in the situation, and I mean "hands on."

The deal was, in March of 1976, dashing driver Hunt had come to L.A. to compete in the Long Beach Grand Prix, and I was assigned to do an extensive series of interviews with him before the race, about Susy and Burton.

The *Enquirer* was so hot for his inside story about losing Susy to the magnetic, hard-drinking Welshman and ex-husband of Liz Taylor, that we arranged to pay Hunt fifty thousand dollars to talk to us. Even today, it's still a lot. Hunt would give us a take on the story that nobody else had. The world was shocked not so much by Taylor and Burton's second split-up, but much more by Burton's instantaneous leap into a September-May romance with the leggy young English model.

I had seen the pictures of dumped husband James Hunt in the papers. A tall, somewhat angular blond chap, he had those very clean, kind of sharp upper-crust British good looks, tinged with a little slyness. He also had a big reputation as a ladies man.

He was ensconced in a stateroom on board the Queen Mary, the historic ocean liner permanently moored at Long Beach, California, and now converted into a stylish hotel. It was serving as local digs for a lot of the Grand Prix drivers during their stay.

As I came on board for the first time to meet James Hunt and set the deal, I cannot deny that because of his reputation, I wondered what, besides the interviews, might happen, and if he'd be attracted to me. If he weren't, that would make interviewing more difficult—and if he were, that might make interviewing more difficult too.

As it turned out, he was but it didn't.

We would have to be huddled for three days in his staterooms on board the hotel/ship, first to agree on the terms of our money deal, then to extract from his brain every intimate detail about him and Susy, plus every intimate detail he knew about her and Richard Burton.

Every day, I'd arrive at the ship and have to track him down. Hunt changed cabins every night, not seeking to avoid the paparazzi, none of whom seemed to have twigged that he was in town a week before the race—but instead, because he was trying to find a room that was big enough, as he said, "to swing a cat in."

I must admit, I found him appealing. Cute, athletic and attractive, he made it plain he liked me too.

The staterooms on the Queen Mary are conducive to closeness. Why? Because they're little. As oceangoing cabins, they had been designed to get maximum luxury into minimum space. The deck which was turned into a hotel, the Promenade Deck, was the poshest one of all during the ship's lifetime. Its burnished first-class staterooms, once seagoing home to film stars and famous politicians, were small compared to a real hotel, but they reeked of glamour and history.

Hunt's first suite had beautiful wood paneling inlaid with a thirties art deco design of lithe girls with long scarves, obviously original to the ship. There was a thick blue spread over the bed, elegantly sewn with a nautical crest, and pale two-tone wood chairs and tables. I wondered if Clark Gable or Spencer Tracy had ever sat around on them. The cabin featured a port-hole with a big screw-type clamp that opened and closed it. Outside, seagulls squawked and flew by at eye level. There was a smaller room adjoining, which must have been for milady's maid during transatlantic crossings of another era. Now it was a sort of dressing room.

James and I sat at a table in the suite and went over the *Enquirer's* offer and the complicated payment agreement which contained all sorts of extra clauses that let us off the hook if we didn't publish. Actually, I thought he was pretty off-handed as he signed it, and I figured he must want to talk. I turned on my tape recorder and began at the beginning.

He leaned forward as we taped, and began to tell the intimate story of his life with Susy. He freely spilled, answering even my most impertinent questions. During the hours of our first interview, he kept pulling his chair in until finally, his muscular leg was touching mine. It was pretty sexy, and I used the opportunity to ask the even more personal questions that were part and parcel of every *Enquirer* story. What was their marriage like? Did the sex go bad? Was he unfaithful? Was she? What led her into Burton's waiting arms? As he told the sad tale of how he'd blown it with the girl of his dreams and lost her to the charismatic Burton, I almost thought he wanted me to put my arms around him and comfort him, and I'm sure it was at least partly true.

James had met the delectable and, I gathered, somewhat naive Susy at a tennis club in Spain two years previous, and they'd hit it off instantly. When it looked like he'd lose her because of all the time he spent away racing, he proposed marriage to win her back, and she accepted.

He lamented about the male dilemma which had confronted him, pitting his devotion to an exciting career against the needs of a devoted wife. While he was off globe-trotting on his grueling racing schedule, she was miserable and pining at home along the Costa del Sol. They'd only been married a year, but things weren't going well. James encouraged Susy to find interests of her own, and she half-heartedly tried tennis and horseback riding. During their Christmastime visit to Gstaad, Switzerland, just three months ago, she had finally obliged him and locked onto an interest. His name was Richard Burton.

Burton at fifty was on his doomed second go-around with the tempestuous Elizabeth Taylor, and they had passed a quiet Christmas at their beloved Swiss chalet in Gstaad that December of 1975. Meantime, the Hunts were popular guests among the glitterati of Gstaad, including Roman Polanski and a host of European film stars.

James moaned that when he jetted off to drive a race somewhere right after New Year, he was so glad that Susy was enjoying herself at Gstaad that he decided to leave her there on her own. As fate would have it, she was eventually invited to the Burtons' home, and the rest, as we say, is history.

It had been well reported that as James continued his world racing travels, Susy went to New York with her famous new-found friends, sharing a suite with another member of the Burton entourage, and finally, openly romancing with Richard. Elizabeth was there too, of course, and the press, including us, had a field day chasing both Burtons and Susy relentlessly.

James Hunt gave me all the first-person stuff from his point of view—his anguished telephone conversations with Susy, not knowing if Burton was standing in the room with her—the weirdness of knowing Elizabeth Taylor was there too, and probably madder than a hornet at Susy—how he knew his prolonged and frequent absences had ruined things for him and Susy—how he still loved her but did not begrudge her a chance for happiness.

Bottom line, Elizabeth and Richard split up, Elizabeth left, the gorgeous twenty-eight-year-old Susy moved in with Burton, and everyone figured they'd get married once his divorce from La Liz was final for a second time.

Ruefully, James admitted to me how Susy told him over the phone that she and Burton were in love and planning marriage. He seemed genuinely near tears relating how his wife announced she and Richard would both get quickie divorces in Nevada. I felt sorry for the guy. I think he was truly conflicted. He hadn't been there for Susy, and that's why she left him—yet he hated thinking of her in the arms of someone else.

At the same time, I also had a feeling that James was a little proud that if it had to happen, the guy who stole his wife was no one less than the world-famous Richard Burton. How flattering that a mega-personality like Burton shared his taste in women. Shared his actual woman, for that matter. Not that James needed more affirmation, being a popular racing star, but this gave him a whole new cachet—the guy whose gorgeous wife Richard Burton wanted and stole.

Could be useful in playing for sympathy, as he'd just done with me.

Presently, Burton was about to open in his starring role in the play "*Equus*" in New York, so the lovebirds would have to wait until he finished the play before they could take time to sit it out in Nevada for six weeks to establish pseudo-residency there, thus qualifying for quickie divorces. Then they could wed. It was now March. They would go to Nevada in May, and, we could only speculate, have a summer wedding.

While it was obvious that James Hunt's macho ego had taken a hit, it appeared he was not planning to curl up and die. From the way he looked at me, checking out details of my figure, I felt even at this moment that he'd recovered somewhat from his broken heart.

Off the record, he told me he was worried that Susy was hitching up with an unpredictable drunk, Burton's fabled reputation as a drinker having preceded him. But apparently, when Hunt finally talked to Burton on the phone, he was impressed with the famous man. It seemed Burton was ready to let Susy help him reform. In the end, all Hunt could do was ask the actor to take care of Susy, love her, and be good to her. Hunt said Burton's legendary velvet voice was very firm and strong when he assured the racer he loved Susy and very much intended to look after her.

I thought that was a nice touch on everyone's part, although it was confusing who was playing caretaker to whom.

Hunt had later met Burton in person, and I was all ears as he described the man's enormous presence and of course, that voice. I eagerly lapped up every detail, as I'd always thought Richard Burton represented the very definition of star quality. I kind of loved all his flaws and his troubled mind, and I thoroughly related to Susy's falling into his needy arms. Be that as it may, Hunt still seemed concerned that Burton might not be good enough for his wife.

Hunt and I dined together after concluding our first day of interviewing, and I could see why the ladies loved him. He was handsome, playful, and charming. We exchanged gay banter in the posh Churchill's restaurant on board the ship, then strolled around the Queen Mary's fabled decks poking into the shops and exploring the public areas. Hunt pushed his arm through mine as we walked, but made no other moves or suggestions. Classy. Still, I reckoned it wouldn't be too tough for any girl he fancied to have an affair with him if she wanted it. All one would have to do is drop a few not too oblique hints.

Hunt was definitely the playboy type, and while I found him appealing, I wasn't into playboys. I had a handsome and reliable boyfriend. It did strike me as ironic, however, that I was interviewing this exciting, attractive Englishman on board a ship, when my real-life English boyfriend just happened to work on board what? On board a ship! Alan Bell and I had met in the months before I joined the *Enquirer,* during my days as the Magician's Assistant at sea. So thoughts about cute Alan, a real officer on a real ship, who'd be in port on Friday as he was every week, kept me focused on the business at hand with no problem.

The signals I gave Hunt were purely those of a professional young reporter.

That's why I was a little stunned when I arrived in his suite on the afternoon before Grand Prix weekend. After our three days of interviews, I'd spent a long hard day and night at my desk writing a twenty-five page account of all James had revealed. He'd been promised copy approval, so I was bringing the finished story to him to read. As usual, he had a new cabin. I knocked on the door, and when it opened, James Hunt stood there in his jockey shorts.

I said, "Oh, sorry, shall I come back in a minute?"

"No, no. Come on in. I was just having a nap. Been driving all morning."

"Well, okay, long as you don't mind. I've finished the story and have it for you, as promised."

The lanky driver had a great body. Very muscular, thin, with a hairless chest, washboard stomach. You could tell he worked out. Unselfconsciously, he walked over to the rumpled bed, got back in under the covers, and patted the edge, motioning for me to come sit down. I looked around the new cabin, and there was no table or chair.

"Hmmm, you don't mind?" I ventured, wondering if he had planned anything more than the reading of my copy.

"No, of course not. It's comfy. Now let's see the story."

I handed him the pages and he began leafing through them, pencil in hand. He made a few changes, poring over the copy for about forty minutes, during which I got up, walked around the room, ordered a tea tray from room service, drank the tea, and sat back down again. Finally, Hunt laid the story down on the covers.

"Hey, that's amazing. It's just what I said, only it's all orderly and makes sense. I've enjoyed this," he complimented.

"Thanks," I smiled. "You've been great to work with. Now let's just hope they publish it and you get the money."

He raised his eyebrows and smiled, "Yes, that'd be lovely."

I ventured, "So now that we're all done, how about tickets to your race? I want to see you do all this exciting Formula One stuff you've been talking about."

"Well, of course. Want some pit passes? Actually, I already took care of it. There are four passes in that envelope on top of the bureau, just in case you want to bring a few friends. Here, all you do is ask for me, and you'll be shown right to our spot on the track. You can watch the whole race from there."

"Hey, James, that is awesome. Thanks very much." That settled, I picked up the story with his scribbled changes and his initials at the bottom of each page, and began to put it into my leather portfolio.

Suddenly, James grabbed my arm and pulled me down onto the bed. He leaned up toward me, and kissed me on the mouth. I was taken aback, began to push him away, and then realized things were going to start happening fast if I didn't extricate myself and head for the door.

"You're very sexy, James, and really attractive—but I gotta go. Florida's waiting for this." I reached for my portfolio, but all the while, he did not release his arms from around me, and began to fiddle with the buttons on the back of my blouse. I could feel him pulsing as he held me strongly against his torso.

"No really, I do have to go. Gotta go, gotta go—bye James—but I'll see you Sunday at the race, no worry. I'll be cheering you on." I shoved his body hard, freeing myself, and got up, smoothing my hair and my skirt. I grabbed the pages, smiled and gave a small wave, and stepped out into the mile-long alleyway of the hotel ship.

"What cheek," I thought. "I *know* Richard Burton would have been smoother."

*****

Two months later, Richard Burton finished his triumphant run as the psychiatrist in *"Equus,"* checked out of Gotham's Lombardy Hotel, and flew straight to L.A. with Susy Hunt for a little rest before Vegas.

Even though the famous lovebirds arrived in great secrecy, a close real estate contact of mine called me at home to convey the inside dope. They'd rented a house high in the secluded hills, at the end of a narrow winding road called Beverlycrest Drive. "I handled it myself," she chirped. "Burton was as excited as a bridegroom."

I immediately rang my editor, a marvelously brainy and intuitive but alcoholic Scotsman. "Burton and Susy are here," I announced excitedly. "A contact just gave me the address of the house they've rented."

"Bloody great," he intoned. "When you get into the office, we'll have a meeting and then I'll want you to go up and doorstep them."

I hated door-stepping. It was the term we used for walking up to the front door of a star's home, knocking, and then trying for an interview cold. If a maid answered, you'd try to get her to let you in. If the star answered, you'd gulp and try anything to get them to answer a few questions. The whole endeavor rarely resulted in anything but rejection or horrified outrage from whomever answered the door. Stars had punched reporters, called the cops, screamed, and generally reacted the way any sane person would. Bad enough we knew where they lived, but to actually come up to the door and knock exceeded most people's tolerance.

Door-stepping was my least favorite approach to a story, and I'd usually do anything to get out of it.

But nobody even knew Burton and Susy were in town, so going through the usual publicity channels would be useless. Their public relations people would never admit they were in town, much less by any remote stretch set up an at-home interview for the *Enquirer.* Still, out of curiosity and thoroughness, I placed a call to Burton's press rep. I was brusquely told that Burton was resting somewhere in seclusion after closing in his play and nobody even knew where he was.

Silently adding, "Nobody except me," I put the phone down and went to meet with my editor. We decided an intimate story about Burton and Susy's life together would make the paper, and I'd have to figure out how to get it. Accepting that I was unlikely to be invited in for tea and rude questions, I resigned myself to a stab at door-stepping.

I headed west up Sunset Boulevard in the brilliant May sunshine. It was a stunning blue-sky spring day, about seventy degrees. Beverly Hills was manicured, green, lush, perfect. No smog in the air. I swung upward into the hills of Beverly and onto Beverlycrest Drive.

Staring out the window at each address as I snaked up the narrow foliage-lined road, I came to the street number my friend had given me for the Burton love nest. It was a rambling ranch house, nestled into the curve of a hairpin turn on the scenic street. The curve wound steeply down past it, so you could look back up a high bluff from round the bend and see the house above—or at least you could see the neat wooden fence that surrounded what must have been the house's back yard.

I drove the whole thing just to scope it out, and saw that the hill behind the house wasn't too steep to climb. Looking up, I saw that if I were to climb it, I could stand at the top, by the fence, and be hidden by all the greenery that hung over and around it. After satisfying myself about the lay of the land, I turned my car around, and drove it back up around the hairpin curve, passing the front of the house again. About a quarter block past the romantically situated home, I pulled over on the opposite side of the street.

I turned off the engine, picked up a newspaper, and pretended to read it as I took a moment to get my ideas together. Just then, a UPS truck drew carefully up the skinny street and stopped in front of the house. I watched in fascination, thinking, "Wonderful, someone else can do my ground work for me."

Out popped the brown-clad driver, holding a box. He bounded up the front walk of the perfectly groomed yard, seeming to take note of its well-trimmed hedges, and hurried to the door, checking his watch.

He rang the bell, and in a moment, the door opened to reveal a plump, older Hispanic maid in a crisp gray and pink uniform. I could hear the guy's voice. "Package for Mr. Burton."

"God bless you, Alice," I praised. My real estate source was right on. It was indeed the Burton hideaway.

"Señor Burton no esta aqui. No hablo inglese."

"Is this *the* Richard Burton?" the driver pushed his luck.

"No esta aqui. Y yo no hablo inglese."

The driver got her signature, then took off with his clipboard, wondering, I was sure, if it was *the* Richard Burton who no esta aqui. Sitting there in my Toyota, I knew.

After the truck left, I got out of my car and walked to the front door. When the maid answered, I said, "I'm here to see Señor Burton."

"Señor Burton no esta aqui," came the not-surprising rejoinder.

"A que hora aqui?" I asked, more or less in her language.

"No se—mas tarde, mas tarde."

"Okay, I'll come back. Me, mas tarde. Okay? Muchas gracias."

I smiled sweetly, gave a little nod, and walked back to my car. I knew what I'd have to do. I could always come back to the front door later for these same results. But in the meantime, I had to climb that hill in back and see what I could see. And I'd have to wait there until something happened on the other side of the fence.

Silently cursing the dressy, bone-colored business pumps I was wearing, I drove slowly back down the hairpin curve, and parked my little car on the straightaway just below the Burton rental.

The hillside was thickly covered with a sea of succulent ice plant, and the heels of my shoes sank deeply into the growth as I clambered up the steep embankment, trying not to slip, and carrying my pocketbook slung over one shoulder. Inside the large bag were my tape recorder, my reporter's notebook, a little camera; on my nose, a pair of huge sunglasses. I grasped onto a low-hanging tree limb as I got to the top, and pulled myself, high heels and all, right up to the slats of the fence, glancing back to make sure no one was around. There were no other houses on the straightaway, no sidewalks, no traffic. I was completely hidden in the lush greenery and nobody could have seen me from below even if they'd glanced up.

I looked along the length of the fence and realized in a flash that there were knotholes in almost every plank, each one a natural peephole. How did I get this lucky? I peered into the nearest one, right before me at eye level, and suddenly knew how archaeologist Howard Carter must have felt when he poked his head into King Tut's tomb.

I, too, saw wonderful things. Big as life before me, I saw Richard Burton and Susy Hunt.

They were so close to me, just across the pool in a den with the sliding glass door open, that I thought surely they must have heard the gasp that came out of my mouth. I tensed, my eyes wide, hoping against hope they hadn't heard this involuntary breath, not to mention my footsteps scrambling up the hill.

I could literally see the color of Susy's toenail polish (bright red), and hear every word they exchanged. The incredibly suave Burton was wearing a white pullover and pale green slacks, she a black bikini printed with yellow and white flowers. I was transfixed, afraid even to breathe, terrified that I'd rustle some leaves or sink into the spongy earth and lose my balance, or that a dog would suddenly appear and start barking at me.

But none of the above happened. I just stood there and watched. This wasn't even fair. It was too easy. All I had to do was stay hidden and quiet as long as I could, or as long as they remained in my view, and take notes. I was in the middle of every journalist's dream. I was a real fly on the wall. The image of myself as such a nasty and annoying insect did not strike me at the time, although in retrospect, I'm sure Burton and Susy would have described me that way if they'd known I was there.

But for now, they had no inkling I existed. They were just relaxing, just hanging around, just as natural as can be. There was no question—they were *not* acting. Burton said, "You have your lotion, darling?" as they both stood near the open sliding glass door of the book-lined den. "Yes, I've already put it on," replied Susy.

Burton sank deeply into the cushions of the yellow-slip-covered sofa and leafed through the pages of a book he was holding. Susy chattered on, with a broad white smile playing across her mouth. She kept looking back at the pool, and it felt as if she were looking straight at me. My eye through the knothole saw everything, and I only hoped she in return couldn't see my large brown orb peeking out, like in a *Little Rascals* movie. She was itching to get into the California afternoon sun to dispel some of the pasty whiteness the wintry months in Europe and New York had bestowed on her skin.

Just outside the den lay the palm-fringed patio with its large rectangular pool glistening in the now-eighty-degree sunshine, all of it beckoning to the bikini-clad Susy.

She stood in front of Burton telling him, "Now you must watch the clock, darling, and don't let me fry."

Burton grabbed both her hands, kissed them first one, then the other, and said, "I'd rather die." And with that, Susy pecked him on the cheek and left him sitting on the sofa with his book. With long-legged strides she stepped outside onto the brown wooden deck by the door, past an iron umbrella table, past several graceful statues of pidgeons perched on the deck railing, down three or four steps, onto the cement pool deck, and into the sunshine on the far side, where she plunked down on an orange towel about four feet from where I secretly stood.

It was amazing. It was surrealistic. Suddenly I felt nervous and embarrassed. I was a voyeur. She stretched out like a cat and almost seemed to purr, with a contented smile still on her face. In a burst of ironic prudery, I hoped to hell she kept her top on.

I looked past her, now almost paralyzed with fear that I would move and make a noise. I could see Burton, my idol, my ideal, sitting there on the den sofa, thoroughly engrossed in his reading. The sofa was positioned against a window overlooking the pool area, so he had only to turn around to see what Susy was up to.

He did not turn around, only turned pages. At one point he slapped at his neck, as if to do in a bothersome gnat, or relieve a sudden itch.

Susy just lay there.

I began to think, "This could go on all afternoon. What if she just decides to worship the sun the whole day while he finishes his book?"

As it happened, I was supposed to catch a plane to Chicago early that evening. My parents were moving to Colorado and this would be my last visit to the house where I grew up. Suddenly it hit me that I might not make my flight. At the moment, I was trapped. I didn't dare move. "If I do, they hear me, I'm a dead duck. They'll get the cops. Or what if someone sees me from the street? Then *they'll* call the cops. I'll be in jail. I'll miss my trip to Chicago."

Silently, I bargained with God, "Please God, I know I'm being naughty, and I'll never do this again, never-never-never, I promise, but *please* help me stay still."

Susy stirred, wiggling her flaming-red-painted toes, and scrunching a yellow towel under her head.

Inside, Burton continued his intellectual pursuit.

At least a half-hour passed, and my body was starting to go numb.

My left leg was asleep, and the heel on my right shoe was now stuck completely into the ground. Still, it was a memorable experience and I tried to appreciate it. Someday, I consoled myself, I can tell my grandchildren about this afternoon spent so close to greatness.

The heat of the L.A. sun finally got to sunbather Susy. She got up and with a grateful glance toward the sparkling cerulean pool, walked to the deep end and dove in.

Startled by the resounding splash, the engrossed Richard turned around, and with a proud grin, watched his young lady through the window as she swam the length of the pool. At the shallow end, Susy stood and shook her head like a drowned puppy.

I suddenly thought, "She looks almost myopic climbing out of that pool, faltering on each step, squinting hard. Maybe she wears contacts."

I was close enough to see that she wore no makeup at all, and our Susy really was a natural beauty. Her facial bone structure couldn't have been more perfect, and she had a swan's neck. Her stomach was flat, her arms willowy. But perhaps due to her sedentary life over the past months, her thighs seemed too dimpled with cellulite to belong to a top model. She had obviously let her once-svelte figure go somewhat to pot since taking up with Richard Burton and forsaking her own life before the fashion cameras.

Still, who was I to criticize? She had Richard Burton, and I had my heel stuck in the dirt, hiding behind a fence.

I sighed and kept watching the show.

Susy groped for another towel and dried off, looking constantly into the den at Richard. She definitely seemed vision-impaired, almost tripping over one leg of the umbrella table as she made her way back to her spot in the sunlight. Down she plunked, just feet from my hiding spot. And there she was again, laid out like a dead body, bronzing languidly in the friendly rays of the California sun.

A butterfly fluttered around some pink geraniums in a clay pot and headed toward my knothole. Susy called out, "Oh Darling, look at the lovely little butterfly," and she jumped up.

"Ohmigod," I thought, "go the other way Butterfly, go the other way Butterfly." But the butterfly kept coming my way.

"Oh Darling, come out and help me try to catch it."

"*No* Darling," I screamed silently. "Don't come out and help her catch it."

The butterfly lighted on top of the fence, directly above my head. Susy was walking straight toward where I was planted. "Not good," I mentally repeated over and over. "Not good, not good, not good."

"Bring the net, Richard."

My luck, she's a lepidopterist. My luck, she's got a net. My luck, the butterfly is practically sitting on my face.

I didn't see him put his book down, grab the butterfly net, or walk out, but suddenly, there he was, Richard Burton, right next to Susy Hunt. If the fence hadn't been there, I could have shook hands with them both.

"Ah yes," came the silvery intonation. "It's a nice one." My eyeball was away from the knothole and back in its own socket. Standing there on unsteady feet, I had scrunched my body over and into as ball-like a formation as possible.

Suddenly, I started losing my balance.

I had leaned too far over—and in the trauma of the moment, got a vertigo attack from looking down the hillside below. I had the horrifying sensation that I was about to fall, and maybe tumble all the way down the hillside below.

"I'll catch it for you," said Burton.

"Yeah, you're about to catch more than a butterfly," I wailed internally. I teetered, threw my arms out like a tightrope walker, swayed; and then the inevitable instant came: I sat down hard on the mossy ground, crumpling and bracing myself with my arms to keep from rolling down the hill.

Just then, at the same split second, **"WHOMP"** came the sound of the butterfly net thumping down hard on the fence.

Susy screamed with delight, "Oh darling, it's got away." I blinked repeatedly, my mouth wide, gulping in air. I thought, "Susy, you only know half of what got away."

Her voice was moving away from the fence, and I got onto all fours and looked through a low-level knothole to see what was going on. "Look, there it goes. Ooh, let's try to get it—come on, Richard."

Burton swung the net smartly over the swimming pool and with a neat turn of the filmy cheesecloth bag, captured the delicate creature inside. Susy squealed again, and started hugging Burton's shoulders from behind. "Oh, you clever, clever darling."

But Burton, taking the bag in his hands and examining the thrashing ephemeral thing within, contemplated for a long moment. He said "Shame, isn't it, to stop it living free? Such a short life."

Susy put her chin down and raised her eyes to him beseechingly. She paused, then said, "May I have a close look? That's all I really want. Then we'll release it."

I used their involvement in this endeavor to recover myself, stand up, shake my bloodless leg back to life, brush the soil off my clothes, and replant myself.

The butterfly was viewed and released, Richard kissed Susy's forehead, and then told her, "You've a kind heart, my darling love. It's why I love you. It's why I'll marry you. By the way, have I asked you lately? Will you marry me?"

What did I just hear? It was the big rumor, the burning question everyone wanted to know. He'd been romancing Susy, traveling and living with Susy, hinting at a hitching, but would he actually marry Susy? Was he really through with Elizabeth for once and for all?

Susy responded very physically, draping herself around him. She said, "You know I will, and you know I can't wait for August. I shall be your child bride."

"Good," said Burton, stroking her hair. "Just as long as I know that, I can endure." Then he kissed her longingly, just like in the movies, there in the sparkling California afternoon.

I let my heels sink back into the ivy and nearly fainted away in a dead swoon.

Apparently, it had been discussed and set. So they would wed in August. They referred to it so casually that I might have missed it if I hadn't been glued to my knothole.

Burton released his intended from their embrace with a charming flourish and a smile. "And now, I'm back to my book, darling love, but I'll call you when your time's up."

"You take such good care of me," she cooed, curling under his outstretched left arm. As he headed back to the den, Susy lay down again on her orange towel, arranging herself in the sun's direct light.

Wind chimes on the deck, shaped like a flock of little birds on the wing, tinkled on a string in the caressing breezes. Now I concentrated on watching the soon-to-be-remarried Burton.

Fascinating guy. Literate, brainy, dissipated, sexy, and all tanned somehow. He was the biggest major mega-superstar I could think of. He was a legend. There was something so troubled and needy and brooding about him. At the same time, he was powerful, he was commanding. Even sitting on that yellow print sofa, he was in charge. Just the way he held his book. I noticed that he didn't seem too engrossed in it any more, that his attention was wandering. He leaned back and stretched. I tried to see if there was a glass nearby, because everyone knew Burton was a two-fisted drinker. But I couldn't see any signs of booze. Maybe it was true that Susy was helping him change his self-destructive ways.

Transfixed, I continued to watch as he lolled on the sofa reading. It was an idyllic afternoon of privacy, and I was secretly sharing it with these two very public people.

Finally, Richard Burton looked at his watch, drew himself up from the sofa, and book in hand, came to the open sliding glass door and stepped out onto the verandah.

His eyes seemed riveted on Susy. It actually made my heart beat faster, just watching the way he looked at her. I thought he looked slender and well, with a hint of gray at the temples. With a smile and again, that affectionate concern, he called out in a voice he could have used onstage, "Angel, time's up now." Golden voice, melodic, rich voice. It almost seemed a waste to use it on such mundane sentences.

Susy gave a tiny, half-meant groan and whined, "Do I have to?"

"Well," said Burton, "do you want to risk another five minutes?"

Susy nodded eagerly, so Richard threw a quasi-chiding glance and, chewing on one end of his glasses, walked inside, obviously really concerned that his fair-skinned lass not burn herself.

I thought it remarkable that the great Richard Burton could be so involved in these humble, caring, everyday rituals of relationship. He was like a father hen clucking around his little blond chick. I thought it was not only remarkable, but adorable, and felt I had stolen an insight into the magic of his other, more famous relationship. I felt sure that at the zenith, he must have been a doting and attentive lover to Elizabeth Taylor. People are what they are.

Susy, clutching her last moments allowed in the sun, again got up from her towel. She mopped her damp brow and neck, walked gingerly to the pool's shallow end and stepped gracefully, with a sigh of relief, into its cooling liquid.

I was feeling pretty sweaty myself, back there behind the fence. That pool looked plenty inviting to me too. However, in the spirit of this whole weird afternoon, I had to content myself with vicarious enjoyment of Susy's cool-down.

One last time, she walked back to her orange towel on the pool deck just a few feet over the fence from where I stood, and lay down on her stomach.

Susy need not have worried about scorching her sensitive skin, for in *exactly* five minutes, I saw Richard stir on the sofa, looking at his watch. He *really cared* about watching that clock for his lady fair. He liked her, he really liked her. Richard Burton bit a pesky hangnail as he stood up and came out onto the deck, standing there like a royal visitor. Undeniably, the man had a noble carriage.

An affectionate grin played across his face, and in his best Welsh accents, he thundered, "All right. Your headmaster says you've got to come in."

It gave me the chills.

It made my day.

I can still see him standing there, looking out over the back garden and swimming pool from his position on the deck, speaking loudly in his most imperious, stentorian Shakespearean style, *"Your headmaster* says you've got to come in." Oh Susy, you lucky, lucky girl.

Susy beamed like a little girl, and I'm sure she felt just as protected and adored as one. "All right, darling," she purred, collecting herself, and with those same myopically tentative steps, off she went, up the several stairs and into the den's open door.

Now like a little girl posturing for her father, she slouched stylishly in a model pose, her wet suit dripping on the floor, dragging her towel behind her like a mink coat. Burton threw his head back and laughed loudly. He grabbed her hand suddenly, and she recoiled like a puppy, running into the next room.

"Come back, I command you," he laughed.

In my new voyeur role, I didn't especially relish participating in anything more personal than I had already seen. I hoped they weren't going to push my curiosity to its outer *outer* limits.

Susy reappeared in the den holding a paper for Burton to see. He made as if to take it from her, then took her off guard and scooped her up in his arms, straining a bit I thought as he picked up her lanky body and carried her into the next room. She was not a small person, and he was, after all, twice her age. He was nuzzling her chest, and who could blame him?

Aaaaah, love in bloom. I waited for a few minutes to make sure they were not going to reappear.

Satisfied that the show was over, I confronted my more immediate problem of getting back down over all that ice plant. The hillside was slippery with it. I pulled my heel out of the dirt, turned, and surveyed the way down. There was nothing for it but to simply descend from my leafy hiding place on top of the embankment and hope I wouldn't fall. I took a deep breath, and cut a sideways traverse back and forth so that I wouldn't gain momentum and end up sliding down like a human toboggan.

I headed back to the office and gave the full scoop to my editor, telling him I'd write it on the airplane and file it by phone from Chicago.

A couple of hours later, as I nestled into my seat on the plane and looked out across the runways of L.A. Airport, the whole afternoon seemed totally unreal. Did I really do what I think I just did?

I spent half of my four-hour flight to Chicago writing up every detail of my naughty afternoon as the spy on the hill. When I got to Chicago, I called back to a tape in Florida and dictated the whole thing.

The next day, I had a call at our family home in the North Shore suburb of Glencoe. It was my editor. "Barbara, all reporters have been given a 37% raise."

What news. All that fun and more money too.

Then he added, "But your raise will be even more, like 46%. The Boss loved the Burton break. In fact, he thinks you're a great reporter, even if you aren't a Brit. Hurry back."

7

Tammy's in Love

I'd been working the story for a week or so, tipped by a Nashville contact who knew Tammy Wynette well. The attractive country songbird was having a secret affair with none other than Burt Reynolds.

It seemed such an unlikely pairing that nobody believed it.

Burt was a cool Hollywood guy, glib and sophisticated. Tammy was salt of the earth, with a definite country twang, a glittering Nashville-style superstar. She wasn't Burt's type at all, as my colleagues kept reminding me. They were friends maybe ... but lovers? No way.

However, I was convinced. I had a great Burt Reynolds source who also confirmed the information.

And this source should know. It was someone who worked in Burt's house. He cooked the meals and changed the sheets. For weeks, he'd been keeping me apprised of Burt's latest breakup with Sally Field. And now, he furtively informed me that lonely Burt had run straight into the comforting arms of good ol' girl Tammy.

Tammy had a pretty speckled romantic history herself. She was on her fourth divorce, from a short rebound marriage. That one had followed her breakup with longtime singing partner, husband #3, the volatile George Jones.

Was it possible Burt might be in line for the #5 slot on Tammy's wedding card?

Burt wasn't talking. Tammy wasn't talking. Their publicists

weren't talking. I called Tammy's Nashville office that morning and posed the question.

Her personal assistant roundly denied the story, and I requested that she ask Tammy, who was on the road, for a personal answer. When I called back later, the assistant said, "I've talked to Tammy herself and asked her for you. She says you can quote her if you want to. She says it's not true."

But sources were talking and I was believing.

About eighty-thirty that October evening, editor Bernard Scott called me at home, from Florida.

Scottie was very low key, a refined Englishman who moved in only the more genteel circles of Lantana social life. No sloppy bars or romantic skullduggery with blue-collar local women for him. He preferred golf, quiet dinner parties in the homes of married friends, or to entertain in lovely Palm Beach restaurants. He was a shy man and great journalist who had cut his teeth on some of England's better papers. At the *Enquirer,* he was known for his professionalism, his wry humor, and his class. I liked Scottie a lot.

But he wasn't my editor, so I was surprised to hear his voice.

"Bahbra, I've called Mike Hoy," (Mike *was* my editor,) "and he's given his okay for me to borrow you for the evening. It seems Tammy Wynette is in Los Angeles. Of all things, she's going to go on the *Dinah Shore* show tomorrow."

This was very ironic, since Burt Reynolds had had a serious romance with none other than much-older Dinah. Dinah finally broke it off saying she didn't want to grow old and gray in the arms of a younger man (Dinah, you silly thing). She had a popular afternoon show of chat, cooking, singing, and celeb guests, sort of an ancestor to today's format shows like *Rosie O'Donnell.*

Scottie continued, "Since the Tammy-Burt romance is your lead, would you like to see if you can get to her?"

"Would I like to? Sure, Scottie." I replied.

"She's holed up at the Beverly Wilshire Hotel. I've got a couple of free-lances over there, but you get in and see what you can come up with. We don't have a room number, unfortunately. Give it your best shot."

That, of course, I would do.

I grabbed my tape recorder and notebook and headed immediately to Beverly Hills and the famous hotel with the glamorous reputation.

As I walked to the front of the hotel, I ran smack into Hal, an older free-lancer who was fine on stories culled out of clips, and great on research, but who just didn't cut it on stories calling for a more inventive touch. I wondered why Scottie had him come out for something like this. He was like a lost soul. He'd apparently been moping around on the pavement in front for about an hour, wringing his hands, wondering what to do, and waiting for Tammy Wynette to show up.

He immediately asked me, "Barbara, what should I do? Shall I just wait here, or what? What are you going to do?"

Frankly, this was one time I preferred to work alone, and my first priority was to shed Hal. Nervous and clinging, he would be a definite liability in any scheme I dreamed up.

"Look, why don't you just stay here and keep an eye on the entrance, and coordinate with whoever else is here. If you spot her, try to nab her for a few words."

I wasn't going to tell him how to do the fancy footwork or the sideways thinking if he couldn't figure it out for himself. In the predatory world of tabloid journalism, you couldn't afford to give your tricks away for free. If you did, the other guy would always take credit for your scheme, and you'd miss your chance to enhance your own stock. At the *Enquirer*, even on a team assignment, it always boiled down to every man for himself.

I said, "I'll go to the other entrance in case she comes in that way."

"How long should I stay?" he pleaded.

"Gee, Hal, let me see if I can find anything out and I'll be back to talk to you, okay?"

Then, leaving the poor guy lurking anxiously around the Beverly Wilshire's street entrance, I headed through the lobby and down a hallway near the front desk, straight for the nearest pay phone .

I had an idea for getting Tammy Wynette's room number. If it worked, at the very least she would open the door and I could have a moment with her.

Checking inside a Beverly Wilshire Hotel matchbook cover I'd grabbed from the front desk, I found the hotel's main phone number and dialed it.

A crisp and pleasing voice answered, "Good evening, Beverly Wilshire Hotel."

It might have been the guy I'd just seen standing there.

"Yes," I answered, stepping into a part. "This is Burt Reynolds' assistant, Carol. May I speak to Miss Wynette, please? I have an important message from Mr. Reynolds."

"Certainly, madam. Just one moment please."

Was this happening? Was this just too easy?

The phone began ringing, presumably in Tammy Wynette's room. She *was* staying there. He'd put me right through. Dropping Burt's name had worked like magic. This was almost too amazing to believe. My mind raced. I almost hoped she wouldn't answer. What in the hell was I going to say if she picked up? "Quick, quick, *THINK*!" I screamed to myself.

A woman answered, "Helloooo?"

Did I detect a slight Southern accent?

"Is Miss Wynette there, please?"

"Why, this is Miss Wynette, dear. Who's this?"

"Oh, I'm so glad I got you. This is Carol, Burt's assistant. I have in front of me the most beautiful floral arrangement that Burt told me to bring to you this evening. It's kind of late, so I wanted to call first and make sure you were in your room."

"Oh sugar, that's just faaahn. Don't you worry one little bit. How sweet. You just come on over. I'm having a girl evenin', just paintin' my toenails and stuff, and I'm here, relaxin'."

"Oh, that's fantastic. Burt would *kill* me if I didn't get these to you, so I'm so glad you're there. He especially asked me to personally hand them to you, sort of directly from him to you."

"Oh honey, he's so sweet. Isn't that just like him?—so thoughtful and caring."

"It really is," I added, off-handedly throwing in, "What's your room number again?"

"638, sugar. You just come right on over. That is so sweet of Burt. How long do you think you'll be?"

My God, I thought, FLOWERS! I'll have to find a florist, and fast.

"Within the hour," I offered brightly.

"See you then, honey," said this nice woman.

BINGO! I practically jumped up and down in a victory dance. My ploy had worked like a charm. I was in! I mean really *in*. She was there, she'd answered, she thought I was Burt's personal assistant, and she was confirming by her very words that they had a liaison.

First, I ran outside and found Hal. "You might as well go home, Hal," I told him. "Looks like she's here, she's in her room, and I'll be talking to her." He seemed relieved to be off the hook, doffed his little hat, and headed down the street.

Now! Flowers. I needed the flowers. It was after nine PM, and the florist in the hotel had been closed since six. I got out the yellow pages and frantically ripped through them for any florist within a fifteen-minute drive. But every one I called was already closed. Panic set in. I had a date with Tammy and I just couldn't blow it for lack of a few posies.

As seems to help me when I'm under the gun, I paced. My heels clicked sharply on the marble floor as I went up and down the elegant hallway, nervously pondering my problem. The clock was ticking. If I didn't get a brainstorm, I'd have to leave the hotel immediately and drive miles away to a corner Conroy's which might, only might, be open.

Suddenly, I heard a man's voice projecting on mike through a room, thanking a group for its attendance, followed by clapping. Something drew me immediately to the open doorway.

Inside was a gathering of about a hundred and twenty people, seated around tables for eight or ten. The mike man finished and a lady speaker took over to give concluding remarks. As she spoke, it all kicked in for me.

I slipped into the room and slithered into an empty chair near the back, keeping my gaze on the podium the whole time, so as not to make eye contact with anyone.

My quarry was before me, in easy reach.

Flowers.

On every table was a huge and splashy floral centerpiece.

As the meeting began to loosen and break up, I tried to look as if I'd been there the whole time. People were starting to rise and gather their belongings. I got up, said to the man near me, "That was so interesting, wasn't it?" and with exaggerated moves slung my bag over my shoulder.

I'd been to enough large Hollywood functions to know that at the end, ladies always grab for the centerpieces and take them home.

Before anyone else had a chance, I lunged for the coveted floral spray standing within my reach just a yard away. With determination in my eyes, I lifted it up, balanced the huge and heavy thing precariously, and headed at a brisk pace for the door, without a backward or a sideways glance.

And I kept walking.

To this day, I wonder what the people at that table must have said to each other as I strode away balancing their flowers in my arms, after brazenly beating them all to the grab.

Down the hall I cantered, flowers teetering, heels clicking, water spilling on the marble floor, all the while hoping no one would follow me and halt me. I turned the first corner quickly and headed for the lobby bank of elevators. Much to my good luck, an elevator door stood open with the green "up" arrow alight over it.

I scuttled myself on board, and somehow managed to push "6" with my elbow. Mercifully, no one else got on, the doors closed behind me, and I felt myself and my floral extravaganza rising upward toward the sixth floor. When the lift stopped and the doors reopened, I stepped out and headed for a large, glass-covered table that stood nearby in the hallway. I set the heavy flowers down, shook my arms in relief, and let out a huge breath, my shoulders rising and then falling—in through the nose, out through the mouth.

I needed a minute to collect myself before heading to room 638. I had to calm down.

Picking the arrangement up once again, I walked slowly down the gorgeously carpeted hallway, going over the plan. Okay, I was Carol from Burt Reynolds' office. Burt cared, so he sent me with the flowers. I'd hand them to her, she'd be gracious and delighted, maybe blush and gush a little, I'd verify that she was in her room and alone, and that would be it.

If she said anything extra at all, it would be pure gravy. Just accepting flowers from Burt Reynolds so naturally would prove she was intimate enough with him to expect such a gesture. I'd do the thing and be on my way. Or I'd do whatever else there was to do.

I stood outside room 638. This was it.

I set the arrangement down to free my hands, and knocked on the door three times. As I lifted the flowers back into my arms, I heard a strong female voice on the other side of the door. "Who is it?"

"I have your flowers, Miss Wynette," I said, unable to spit out my newly assumed name.

The doorknob turned, the door opened inward, and there, in a fluffy white bathrobe with her hair in pink sponge rollers, stood a smiling Tammy Wynette.

"Hi honey. Isn't that nice of you to come on over."

"Well, these are kind of a special order, you know."

"Why, aren't they spectacular?"

"Where would you like them, Miss Wynette?" I asked. It seemed appropriate for me to offer to set them down, rather than just push them through the doorway at her. They were very heavy.

"Oh honey, just bring 'em on in here."

I stepped into her plush suite, with two double beds, a lot of lighting, and pretty clothes strewn across the chairs. Tammy's bed was rumpled, with five or six pillows plumped up against the headboard, and she had the TV on an in-room movie.

"Here," she said, clearing the hotel brochures and menus from a table. "Just set that lovely thing down here."

Tammy started preening the blossoms, and sniffing the orchids and roses so artfully arranged. I suddenly realized she'd start looking for a note from Burt any second, so I leapt to distract her.

"Oh Miss Wynette....."

"Please Carol, you call me Tammy."

"Thank you ... that's so nice of you. Well Tammy, I have orders to tell you these come with all his love, and he wishes he could be here himself."

"Well, ah'm just glad to meet you, Carol. When he called me earlier, he didn't say a thing about these, so it's a lovely surprise."

I nearly choked. He'd called her earlier. No wonder the hotel put me right through. Sputtering inside, I managed, "Oh, you know Burt. Always one for the surprises."

"Yes, he's really very romantic and very sweet. This is just like him."

How did I know that already? "Yes, people don't realize what a softie he really is," I encouraged.

"Well, I realize it, and sometimes, I just ache over this whole thing. Burt is the best, most terrific person I know. He's been through a lot. We both have—health-wise, love-wise, work-wise. Well, I don't have to tell you, do I?"

I shook my head knowingly from side to side, in girlish confidence.

"Gee Tammy," I wanted to say, "you don't *have* to tell me, but I wish you would."

Instead, I softly murmured, "Burt Reynolds is a wonderful man ... although of course, I don't know him the way you do."

Barbara Sternig, I mused to myself, you Mistress of Understatement, you.

As I sat there on the side of her extra bed, the loquacious Tammy inexplicably continued pouring her heart out to me.

It was a genuine girlfriend talk. At first it made me so uncomfortable that I found myself looking toward the door for a way out. Part of me wanted to tell her to zip her lip. Part of me, obviously, didn't.

On the one hand, I was embarrassed I'd deceived this nice women about my identity. On the other hand, I never dreamed it would go further than a hello at the door. On the third hand, I was stunned that she would just open up this way. And on the fourth hand, I was thinking a million miles a minute of ways to remember everything she said.

Forget the tape recorder I had in my purse.

Or take notes? I think *not*.

I frantically tried to use memory tricks I'd learned in a course one time. I attached one subject she covered to each finger of each hand and then tried with all my might to attach details to knuckle, fingernail, phalanges.

"I must say, we are so close. We are just so close. I guess I can tell you, because you're obviously aware of all this—but I've never felt about anyone as I do about Burt. I've never felt that close to anyone in my life. "

What was I supposed to respond? What would Carol respond?

"I know he thinks the world of you, Tammy ... the world."

"Really?" she asked sincerely, searching my face.

"Really."

What could this hurt? She was a special person, and who wouldn't think the world of her? Heck, *I* thought the world of her and I'd just met her.

"You know I thought I'd wrecked everything when I ran off and did that silly ol' rebound marriage. So many awful things had been happening in my life. Burt knew about them—people kept breaking into my house—you know, like stalkers. Then when the bedroom wing of my home burned down, with all my trophies, show clothes, even regular clothes ... I kept getting scary phonecalls at home, and I was just scared to death. I'm just an old-fashioned sort of Southern girl. I thought it'd solve my fears and my problems to have a man. I married someone I knew, just to have a man's protection."

"I know how stunned Burt was," I said.

"Honey, I tried calling Burt fifteen times the night before. He knows. We were on the road, and I couldn't reach him. Some of my singers knew Burt and kept telling me how much he cared about me. They all told me to call off the wedding. I went way in the back of my bus and cried. I knew it was a big mistake, but I said it was too late.

"Burt called me three weeks after the wedding and said, 'Thanks a lot. It's nice to read it in *Newsweek*.' "

"Oh, he was terribly upset," I interposed.

Tammy went on, "I know he was upset, and I was too. I told him how sorry I was. You know, Carol, if I'd reached him that night, I never would have done it. I never would have gotten married. I cared about Burt so deeply."

"Gee, what a tragedy that you two didn't really get together before it got to you being so frightened," I offered.

"Well you know, it's just that after our first two dates, Burt said to me, 'Call me.' But it's not my upbringing, so I didn't. So when he finally did reach me, I had the kids with me and told my housekeeper to tell him I wasn't there. I thought that'd be good for him."

I interjected, "I'll bet that hasn't happened to Burt much in his life!" I opened my eyes wide and smiled.

Tammy continued, "When he did get me on the phone, he said, 'Look, I don't chase.' I said, 'Neither do I. It's what my mama taught me.' I guess I felt he wasn't a possible mate for me. I needed someone who simply wanted to be with me right now, and that's why I went ahead and married someone who was available. I was scared and weak. And of course, it wasn't long before that marriage all fell apart.

"But you know I love Burt dearly, and we have an understanding because of our careers. He does need someone, and if he ever marries he'll get a girl of maturity who's on his same level and he can give the same things to her she gives to him—someone who adores him and who he can adore back,"

Tammy went all quiet, so I said, "Well, what about you two? Burt doesn't tell me anything about his inner soul feelings, but you seem like that woman. You seem so perfect for him."

I could see tears glistening in her eyes as she said, "I don't know if it'll ever be us. I don't really hold out much hope. But it doesn't matter, because no matter what, we have so much together. We're always in phone contact as you know, and we see each other as often as we can, and it's great just knowing he's there.

"I could have him sitting there next to me on the bed right where you are and we'd just talk for four hours and be perfectly happy and he'd never touch me. Just to talk! He can't trust most women like that and he always tells me he never knows why people like him—for himself or for his image. You know dear, I don't need him financially or for the fame—I have my own and I couldn't care less about his.

"Our trouble is we're both workoholics. My whole life has been work and my girls. They keep me working." Tammy was referring to her five beloved daughters. "If it weren't for them, I'd stop working and maybe Burt and I could be together.

"He wants a son in the worst way, and could give such devotion—but they won't let him adopt one as a single parent because of his travels and his Hollywood sex image. It's kind of sad. Burt's never had the ideal relationship. But you've probably seen more than I even know about," she fished.

"Well, he goes out a lot, but I don't think anyone means anything to him," was my helpful venture.

Tammy continued. "I just hate the girls who go out with him once, and then spill their guts about him. He doesn't need that, and I never want to do that to him. I hate reading all this junk about Burt and me, all these guesses. People bug me all the time. I got a call today from that silly dumb newspaper the *Enquirer;* a girl called me. I denied it all. I won't say a thing."

Gulp. That silly dumb *Enquirer.* A girl. That would be me.

Tammy was rolling. "Carol, I am *so nervous* about going on *Dinah* tomorrow. I'm petrified. I've stayed in my room all day without makeup and I've only seen room service. I just know she's going to ask me about Burt. I'll deny it on *Dinah.* If she asks me if we date, I'll have to admit it. But if she asks if there's more, I'll deny it and tell her my life's an open book. She might not ask at all, since she used to go with him. I know she hated Lucie Arnaz for going out with him."

Was this the hot seat or what?? I don't mean Tammy. I mean *me.*

Tammy Wynette wasn't telling her story to anyone, but she was sitting here in her bathrobe and her rollers telling it to me. And I wasn't who she thought I was. And she'd die if she knew. And she was a nice woman. And I felt bad.

It was a horrible dilemma for me—caught between my wacky job and my self-image as a nice person. One thing is sure: I didn't feel too nice at that moment. I started to edge toward concluding things and getting out of there. I was feeling like a thief in the night. I *was* a thief in the night.

But Tammy needed a friend to talk to, and I was it. She didn't want me to go. On and on it went, all about how she had surgery just a couple of months ago, and right afterwards, Burt ended up in Century City Hospital too, with a heart problem. Tammy revealed with great emotion how she had them bring a rollaway bed into Burt's hospital room and then she slept next to him just to give him comfort and company .

"Honey, I know how scary it is to be in the hospital. I didn't want Burt to wake up all alone without a loving person in that room with him. I used to get in the bed with him and just snuggle with him, just to give him some home warmth."

Tammy, I thought, I want to hug *you.*

Tammy told me how Burt's mom became ill while Burt was in the hospital, but Tammy couldn't bring herself to tell him for fear it would make his own condition worse. She revealed how his pals pleaded with her to influence Burt to slow down, and how useless she thought that idea was. "No one can tell Burt what he should do about his career. I wouldn't dream of doing that."

And Tammy wistfully gave me the whole story of how rabid Dinah Shore was about any of Burt's new girlfriends, how she feared Dinah's wrath coming down on herself if she found out Tammy and Burt were so close, and on and on.

It was getting late. Tammy had to get up early. I told her I'd give her love to Burt, she gave me that great big hug I wanted, I gave it back feeling like a heel, and then I beat it.

I lickety split down the carpeted hallway, chafed at waiting for the elevator, and once in the lobby, practically flew out the door to my car. I jumped in, talking to myself, repeating key words, turned on the dome light, grabbed my notebook, and going from finger to finger, wrote down every particle of info I could recall. Index fingernail: he wants a son. Right hand pinky tip: nervous about *Dinah* taping. Left hand middle finger knuckle: rebound marriage.

You know, those memory tricks really work.

At home, I called Scottie even though it was nearly three AM in Florida. He was over the moon.

I got a hero-gram from him the next day, noting, "Don't want to sound corny, but I think it was one of the most enterprising pieces of tabloid journalism I've seen."

He signed his note, "With ever-increasing admiration."

It's a silly story I have often remembered, the brazen flower escapade, the lousy trick I played on a gracious and true lady, Tammy Wynette.

But it was the *Enquirer* and it was war. My job was to find out the truth behind the rumors and get around lies that even Tammy was telling.

I wonder to this day what Tammy must have thought when the next week the *Enquirer* blared with such certainty that she and Burt Reynolds were closerthanthis, that he could and probably should have married her when she needed him most, how upset he was when she married someone else, that she'd even slept in his hospital room with him.

I always wanted to meet Tammy again and apologize to her. Now I'll never get the chance, because she passed away in April of 1998 at the unspeakably unfair age of 55.

Such a wonderful woman. After this little caper, it may be presumptuous of me, but I hope I end up where Tammy is, so I can finally ask her to forgive me.

8

Frankie Pops the Question

hen I say
that Frank
Sinatra and Da Boys
weren't through with
me after Lake Tahoe,
nor I with them, it's
an understatement.

Six or seven months
after the Sinatra/John
Denver story ran, it turned
out that Frankie was about to pop the question to his big blond ex-
showgirl squeeze, Barbara Marx, and with my new reputation as the
Sinatra Genius, I naturally got the assignment.

On very short notice, I was flying to Las Vegas, and by that
night, I again found myself working undercover, nose to nose with
Spider, Frankie Eyelashes, assorted additional bulldogs, plus the
Chairman of the Board himself.

Since my kneecaps had remained intact after the Tahoe tale was
published (mercifully under a house byline and not my own), I felt fairly
confident that the Sinatra crowd was still in the dark about my charade.

I'd gotten away with it. Once.

But if I surfaced again on the periphery, snooping, fawning and
questioning, whistles were going to go off. These street-wise guys
would put it all together in a flash. And Spider, even if he still didn't

realize he'd been had by a reporter, would at the very least be on a blood trail for the big-eyed broad who'd disappeared on him at payoff time.

There was definitely the possibility of peril to my person.

This time, if Da Boys were indeed with their Bossman again, my main problem would be to either avoid them, or to look so different that they wouldn't recognize me.

My cohorts on the assignment were Al Coombes, short, stocky, self-possessed, ex-Fleet Street, seen and done it all, a lapsed barrister; and our photographer, Bob Aylott, slender, baby-faced, genial, British, a little boozey, but competent and tenacious in the pinch.

The deal was, Frank either already had, or was about to propose to the forty-eight-year-old Marx.

According to a close friend of hers who was confiding in me, Marx had set her cap on Frank at least ten years earlier. All her girlfriends knew it.

He was the ultimate embodiment of her husband profile. Even as a young model she'd told her then-unknown boss Mr. Blackwell (he of the Worst-Dressed List) that she was determined to marry a man of means. In 1986, Blackwell was quoted in a *People Magazine* book excerpt summing up Barbara's allure for a rich man. "Barbara is not a woman of humor, nor is she very intelligent, but she's beautiful, she's sweet, and she's incredibly patient. She was very ambitious even in the early nineteen fifties about marrying a man of position."

She scored in that department on her second marriage, by snagging the youngest Marx Brother, Zeppo. He was rich, he belonged to a show business dynasty, he denied her nothing, and he was good to her kid. She stayed with him for fourteen years.

Zeppo was twenty-seven years older than Barbara, a funny little guy, short and balding. In his youth he was the suavest of the Marx Brothers, but now at seventy-five, he appeared completely out of context with the stunning, statuesque ex-chorine. For Barbara Marx, there was bigger game out there and the time had come to go hunting.

Barbara and Zeppo lived on the Tamarisk golf course in Palm Springs and as members of the elite desert community's show biz crowd, knew Frank Sinatra socially.

Barbara's excellent tennis game put in her Frankie's company often. Over the years, she'd been a frequent doubles partner for his pal, ex-Vice President Spiro Agnew, and she used that intimate proximity to learn everything Frank wanted in a woman. She then methodically set about molding herself to become that woman, even though she was still married to Zeppo.

Through tennis, Barbara and Frank got tighter and tighter, and over a two- or three-year period, she began spending more and more time with him, then all her time with him.

Zeppo looked the other way at first, then became sick with jealousy, and finally resigned himself that his wife had dumped him.

It had been a year since he'd let the former showgirl have her divorce. She immediately moved in openly with the sixty-year-old Crooner, never to move out again. Despite the open affrontery of Sinatra's relationship with Barbara, Zeppo wouldn't say a bad word about Ol' Blue Eyes. Zeppo had been cuckolded, but no matter how it galled him, he couldn't afford to have Frank as an enemy. Not in Palm Springs, not in the world. Show biz is after all just a small town.

A restaurateur friend of mine, a famous lady herself who had known Barbara Marx as well as Frank Sinatra for years, told me at the time, "Kind of like Jackie-O, Barbara always loved power, and I know it's been her dream for many years to be Mrs. Frank Sinatra.

"But he would not be an easy husband for any woman, because he's totally a man's man. To be part of his life, you have to become part of his anatomy, because I doubt you could become part of his emotions. The guys and his own pursuits will always come first, so the only way to him is to just be there, be there, be there. Never leave his side, be at his disposal. Frank is very insecure and wants his woman totally devoted. To make it a success, it will have to be ninety percent on her part. But being Mrs. Frank Sinatra is her ultimate full-time dream job. This is what she really wants."

Well, now it seemed this is what she would really get, and I was there to glean every detail, once again concealing my identity as a reporter.

Hotel rooms were scarce in Vegas and we couldn't get into Caesar's Palace where Sinatra always stayed and was appearing. As I checked into my second story room at the Bali Hai Blair House Motel, I was glad to be off-strip.

Like in Tahoe, I felt safer here.

As always with Sinatra, a lot was going on.

He was performing two shows a night at Caesar's. He was slated to skip his early show that night to headline the SHARE show in L.A., an annual charity extravaganza staged at the Santa Monica Civic Auditorium by the wives of stars. His appearance would make a hero of his girlfriend, who was a member of the high-stepping money-raising group. Then they'd hop their plane back to Vegas for his midnight show.

Next, he was getting engaged this weekend, or so we thought.

And then on Sunday, as I read by chance in the local Vegas paper, Frank Sinatra was going to receive his doctorate.

Busy guy.

Seeing this blurb in the paper was a great piece of luck. For sure, part of our weekend's activities would now have to be Frank's appearance at graduation ceremonies for the University of Nevada, Las Vegas, where the singer, who barely made it out of high school back in Hoboken, would be recipient of an honorary Doctor of Humane Letters degree.

It seemed amazing, but this was the first time in his sixty years that Sinatra had ever received such an honor. He was apparently very excited. The regents of the University would bestow it upon him.

The article said that presidential hopeful Senator Frank Church of Idaho was also receiving an honorary doctorate and would deliver the commencement address.

My first order of business was to get invited to that graduation ceremony by hook or by crook. It proved easier than I imagined.

A few calls to the University and I learned they were not passing out press tickets, but that Senator Church had a press room set up and that's where I could get credentialed.

Frank Church was a ruddy, smiling, charismatic, outgoing man whose work would be cut short just eight years later, when he died very suddenly and too young at age fifty-nine. But that spring he was full of sanguine energy, and this event would help him get a lot of publicity for his candidacy, due to his dais-mate, Frank Sinatra.

It was a perfect sideways entree for us whose real quarry was that other Frank. For sure, Barbara Marx would be there to cheer her man on. Don't forget, she was part of his anatomy. Maybe I could get next to her, close enough to check out her ring, close enough to have a word.

And who knows, there might even be a bonus fracas, since the news blurb especially noted that Frank's beloved mother Dolly would also be in attendance. Dolly hated Barbara. Barbara wasn't good enough for her Frankie boy. Of course, in Dolly's studied opinion, no woman on earth was.

In Senator Church's press room, I soon chatted up some of his youthful workers, showed my *Enquirer* press pass, explained we could deliver twenty-five million readers, and walked out fully credentialed not only for the graduation on Sunday, but also for a cocktail party Church was tossing that evening. I arranged for credentials for Al and Bob too. All they had to do was show their press passes at the door tonight to collect them.

So that evening at cocktail time, the three of us kicked off what would prove a long night by socializing with the admirable Mr. Church, and getting to know some of his close aides.

My men and I arrived in two cars, and when the reception broke up about eight o'clock, Al said, "Are you as hungry as I am?" It was decided we'd reconnoiter in the coffee shop at Caesar's, fortify ourselves with some dinner, and plot our evening's endeavors.

A short run up the Vegas Strip and we swung our cars into the long, statue-lined driveway at Caesar's Palace, with its huge and ornate fountains splashing high and spraying sparkling curtains of water over the center median.

The old journalists' trick, self-parking for a quick escape, was our choice. Then we strode, three abreast, into the huge and noisy casino at Caesar's.

As we entered, my mind was transported back to my Tahoe adventure, by the distinctive background music of gambling—the "thunk" of a slot machine arm and the clinking of change, the ringing bells of a jackpot, the smooth click-click-click of roulette wheels, the excited cries of winners, and the seductive plop-plop of stacked poker chips and playing cards changing hands on green felt.

Who knew whether it was day or night? Who cared?

We did. We had work to do.

Heading for the coffee shop, we settled into a big, high-backed booth and ordered drinks and food. I told the guys of Sinatra's Tahoe casino habits.

"He likes to come out onto the floor after his last show to let the public see him, and to hold court with his pals. I figure it'll be the same only more so here in Vegas. This is his primo stomping ground, and he's famous for his casino antics when he's here."

Al said, "OK, you hit the casino floor first and see what you can come up with. Bob and I will get out to McCarran Field and check out exactly where his plane from L.A. will pull in, and how we can get close enough to get some shots of him and Marx as they walk off.

"So Barbara, do your thing here for a couple of hours, then join us in the private terminal at the airport. We should all be there when they arrive back from the SHARE show."

"Right," I said, adding as an afterthought, "Listen, if anything goes wrong for anybody, let's use Cleopatra's Barge as our designated meeting and message point." This was before the world got cell phones. "If we get separated, or whatever happens tonight, leave word or a note with the bartender, check?"

"Check," the guys agreed. We all gave a thumbs-up and then rose from our booth.

It was Saturday night, it was Vegas, it was Showtime.

Al and Bob went one way, and I went the other, out onto the casino floor.

First stop for me, the ladies room. Something told me that even though it was still early in the evening, I'd be wise to alter my appearance from the long-haired look I'd espoused in Tahoe, just in case I encountered Da Boys. So I teased my hair until it was huge, then twirled it all into a French twist. Light lipstick, and I was out the door.

Tonight, I was sophisticated in a two piece dress with flared skirt, subdued jewelry and expensive but conservative shoes. Nothing at all like the sexy tops, tight jeans, platform boots and big hoop earrings I'd donned to crack the inner circle last time.

A security guard near the showroom began giving me the eye as I walked past, and I flirted back, sidling over to him for a chat.

"So are you here alone, a pretty lady like you?" he asked, interestedly.

"Well, my friends had to go to the airport to get someone, but me, I'm on a mission."

"A mission?" he smiled. "What kind of mission?"

"I'm determined to see Frank Sinatra tonight. But I'm upset. I saw on the sign over there that his early show is cancelled, and I wondered if he's sick, or what?"

"No, not sick. He had to go down to L.A. to do a special show for some charity, but he'll be back for his midnight show."

"Oh well, that's lucky for me. Does he ever come in here, into the casino?"

"Ever?" exclaimed the young man. "Ever? Only like, every night!"

"No, you're kidding."

"No ma'm, I am *not* kidding. Sits right over there."

He pointed to a special VIP cocktail area with a railing around it, one step up off the casino floor. It had a *"Reserved"* sign in front of it.

"After his second show, Sinatra always comes into the casino and sits over there. Always. Every night."

Suddenly, despite my grownup clothes, I became gushing little Barbara Brown Eyes again, laying it on thick to get the full skinny. I oohed, I aahed, I sighed.

"Oh yeah," continued the guard. "He sits with his pals and gals right over there every night. That's why that long, long table is set up. That's Mr. Sinatra's domain right there."

Big eyes. "Nooooo, which chair does he sit in?"

The guy pointed to the middle chair. "Oh yeah. And every night he's got his babe with him. This real tall blonde. Older, but man, she's gorgeous. Oh, she's beautiful, all right, a real looker. And she's on him like Lincoln on a five dollar bill."

"Wow," I said, "that's so exciting. I *have* to see them."

"So, you gonna be around later?" asked my new friend.

"I sure am. What time would he come out and sit there?"

"Probably not before two AM. He and his group usually come in late and stay for a couple of hours, or even longer, depending."

I couldn't wait to tell my cohorts. The chances of Bob grabbing a picture, however, with his full-size equipment and professional strobe lights, were slim to none. But at least we knew where we could find our lovebirds.

As the security guy stood at his post with his hands clasped behind his back, smiling at me a little proudly, I walked away, over toward Sinatra's VIP playground. Around and around the railing I paced, looking for good camera angles to Sinatra's chair, checking nearby tables as potential vantage points, searching for a potted palm or some other obstacle that might hide Bob and his big camera.

I sat down at a table near the railing, then got up again and sat down at another one, like an artist striding around to get some perspective.

As I sat and scanned the area, engrossed in my own thoughts, I was oblivious to the gaze of a short wiry man in a barely detectable toupee, gray hairs and black, with a large diamond ring flashing on the pinky finger of his powerful hand. His features were sharp, his skin tanned, his eyes narrow and vigilant behind aviator glasses, his predatory look pure Vegas.

"You lookin' for somethin', sweetheart?"

My body visibily started at the words, at the voice, and my head whirled around. I'd been miles away in my own mental machinations, but the accent, the tone, the verbal leer pierced through my busy thoughts, and in a chilling instant, sent my heart into my throat.

I looked up and before me was none other than Spider.

Yes, *that* Spider.

I could feel the heat as my face flushed red from my chest up, and I blinked a couple of times looking at him standing there before me. Did he see me flinch? Did he sense my inner trembling? Could he detect that the hair on my arms was standing on end?

But most important, did he know it was me?

"What? Oh no, I'm just waiting for my husband and kids to get over here so we can go to Circus Circus. What's it to ya, anyhow?"

It took every bit of will within me to make my voice sound sharp and hard and confident. I tried with all my might to give myself an accent, calling up the flat nasality of my native Chicago and laying it upon every word. I moved my jaw as if I were chewing gum.

Something passed over Spider's face, and I hoped it was confusion, a sense of mistaken identity.

"Hey, wait a minute. Don't I know you?"

My heart was now pounding so fast I was afraid I wouldn't be able to speak at all. I felt trapped, like a helpless moth stuck in a Spider's web. Did it show in my eyes? I called up my childhood drama classes and cleared all emotion from my face.

"Huh?" I said, lifting my lip and squinting as if in disbelief. "That's a great line, man. What is it, about number fifty-seven? But sorry, bub, I'm married."

Spider paused, narrowing his beady eyes further, almost to slits.

"You, uh, you been in Tahoe recently?"

"TA-hoe? Naw."

"You remind me of someone. Barbara. Yeah, Barbara. Is your name Barbara?"

"Naw, Janine."

"Where you from? You from L.A.?"

"Naw, we're from Ohio."

Was he buying any of this?

Still sitting and chewing, I craned my neck, looking around the casino for my phantom family.

Spider's eyes were locked suspiciously on me, and with my peripheral vision, I could see he was scanning me up and down, back and forth. The expression on his face scared me, really scared me. It was like a lion glaring at its prey and about to pounce. Was he going to nail me? Was he going to grab me hard and hurt me? Did he *know*?

He looked at me. I looked straight back at him. Then I could tell. Spider wasn't sure.

The flatness in my voice, the different hair, the more conservative clothes, the missing gush quotient, my body language, and finally, the line about being married ... he just wasn't sure.

My other advantage was that he and Da Boys met so many dames that even a luscious tomato like Barbara Brown Eyes didn't stand out.

He really couldn't remember *exactly* what I looked like.

Frowning up at him, I crossed my arms in front of my chest,

hunched my back and bent my torso over my knees in a protective posture. I hoped and believed I looked and acted entirely different than the playfully inviting ding-dong from Tahoe.

"OK, sorry," said Spider, taking a step back, palms open and up toward me. "But you looked like a broa ... like someone I met before."

"Yeah, well, you didn't, buddy, and you can tell it to my husband in a minute if you want to."

I was laying it on, and as Spider walked tentatively away from me, taking out some Binaca, spraying it into his mouth, and glancing back over his shoulder, I got a little burst of power.

Only because this close encounter came out okay, I got the power. Otherwise ... well, otherwise, I'll never know.

That made two times I'd escaped the Spider's web, once avoiding becoming a Spiderette, and this time, a dead fly.

As Spider blended off into the casino crowd, I got up and walked briskly in the opposite direction, toward Cleopatra's Barge, just to get away, just to go someplace where I knew I could leave a message if I needed to.

As I pushed through the casino crowd, a group of men hooted loudly around a craps table. One of them yelled, "Fever in the south, here come da doctor!" And then a blubbery, slick-haired mountain of a guy slammed the dice across the green playing pit, his beautiful lash-lined eyes bloodshot and wide.

I veered sharply, doing a one-eighty away from that place, as Frankie Eyelashes jiggled and shook, waiting to see the numbers he'd rolled. Craps was his game.

So Da Boys were back.

I'd have to be careful this night, very careful.

****

Time was running on and I had to leave for the airport soon. Even though Sinatra and entourage probably wouldn't be landing for a couple of hours, we all needed to scope everything out. That way, we had the best shot at Frank and Barbara Marx, and the best chance for that photo, that private moment, those words.

Personally, I felt anxious because now it was obvious Sinatra's gang was on duty. There was every chance Spider and Eyelashes would go out to the airport to meet their boss, maybe even drive him back. Pure and simple, after this casino encounter, I was dogmeat if Spider saw me not only again, but specifically around Sinatra. Could I try a disguise? What disguise?

Thinking on my feet, I walked around, and then into the hotel gift shop, looking for ideas. There, in a corner, was my answer—a large rack of lovely hats.

Hats. Of course! I'd buy a hat, one with a brim, and I'd stuff my head into it, morphing even further from Barbara the Tahoe Tart. Then on my way to McCarran airport, I'd stop at my room and change into jeans and a T-shirt. I'd put on the hat. I'd put on sunglasses. Well, maybe not sunglasses.

Maybe I was just kidding myself, but I really felt I could pull off enough of a transformation to bamboozle Spider. If by chance he didn't come out to McCarran Field to meet the Boss, nothing lost.

I chose a black gaucho-style chapeau, very smart, and charged it to my company credit card. This might be a little hard to explain to payroll, but it was a necessary purchase. I quickly left the hotel and sped back to my room where I stripped off my dress, changed into jeans and a black shirt, settled that black hat low on my forehead with all my hair under it, and for good measure, grabbed another dress, a clingy black one with long skirt, folded it, and took it with me.

At McCarran, I rolled around the terminals until I came to Butler Aviation, the area reserved for private planes. I parked, and walked into the small private terminal.

Al Coombes surreptitiously appeared inside the terminal and came over to me to deliver the news that he'd met with success.

"Sinatra will be pulling in soon, and I've got the security code that'll get us all onto the field."

Al had ascertained the access code needed to open the chain link door that led right out onto the tarmac. He'd paid a "ramp rat" fifty bucks.

"They could be on approach any time now. When I see the plane, I'll knock on the terminal window and you come out. Then we'll all go through and approach them as they de-plane."

I could see Aylott in the shadows just outside the terminal door, his cameras ready to go. He'd be the first one in their face with his lenses. Al and I would try separately for words.

For now, Al and Bob stayed outside, hanging around the perimeter and watching the runways for Sinatra's plane, while I covered inside the terminal to see who'd show up.

I could only hope it wouldn't be Spider and his blubbery companion.

Feeling totally exposed inside the brightly-lit waiting area despite my hat and my change of clothing, I plunked a quarter into a vending box and bought a newspaper. Then I opened it up full-sheet and hid behind it as if I were reading it.

It occurred to me that while no one could see me, I also couldn't see anything from behind the opened pages, so I took my rat-tail comb out of my bag and used the pointy end to poke a few peep holes through the paper. Now by shifting the sheet from side to side, I could scan inside the terminal, and also see outside, where the action was going to be.

An older man chomping on a cigar burst into the terminal. I rattled my newspaper back and forth to line it up on him and see if I recognized him, then peered through. He didn't look familiar. Still, he fit the Sinatra pal image—slick hair, slick clothes, pinky ring. I decided not to emerge from behind the pages of my *Las Vegas Sun*, but to keep it open very wide in front of me.

It was a good call, because a moment later, the terminal door opened again, and through my peephole, I saw a fleshy mass surge into the small space, garbed in dark shiny suit, Italian boots, trendy white shirt open at the collar, gut protruding over his belt line. It was Eyelashes.

I froze. Could Spider be far behind?

Frankie Eyelashes made a beeline for the guy with the cigar and said, "Da plane should be here. Dere's no problem, is dere?"

"Naw, no problem. They probably landed awready. You and Spider, did youse get the limo stocked?"

"Yeah, it's stocked. We got extra too, and went for a leetle ride for a few shots with dose chicks."

"Yeah, well dat limo better be prime, you knucklehead. You know how da boss likes everything da way he likes it. He better not find any panties in dere."

Frankie Eyelashes guffawed and the cigar man came down on him again. "I ain't kiddin', you bastard."

Frankie whined a few crude barbs back at him, and they sat there trading comical insults that reminded me of a pair of prepubescent schoolboys learning to talk naughty.

The terminal door opened again, and from behind my flimsy fortress I trained my gaze on the wiry form of none other than Spider, walking quickly toward his comrades. I couldn't believe that everywhere I was, he was. Or was it the other way around?

"OK, Boney, you better get out dere by da limo. All clear?"

"Yeah Spidah, it's all clear." Boney got up and started for the door back out to the parking lot. Spider and Frankie Eyelashes started punching each other in the arm good-naturedly, then Spider fumbled for change and walked over to a coke machine. As for me, I sat immobile, gazing through my peepholes and wondering how this was going to turn out.

Suddenly, there was a sharp rap on the terminal window. I cringed. Would Eyelashes and Spider look up at the noise, watch me respond and get up, see through my disguise, and end my adventure? Or would they hear the knock, spot Al, and descend on him? Would they go for both of us when I followed Al onto the tarmac?

Behind my paper, I slowly donned the sunglasses I'd thrown into my bag, made sure all my hair was stuffed under my hat, pulled the brim even lower on my forehead, then calmly folded the newspaper's pages, laid them on the table, and walked at a relaxed pace out the door .

As I stepped outside, Da Boys were bending down, pulling their coke cans out of the machine. Safe on the sidewalk, I shot a glance back and saw them taking a few quick swigs, then tossing the cans and heading out of the brightly lighted waiting room, toward the door, and presumably toward the same arrival pad where three people from the *Enquirer* were heading.

I was at the chain link gate. Al, who'd already punched in the door code, pushed it open. Aylott went through first, cameras down, Al followed, and then I went through, moving quickly off to a less lighted area on the side.

It all happened fast. The plane swept into the arrival area like a hornet with its wings back, and pulled to a smooth stop right in front of the terminal. Its doors opened, and Sinatra stepped off the little Lear jet smiling, then turned around extending his hand into the hatch, offering it to Barbara as she de-planed down the steps. As we watched, it was all joy, at least for that instant.

But then Photog Bob stepped quickly up to them. I could hear his pitch. "Mr. Sinatra, could I impose on you and Miss Marx for a picture on this happy occasion?"

Sinatra's mood immediately changed, a scowl spread across his face, and he became the difficult and cantankerous opponent known well to members of the press.

Fist raised at the obsequiously petitioning photographer, Sinatra screamed, "Where the fuck did you come from? Get outa here, you bum!"

Bob's tenacity kicked in. "Please, Mr. Sinatra," he continued respectfully, not moving even one inch, "I'm only doing my job. Just one happy picture of you and your bride-to-be."

Sinatra raged, "I couldn't care less about your job, you cocksucker. Get out of here or I'll bury that camera in your head." His face was a mask of anger as he shook his fist and lurched at Bob, who manfully stood his ground, ready to risk all for his picture. Sinatra was coming right at Bob, ready to give him a hiding to hell.

As Sinatra went for Aylott, Al stood off to one side and I stood to the other, unnoticed so far in the fracas.

Just then, a short round balding man in glasses bustled nervously up to Aylott. I immediately recognized Sinatra's longtime publicist Lee Solters. I'd worked with him and his office throughout my days with Rona Barrett, although I had never before seen him angry. He was one of the biggest names in Hollywood publicity and he'd been on the Lear with Sinatra.

Solters put his hand up over the snapper's camera lens and muttered, "I understand you have a job to do, but take my advice and get out of here fast."

Just then, like a shot, Spider and Frankie Eyelashes flashed in front of me and were on the tarmac in an instant, closing in on our guy, grabbing him roughly by his arms and yanking his cameras away from him. Bob played it cool, submitting to these strong, well-used hands but keeping his grip on his camera strap lest Da Boys smash it to the ground. Bob would be black and blue tomorrow.

Al went over to Solters, introduced himself as an *Enquirer* editor, and played the voice of reason while Spider and Frankie roughly continued to manhandle Aylott, pinning his arms behind his back, with Bob continuing to grip his camera strap for dear life.

With Spider and Eyelashes otherwise occupied, I kept my distance and watched from under my hat, as Sinatra, still mumbling obscenities, grabbed his lady fair by the arm and hurried with her toward the waiting limo which by now Mr. Boney had pulled onto the tarmac.

You might say I thought it an inopportune moment to approach them for a word. So I watched from the shadows, saving myself for later.

Into the limo they jumped, speeding off across the airfield into the black night in the general direction of Caesar's Palace, leaving Solters by the Lear jet to deal with this little glitch.

This is where I decided to make a quick fade, unnoticed I hoped. Head down, I slunk back through the terminal and once out the other side, sprinted to my little rental car. No one had noticed me before, during, or after and I wanted to keep it that way.

I hightailed it back to Caesar's Palace, ducked into the first ladies room, shoved open a stall door, and once within, stripped off my jeans and T-shirt and changed into the black dress I'd stuffed into my bag. Juggling my belongings, I emerged from the stall and stood before the mirror. Since no one had noticed me or my hat at the airport, I readjusted the brimmed chapeau back onto my head, and mentally assessed the events at the airport.

Now Da Boys not only knew Bob Aylott was a snapper, but might even have put him out of commission for the night, hopefully not in an alley or a dumpster. In any case, I had to assume there was no prayer of Bob getting a picture in the casino this night.

Yet, Sinatra was definitely about to materialize before our very eyes after his midnight show, ripe for a photo.

There was no other choice. I would take the picture myself. I actually had a better chance of getting it than our photog would have had, with his big professional cameras, plus which I had already assessed Sinatra's VIP area for camera angles.

That was it. I'd pop into the gift shop, buy one of those little pocket cameras, wait until Frankie and group got all settled in their seats behind the railing, then I'd rush up like Jack Ruby, shoot and run. Hopefully, I would escape the kind of consequences Ruby suffered after his rush at Lee Harvey Oswald.

I ran to the gift shop and selected a small Kodak one-step camera and a roll of film. These, folks, were the days before cheap disposable cameras. Everything was more of a challenge then.

I thought, "First the hat, now a $100 camera. Payroll is going to go apoplectic when they see another weird purchase on my expense report, but if I get these pictures, my editor will back me up, and everyone will kiss my toes in gratitude besides."

Purchase in hand, I headed back to the ladies room, sat down in the lounge area, tore the camera out of its box saving only the little instruction book, and loaded the film. I snapped off a couple of shots, just to make sure flash and camera worked.

Where were Bob and Al and Spider and Eyelashes right now? I wondered to myself. Had injuries been inflicted? Had choke holds been applied? Would I see photographer or editor again tonight? Or ever? And would I see Da Boys again tonight?

There was no need to disrupt my own cool by worrying about any of that right now. There was nothing I could do about it. As for what I *could* do, I'd done it. I'd altered my appearance, parked myself where Sinatra and Marx would be, and armed myself with a camera. Words and pictures, pictures and words.

"Get back in that casino," I ordered myself.

I hid the little camera in the folds of my skirt as I again cased the VIP area where Frank would soon be sitting. He was onstage right now, but within the next hour or so, he and his "gals and pals" would be arranging themselves at that long, long table.

I had my large zip pocketbook slung over my shoulder and pretended to be fidgeting with it as I lifted the small camera to my eye to see how wide the angle was and how close I'd have to be to get both Frank and Barbara in the frame.

Silently praying that Da Boys wouldn't show up, I sat down at a cocktail table within a few paces of the railing and ordered a drink. The table was as close as you could get to the VIP enclosure. I could almost take the picture from my chair.

After my drink arrived, I stood, looked at the second hand on my watch, and timed my run-through. I walked up to the railing, eyes straight ahead. My right hand was at my side, and in it, hidden within the folds of my skirt, was the camera. Looking down, I was satisfied that no one could see it.

I stood outside the railing opposite Frank's chair, raised the camera from its hiding place in my skirt, aimed it, looked through the viewfinder, pretended to snap the shutter, then slipped it into my bag and zipped the top.

Stepping back to my table I looked at my watch. The whole operation would take no more than five or six seconds, after which I would calmly walk away and disappear into the crowd.

I practiced the whole maneuver three or four times, then sat, sipping my icy drink and waiting.

Feeling slightly paranoid, I kept my head down so the brim of my black felt hat hid my face, but by tilting my head, I could still see to one side or the other. I was glad when several other couples drifted in and occupied the tables right next to mine, so I didn't stand out so much, a lone woman in a black dress and black hat, head down, like Mata Hari or something. The growing crowd must mean the midnight show was over.

"Hey, Spidah!"

I froze, instantly recognizing Frankie Eyelashes' less than dulcet tones.

Tipping my head, I saw the lower portion of his unmistakably massive body moving into my field of view. He was calling over my head, so Spider must be close too, on the other side.

"Hey Spidah! He's comin' out. Everyt'ing okay?"

"Yeah, yeah, it's cool, baby." Spider's voice was so close I could almost smell his Binaca breath.

Ohmigod, were they going to stand there until Sinatra came out? This could turn ugly, very ugly, when I got up to make my moves.

I've always wondered what quirk within me sparks my decisions in these pinches. I sat and thought about Spider and Eyelashes and how they'd react when I stood and snapped, after which they'd recognize me.

Theoretically, I could have faded away to protect myself. But it never occurred to me to abort my self-appointed mission. It never did. Ever. I always went forth. And at that moment, with Sinatra's goons talking over my head, it was strangely intoxicating.

I took a deep breath, surrendered to the outcome, and sat there, knowing I was probably going to take some bad lumps when I got up and took that picture.

"Hey Spidah, come wit me. He wants us to go out to da limo. Dere's some kids or sumt'in and he wants us to go and check it out. Jimmy in da parking lot called da suite. He wants you and me to go."

"What are dey doin'? Sprayin' or what?"

"I donno. Maybe dey're whizzin'."

The two men broke up, suppressing their prurient laughter so it came out in little gasps through their teeth.

The other couples around me blithely sipped their beers and their rums and cokes, engrossed in their own conversations, but I sat craning my ears to hear every word Da Boys said.

"Okay, let's make it snappy."

Tipping my head to the side, I saw their four legs walking away, and breathed a silent prayer of thanks. But how long this reprieve would last was anybody's guess.

Long minutes ticked by.

Then all at once, I felt the vibration in the area change, and a surging energy began to engulf this corner of Caesar's casino floor. A large group moved forward and assembled inside the VIP railing. I raised my head and watched. In the center of the action was Frank Sinatra, and at his side, the beautiful blonde ex-chorine Barbara Marx. They sat, like a relaxed and beneficent king and queen surrounded by attentive courtiers. Quickly scanning the group, I spotted a familiar face. Pat Henry sat near Sinatra, cracking dirty jokes and pawing a buxom brunette.

I had to move fast. Spider and Eyelashes could return and take their places at the table at any moment.

I waited agonizing seconds as Frank and Barbara got their drinks. Sinatra had his arm around her and was whispering in her ear, and

Barbara was responding like a delighted puppy.

Then, lo and behold, as they sat there, Barbara began brandishing her left hand. She waved it across the table, and then over toward Pat Henry—and every time she moved it, something glinted with prismatic flashes. I could see it. On her ring finger was a huge diamond, must have been ten carats, seemed to be marquis cut.

She was engaged! They were betrothed!

And they looked pretty happy, I had to admit. Frank kept nuzzling his fiancée, leaning over to her and circling her shoulders within his arms. She purred and nestled into the space between his cheek and his shoulder.

For me, this was it.

It was a front page picture.

They were face forward, they were cuddling, they were in love, and most of all, they were engaged. If I waited around much longer, Spider and Frankie Eyelashes might reappear and spot me, then my chance would be gone forever.

I took in the scene for just a few more moments, pushing my luck as I memorized details so I could report them in my story.

Then I took a deep breath, stood up, walked briskly to my mark by the railing, raised my camera from my side, took perfect aim capturing Frank and Barbara in mid-nuzzle with her ring showing on her raised left hand, snapped fast, saw the flash go off, put the camera into my open bag, and started walking calmly away while I quickly zipped the bag completely closed.

Calmly I walked.

"So far so good, so far so good," I thought, my head swimming with nerves, my thoughts jumping crazily, in time with the blood that rushed at every pulse point. Calm on the exterior, walking normally, exploding inside, I headed away, away, away. "Please God, no Spider, no Eyelashes." Just like during the tape recorder caper, I was clenched.

And just like then, I heard no exclamations, nobody ran after me, nobody reached from behind to grab me. I kept walking. My eyes were straight ahead, and I was hoping they wouldn't land on Da Boys. The camera was in my purse. It was safe, and maybe I was too.

Wrong.

Like an instant roadblock, a towering figure in a tan suit loomed into my path. The guy must have been six-feet-eight at least. Braced as I was for the dreaded Spider, this man almost qualified as a piece of cake. I noticed his blond, perfectly razor-cut, almost militaristic moustache. He just stood there.

"Ma'am?"

I looked up. And up.

"Ma'am, I believe you took a picture. There are no pictures allowed in the casino."

He was not smiling. He was very large. He was very solid.

"Oh?" I said, trying to put a little substance into my attitude.

"I'll have to ask you to give me your camera."

"Give you my camera? Why would I do that?"

"Ma'm, there's a sign over there specifically saying there's no photography allowed in the casino. You took a private picture, a picture of Mr. Sinatra, and you especially cannot do that."

"Well, I'm a fan. Fans like to take pictures."

"Ma'm, I will have to confiscate your camera."

"Well, just who are you? Are you a policeman?" I asked, taking the offensive.

He said nothing, but silently reached inside his jacket and pulled out a small leather holder which he flipped open to reveal a silver badge. I grabbed his hand and pulled the holder closer, taking him totally by surprise, and I got a good look at the badge as he quickly yanked his hand away from me and flipped the thing closed.

"You're not a policeman," I said. "That thing says Hotel Security."

"Ma'm, I'm asking you for your camera *now*."

"Well, I'm sorry," I said ruefully. "It's my personal property, and I'm not giving it to you. You're not a policeman. If you want to call the police and get a search warrant, I think that's what you need."

"You know ma'm, there's an easy way and there's a hard way to do things. Since you don't want to do it the easy way, you're going to have to come with me."

"Fine," I said boldly, wondering where we were off to, how long we'd be gone, who else we would see when we got there, if I'd ever come back, and how anyone would ever find out if something bad was about to happen to me.

That's when I noticed his hands. They were the size of baseball mitts. And one of them was now grabbing my left elbow and pulling me along like a little rag doll through the casino.

As we marched along, another burly guy fell in with us, this one in a white polo shirt, with a big ring of keys jangling from the belt loop of his black trousers. An emblem on his shirt pocket said "Caesar's Palace Security." He grabbed my other elbow.

I was now practically off the ground as the two men hurried me through the labyrinth of the casino, past the slots, past the tables where I'd seen Frankie Eyelashes earlier, and then, past Cleopatra's Barge.

Cleopatra's Barge! Our message center!!

Like a death row prisoner searching for his last chance on the way to the gas chamber, I scanned the floating lounge. It was a desperation scan, but maybe, just maybe Al and Bob had returned and parked themselves there. I slowed down, only to spot, over in a corner, Bob Aylott and Al Coombes, hunched over their drinks, engrossed in conversation, looking a little the worse for wear.

If only I could get their attention, at least they'd know I was now the one in trouble. What could I do? What can any damsel do? Go to distress mode!

I started crumpling as if in a faint, letting my full weight fall into the two guards' grips, and moaning loudly, "Nooooo, you *can't* take me away. Noooo!" I was really giving it my all, yelling and falling at the same time.

We were directly opposite where Al and Bob were sitting. "Come *on* guys," I thought frantically, "stop talking, and hear me, and look up for just one second!"

I started waving my arms, but this just resulted in each of my captors grabbing even more tightly to restrain me.

"HEY! HELP! YOU'RE HURTING ME!" I meant it.

I really shrieked this time, screaming my pain, much to the consternation of some tourists in shorts walking toward us. But as for my colleagues on the Barge, they neither heard nor saw. Al and Bob didn't even glance my way.

Now we were past their line of vision, so my little show became pointless and I ended it as abruptly as I'd started it. I simply resumed walking calmly between the large men, as resigned and limp as the Wolf after Peter had strung him up between two poles. The tan-suit guy looked at me very, very quizzically, trying to figure out what was up with me.

Only a short distance on, we arrived at an unmarked door, which Mr. Tan Suit pushed open, and we all stepped through into a cramped, brightly fluorescent-lighted office.

"Siddown," ordered Mr. Tan curtly.

I saddown.

"Now I think you ought to give me your camera, don't you?"

I placed my zipped-up pocketbook squarely in front of me on my lap, crossed my arms over it, and said, "No, I don't think so."

"Ma'am, I don't want to get rough with you, but you've taken a photograph that's not allowed under any circumstances, and we can't let you do that. Mr. Sinatra doesn't want that."

"Well, it's already done. Besides, I'm a fan of Frank Sinatra. He should be glad he has young fans like me who'd even want his picture. It's a souvenir. I've been to his show three times. You should be nice to me, you know. I'm a paying customer, and I'm his future."

"Yeah," said the gigantic man, sitting on an edge of the desk, with his huge muscular leg slung over it diagonally, "well, lady, you may be a fan, a customer, whatever you say, but you'd be surprised at what happens to pictures that get taken of Mr. Sinatra. They have a funny way of ending up in all kinds of places—*like the front page of the National Enquirer*. And even worse rags than that. People who look just like you and who say they're fans just like you, are really slimy reporters on assignment."

"Well, I wouldn't know anything about that," I lied with big doe eyes.

I gulped and looked at the floor. Almost nailed twice in one night, or was I up to three by now, or did this count as number four? And if they got inside my purse, forget the "almost." For in there, besides the camera containing my *Enquirer* front page color close-up of Sinatra and his intended, I also had my *Enquirer* press pass, signed by The Boss, identifying me as a reporter, and accompanied by a good likeness of myself.

The irony was not lost on me that the purse in my lap was the self-same one I'd used in the tape recorder caper up at Tahoe. I only hoped it would be as lucky for me now as it was then.

I silently vowed that they'd have to call out the National Guard to get me to open that bag. Once it was unzipped, I was undone. Anything could happen. But as long as I kept it shut, it was off limits, private property, sacrosanct, and I could sit there and banter with them all night if they wanted to.

It seems they wanted to.

"Okay miss, you can just sit here and think about it, how's that?"

I replied, "Well, if you're going to hold me prisoner here, I believe I'm allowed one phone call, just like downtown, no?"

"Yeah, you can make a phonecall. So who are you planning to call?"

"My lawyer of course, who also happens to be somewhere in the casino right now." Al Coombes, it had just dawned on me, was a barrister.

Mr. Tan Pants merely shrugged and handed me a house phone.

Although he'd missed my noisy theatrics, Al did hear my page and soon came on the line.

"Hi, it's me, Babs. Some men have got me locked in a room back here and they won't let me go. I took a picture of Frank Sinatra —you know how much I love him—and they tell me they won't let me go until I open up my purse and hand over my camera to them. I told them I had to speak to my lawyer."

I listened passive-faced as Al nearly gagged on the other end of the line, then started chuckling. "Oh, this is rich. This is rich," he went. "They've hauled you off, they just dragged Aylott outside, and they're right on my ass too. They're fairly decent bloodhounds, wot? Who's got you?"

"They're hotel security, but they're not the police," I answered looking up at the khaki giant.

"Al, you're my lawyer, what should I do?"

Al composed himself and said, "Oh, of course, you told them I'm your lawyer. Good thinking. You're doing fine, bloody fine. But do not—repeat—DO NOT—open your bag. You've got the picture, you've got the camera, and they can't take it from you. As long as they're not using force, just stand firm. Whatever you do, do not open that bag and do not hand over that camera."

"But they won't let me go," I pleaded, trying to sound naive, not like a reporter in conference.

Al instructed me, "Tell them they are in violation of your first amendment rights by holding you against your will, and your lawyer says the hotel will be sued if they don't release you immediately."

"That's all I needed to know. Thanks." And I put the phone down, empowered.

Breezily, I announced, "My lawyer says you're holding me in violation of my first amendment rights and that if you don't release me, the hotel will be sued."

The big guy raised his hands and said, "Lady, we're *not* holding you against your will. You're free to go any time."

This was a curve ball. "I am?" I asked, suspiciously.

"Yes, you are," he replied, poker-faced.

"In that case," I said, standing and tucking my shoulder bag safely under my arm, "goodbye."

I stepped lively for the door, bouncing and elated, and one of the guards opened it for me with a little smirk.

"Thanks," I said, smiling sweetly, and stepped out the door and back into the soft lighting of the casino. The feeling of freedom was a relief, though a niggling sense of being watched remained. Up the wide aisle I went, heading toward Cleopatra's Barge, in hopes Al would still be there even though poor Bob had apparently been grabbed off the floor again and ejected. How to talk to Al without pinning us as colleagues would be my next problem.

So engrossed was I in that thought that I gasped in genuine surprise when suddenly, another gigantic man stepped directly into my path and stood unmoving before me. He was neatly tailored in a white shirt, subdued tie and dark suit.

"You can go, miss," he gravely intoned, looming there, "but you've made an enemy of Mr. Sinatra tonight. Always remember that. Mr. Sinatra is very unhappy about this."

"Well," I sniffed, "he shouldn't be unhappy. He should only be glad he's got a loyal fan. I'm not against him, you know. I love him."

"Just remember, you may love him, but tonight you have made Frank Sinatra very, very unhappy, and he don't forget. He don't ever forget."

Before I could come up with a snappy reply, the guy dissipated into the woodwork. It gave me the creeps to be warned this way, knowing Sinatra's reputation for underworld affiliations, not to mention the very apparent presence of his strong-arm henchmen. And it might get even creepier when the picture I'd snapped turned up in the *Enquirer.* I wouldn't be too hard to find back in L.A.

I steamed forward, thanking my lucky stars that it wasn't Spider or Eyelashes who had gotten the assignment to scare the broad with the camera. There was no telling what might have happened then.

I saw Coombes coming toward me, and just as my face lit with recognition, a bull-necked older man wearing rose-colored glasses appeared from the side and cornered Al. Immediately, the man was joined by a Caesar's security guard who pumped himself up like a bear as he stood to Coombes' other side.

Almost in mid-step, I changed courses. Instead of greeting Al, I swerved to the side keeping my head down, and stepped up into Cleopatra's Barge where from behind a pillar, I observed Jilly Rizzo himself on the attack with Al. He stood, he growled, he glared, he put his gigantic hands on his hips, he leaned back, legs wide apart, and roughly, he began to interrogate Al.

"How 'bout some ID, asshole?" I heard him say, clutching Al's upper arm.

"What's this about?" responded Al, shrugging laconically and shaking his head.

Jilly didn't really have to give him an answer, but he did. "ID, asshole, ID. We seen you talking all night to some punk we just kicked out of the hotel because he was acting suspicious. We yanked him right out of the men's room and he's in a cab right now. Give us some ID and we'll figure out if you go out the door too."

"Gentlemen, I'm sure there's some misunderstanding," said Coombes, as cool as a cucumber. "I'm a patron of the hotel and I've been standing around with a lot of people. I have no reason at all to show you any ID. I've done nothing."

Jilly pushed out his huge barrel chest, towering to greater-than-full height and glowering down at the docile Al, who simply stood his ground with a bland look on his face and without apparent fear.

"We're on your tail, sucker, okay? You try anything and you're dead meat."

I watched Al trundle away and head across the casino toward Sinatra's group. Jilly and his pal followed. It was amazing that presumably, none of the Sinatra personnel here at the hotel had seen Al or Bob at the airport, but still, they smelled a rat. I wondered if Spider and Eyelashes had phoned in descriptions, and if anyone had yet attached me to Al and Bob. Obviously, I mustn't be seen talking to Al, nor he to me, so I just kept my distance and observed.

Stopping at a slot machine to drop in two or three quarters, I kept behind the group. From a safe distance, I watched Al duck into a men's room. Jilly and the guard waited outside the door for him, then remained on his tail as Al headed over toward the railing behind which Sinatra and pals laughed and drank.

I sat down at a blackjack table with a clear view of the Sinatra group and plunked down a twenty dollar bill for some chips. Then I just watched, in between playing half-hearted hands and not even caring each time I lost. Every time Al moved a muscle, or got an inch closer to Sinatra, Jilly or the guard pushed up to him and told him to move on.

There were literally hundreds of onlookers milling around watching Sinatra, even some with cameras, even one or two who took snapshots, but the gang harassed none of them. They'd carted me off, they'd kicked Bob Aylott out, and now they were going to worry Al until he gave up. Their sixth sense was sharp, extremely sharp, and I wondered if the canny Jilly would find me next.

Finally, just as my last chips were collected by the dealer, I saw Al pack it in and walk out of the area.

Jilly and his pal were on Al like glue, so I waited around a bit, just to see if anything else was happening in the Sinatra group. They were in their own world, just unwinding. No fistfights, no drunken spats, no obscene gestures. I got up and headed out too, toward the hotel exit. I went straight to my car, and as I approached it, Bob Aylott stepped out of the shadows nearby. He glanced each way, then whispered to me under his breath.

"There are eyes around. Get in your car and drive to our hotel parking lot. We'll meet you there."

Without looking him in the eye, I stage-whispered, "They've been tailing Al, but he's coming."

"He's okay, he's in the car. See you at the motel."

I jumped in my rental and sped back to my hotel, thinking all the way over about Sinatra's goons, especially the one who told me I'd made an enemy of Frank Sinatra.

By the time I swung into my motel parking lot, I was sure I was being followed. A pair of headlights had been right behind me since I'd left Caesar's. I turned, they turned. I stopped, they stopped. I slowed, they slowed.

Silently, I pushed down the doorlocks of my car, slowly pulled into a parking place, then sat there, engine idling, headlights still on. I didn't look to the left, I didn't look to the right.

I was terrified.

"TAP TAP TAP!" came the knuckles on my car window. I jumped so high that I actually bumped my head on the roof, and like a trapped deer, looked up, expecting the worst. Expecting Spider.

Instead, I saw Al Coombes' smiling face.

My open hands went to my chest, my eyes rolled, and I practically fainted.

"DON'T DO THAT!!" I exclaimed, rolling down my window.

Al laughed, and then said, "Who did you think it was? SPPIIIDDDEERRRRR??" wiggling his fingers in front of my face.

"As a matter of fact, *yes*," I said, getting out of my car.

"Quite a group," understated Al. "So now they've got a make on us all. Years of practice for that kind of intuition, yeah?"

"They don't even *know* how good their intuition is," I said, reaching down to unzip my bag, and pulling out my priceless little camera.

"They had us tonight, but we got away with it." We all shared our war stories of the evening.

It seems Da Boys had given Bob a punch in the stomach out at the airport as he unyieldingly clutched his camera. They'd finally let him go with a warning that if they saw him with the camera again, they'd smash it over his head and cut him besides.

Al told how Lee Solters had warned, even begged him, not to mess with Sinatra's boys, that he couldn't win, that he was a marked man; and about how he'd then been tailed and harassed in the casino the rest of the evening.

I told of my close encounters of the Spider kind—how I'd confused him about my identity in the casino; how he and Eyelashes had later talked right over my hatted head; how I'd peeked at them through my newspaper at the airport; about my capture and detention; and about the veiled threat I'd received as I left the hotel's impromptu interrogation unit.

"I feel very uneasy right now," I admitted. "They could have tailed any one of us here. They suspect us all—but me, they know I have this picture. What if they find me and break my door in? Or my *head!* They'd do it, you know. In a *heartbeat!* Sinatra's my enemy now, they *told* me, and those guys play hardball."

"Well, you probably don't have to worry, but still, anything could happen," Coombes agreed. "I'd like to think they wouldn't care once we made ourselves scarce, but who knows?"

In deference to my fears, and maybe even his own, Al actually changed rooms, moving right next door to mine, and I promised to scream as loudly as I could if anything untoward, anything at all, happened.

Even with a protector right next door, I hardly slept a wink through what remained of the night. There was no dead bolt on my door and every time I heard footsteps on the stairs outside, or voices in the parking lot below, I sat bolt upright.

What small, fitful slumber I achieved ended in nightmare visions, and I lay there convinced Sinatra's mob would find me and do something bad to me. I got up in a cold sweat at five-thirty AM and propped a chair against my doorknob, but I still shook like a leaf in my bed.

I was glad when the sun came up at last and we had a whole new day to work with.

****

And a better day it was. The two Franks were getting crowned with doctorates, and we'd be there. We had tickets. We were invited press. Presumably, nobody could turn us away. It was a university function, totally out of Sinatra's usual realm.

The graduation started at two o'clock at the University of Nevada at Las Vegas stadium, but we'd been told to get there by one.

It was a blue-sky, brilliantly sunny day, and after my sleepless night of fear, the warmth of the sun felt good on my slightly aching body, especially with my dark silk jersey outfit attracting the hottest rays.

Enhancing these good feelings, our press area had great possibilities for access to Sinatra. We sat on a raised platform in front of the stage, and as the dignitaries entered in procession, they would go right past us.

Before things got rolling, I spotted one of Senator Church's aides from the press party the day before, a friendly young ivy league chap, and asked him, "So what's the program? Who's on first?"

"No, 'Who's On Second,' " he quipped, taking off on the old Abbott & Costello comedy routine.

"Boom boom," I laughed. "But seriously folks," (while de-ashing an imaginary cigar) "will Senator Church speak first?"

"Well, no. Frank Sinatra will actually be getting an honorary degree too, and he'll go first because I guess he's got to leave right afterwards. Then, the senator will receive his honor and will deliver the commencement address. And we guarantee, it's a goodie."

"And when Mr. Sinatra leaves the stage, which way will he go?" I ventured.

"Oh, I believe he's going to go off that way, to the left across the field, and over to that gate where his car will be waiting."

This was almost too much to ask. Sinatra would not be escorted out a back way, but would have to walk all the way across the football field to that gate. If he wasn't totally surrounded by his staff, it would be an easy matter for a press member to leave her seat on the platform and simply walk with him across the expanse of turf.

I parked myself on the last seat in my row, right at the edge of the platform, with a perfect view of all that would transpire, and a perfect exit. I could step right off without having to crawl over anyone, and make a quick beeline for Sinatra as he walked off with his doctorate in hand.

I looked around as parents and well-wishers streamed into their bleacher seats above the stage where their offspring would soon be graduated. Then it was two o'clock. Right on time, the students began marching in, swathed in their caps and gowns, smiles on their faces.

My eyes narrowed to scan the bleacher crowd carefully, in search of a particular well-wisher, but I was unprepared for the windfall which soon greeted my intense gaze.

Right in the front row of the bleachers, wearing huge Mrs. Bug sunglasses, with a scarf tied around her blond bouffant hairdo, sat a beaming Barbara Marx. And right next to her, as an added bonus, was the plump and savvy Dolly Sinatra, Frank's street-wise, bespectacled, beloved mother.

Garbed in a print dress and a hat, Dolly had come to see her adored only child receive the ultimate academic recognition, even if it meant she had to sit next to Barbara Marx.

Everyone knew how Dolly hated Barbara Marx. In fact, Dolly hated any woman who wanted her boy. Dolly thought no woman was worthy of her Frankie, especially not (in Dolly's mind) a gold-digging, ex-chorus girl who'd already used up a Marx brother. And Dolly's resentment must only be more so now that Barbara had indeed snagged her boy, and sported a big diamond ring to prove it.

Yes, Dolly's historic presence next to Marx seemed yet more proof that a wedding was coming. Barbara was indeed being welcomed, grudgingly or not, into the clan.

I visually backtracked from them to me, to see the map of how to get to them. There was high scaffolding in front of the bleachers and my eyes followed the structure to its edge, where a set of stairs led up onto a walkway right in front of the first row. It's how everyone had gotten up there, and it's how I was going to get there too.

Tape recorder at the ready, I slid out of my chair onto the field and headed for the stairway up into those bleachers. It was Showtime once again.

I couldn't see where Aylott had been seated, since they'd put reporters in one area and photographers in another, but I hoped he was seeing what I was seeing and would get a picture.

Stepping gingerly in my high strappy heels up the open wooden steps, I headed right for Sinatra's women.

It struck me once I got close how beautiful Barbara Marx actually was. At forty-eight, she had hardly a line on her face and hardly a flaw in her figure. Plastic surgery or no, she looked like a million bucks.

"Mrs. Marx, I'm with the paper here in Vegas," I smiled. "Congratulations on Mr. Sinatra's doctorate." Her face went on high beam.

"Oh thank you, dear. I'm proud of him, very, very proud."

"And you're engaged! Is that your gorgeous ring?"

She was like a schoolgirl, glowing, smiling broadly, and holding up her hand to me. "Yes, it just happened. Lovely, isn't it? I'm very happy." She tweaked her ring finger right at my face, so I got a really good look at the thing. It *was* a marquis cut. It *was* about ten carats. And it *was* lovely. I learned later Frank had dropped about three hundred and sixty thousand dollars for it.

I turned to the elder Mrs. Sinatra, who was almost smirking as Barbara effused.

"Congratualtions on your son's wonderful honor," I smarmed. "You must be very proud."

Dolly begrudged me a patronizing smile and said, "Very proud. He's a fine man and he deserves it."

Quick, I tried one more question on Barbara. "So when will you two tie the knot?"

Suddenly, she seemed to go cold. She'd suddenly realized she was being interviewed without Frankie's permission or presence, and with a steel-eyed Mama sitting right next door.

"That's all," she said. "There's no more." And she waved me aside.

It didn't matter. I thanked her, turned away, and was gleeful hurrying back toward my seat, just as the parade of university dignitaries began. Marx had confirmed it all, displayed the ring, and actually spoken to me. Before she got wise and caught herself, her sense of joy, maybe even triumph, had glistened through.

I waited at the bottom of the bleacher stairs as all the draped bigwigs of the university marched right past me, bedecked in their academic robes, festooned with colorful sashes, tassles and medallions of esteem, paragons all, of princely scholasticism.

Splendid they were, walking in measured steps as Elgar's "Pomp and Circumstance" blared over the loudspeakers.

And at the end of the parade, decked in a flowing black robe, a mortarboard perched on his head, a ruby red sash of honor draped around his shoulders, was Dr. Frank Sinatra.

He had a somewhat silly smile on his face, a combination, no doubt, of embarrassment, the strangeness of the getup, the unfamiliarity of the occasion, and being trapped in the middle of a formal daytime ritual.

He walked right past me without seeing me. Instead, his eyes were looking up, into the front row of the bleachers I had just descended.

His searching gaze (as well as mine) ended squarely on the person of Barbara Marx. She was madly blowing kisses to her betrothed, over and over, across the open palm of her hand. And Dolly was smiling expansively, approvingly, as she waved her right hand up and down, up and down, toward Frank. I realized the silly smile on Frank's face was that of a little boy who "done good." Mom was watching—both moms were watching—and he "done good."

He looked kind of sparkly after finding Mom and Barbara.

All the brainies of the university seemed to become a little brainless in Sinatra's presence, undoubtedly feeling even more honored over the whole thing than Frank himself was.

During the singing of the National Anthem and opening words, one of the bigwigs kept passing a word or two to Frank, as if fearful he'd leave if no one talked him through it.

And, as I'd been advised, the university president put Frank at the top of the program, bestowing his doctorate upon him immediately, evidently not wanting to impose the whole dull graduation ceremony on such an eminent guest.

Sinatra gave a few humble remarks afterwards, along the lines of "Who'd-a thunk it back on the streets of Hoboken?" He seemed completely sincere. Everyone cheered, Barbara blew more kisses, Dolly waved more waves, and then, as the crowd cheered, Frank Sinatra proceeded, just as Frank Church's aide had said he would, off the stage to my left, off onto that big, big field.

Accompanying him was a top regent of the university. No bodyguards, no entourage, no Spider, no Jilly. Just one beaming educator wearing a black academic robe and mortarboard, accompanying the newly-minted Dr. Frank himself.

I liked it. Frank was trapped. I had him.

Normally, I wouldn't put any obscenity toward a lady of the press past Frank. But I couldn't imagine he would dare castigate me or melt the air with profane invective while walking beside a gentle man of learning who'd just proclaimed him a Doctor, of Humane Letters, no less.

No, I thought, I had Frankie boy this time and he would just have to go along with it. Heck, I could even announce who I really was.

I turned on my tape recorder, slid off my chair onto the ground, and headed across the field at an angle that would intersect with the path of Sinatra and the regent.

Then it was beautiful, like a ballet. Just as I reached Sinatra, Bob Aylott appeared out of nowhere, walking backwards fast, in front of Sinatra and the official and me, snapping picture after picture of Frank, and of me walking with Frank, interviewing him with my tape recorder in his face.

Not even under his breath did Frank Sinatra abuse me, even after I told him I was "a reporter from the paper here." He answered my mundane questions about his new doctorate politely, if succinctly.

"It makes me very happy, very proud. I was never much at school, so it's a thrill."

While I had him by the short and curlies, with that nice regent walking right beside him, I gave him the questions he'd hate, about his engagement.

"Yes, we're engaged. Thank you." He looked straight ahead, a clenched smile on his face as Bob kept snapping. No dummy Frank. He didn't explode while the camera was on him, he didn't curse me away and he didn't make a run at the photographer as he walked with that scholar. He just submitted to the photos and answered small.

But he talked. Civilly ... courteously, even ... and knowing I was a journalist ... and seeing I was a hated "broad." It was a miracle.

I don't imagine any female journalist before or since has ever had Frank so inescapably hog-tied. Everything else was worth that moment.

I've marveled about it for years.

****

After this Vegas escapade, Bob's picture of me interviewing Frank Sinatra appeared on the pages of the *Enquirer,* along with my byline blazing across the top of the story. Seeing my name on this latest Sinatra coverage, would it finally dawn on Spider and Da Boys who dat Barbara broad really was? What's more, now that I had jammed my tape recorder right at Frank Sinatra's face as he walked across the football field, he was not likely to forget, if I ever came close again, that I was a press dame.

I figured my days as an undercover Sinatra babe were over. I was made with Da Boys for good.

I couldn't believe the *Enquirer* sent me after Sinatra one more time. Engagements lead to weddings. I would be there for Frank's. But that's another tale for another time.

****

I wondered for a long time if I'd run into Spider or Eyelashes some night in a dark alley, or hiding in the back seat of my car, or possibly lurking in the shadows of my entrance courtyard. It never happened.

I recently learned that it probably never will. My pal Spider died in the late eighties after suffering a series of heart attacks. At this writing, Frankie Eyelashes is still around, living in Vegas, working, I'm told, as a croupier, which is how he started.

But most of Sinatra's once-inner circle is gone—Pat Henry, who suffered a fatal heart attack in February of 1982; the unique Jilly Rizzo who died in a fiery car crash in May of 1992, under possibly suspicious circumstances; and Frank's beloved mama, Dolly Sinatra, who perished in a chartered jet crash in a turbulent mountain snow storm while on her way to attend Frank's opening night in Vegas. That was in January of 1977, just seven months after her boy's marriage.

Twenty years later, by 1997, the Chairman of the Board himself was eighty-two years old, and failing.

But while he still felt like his old self, he'd gone to his legendary musical home at Capitol Records in Hollywood to give the world one more recorded work, "Duets." Sinatra stipulated that he would not enter the building for his recording sessions until every door to every office was closed. He walked privately into the studio and no one but the recordists saw him. None of the secretaries, none of the A&R guys, none of the honchos. And none of the famous singers who dueted with him laid down their tracks in his presence or laid eyes on him either.

Indeed, the Noblest Roman of Them All was proud to the end. He wanted everyone to remember him as he was in the very good years.

But the great man, still the ultimate icon of Cool, was reportedly suffering with Alzheimer's disease and cancer, and from then on, he stayed out of the public eye. No more music, no more Vegas, no more Rat Pack shenanigans or White House honors, no more contretemps with the press and no more punchups with photographers. Just home, bed, the occasional card game with close friends like Gregory Peck, Jack Lemmon, and his loyal opening comic Tom Dreesen. And of course, Sinatra's daughters Nancy and Tina, and son Frank, Jr., gathered closely around him.

That's life.

He died in May, 1998.

And as that restless paradoxical life drew to a close, Barbara Marx Sinatra was still at his side. In the end, he called her "the love of my life."

So long, Frankie. It sure was fun. Please give my fond regards to Da Boys.

9

I Confess

Many people thought I had a fantasy job. In many ways, I did. I got to meet famous people, people everyone wanted to know about, and my job was to ask them the most intimate questions about their lives, on top of which, at least in sit-down situations, they had to answer.

Since I had not grown up star-struck, I considered it not so much a dream come true to meet these exciting and famous people, but instead, a privilege and novelty of my job. A thrilling novelty, for sure, but essentially, my goal was more about doing journalism than meeting movie stars.

But I have to admit, there was one star whom I had always adored.

As a kid growing up, I'd dreamed about him. In fact, I believe to this day that in my own little girl way, I was truly in love with him. I ached and pined over him, and whenever I saw him on television, I experienced the same exquisite pain and longing which I later learned came with real love. Something about him touched me and had an indelible impact on my heart.

I hadn't thought of him for years.

The series which had made him an American icon was long gone. The second frontier series he did, which introduced a whole new generation of kids to his noble and lanky presence, had finished a few years prior. You never heard his name mentioned any more.

But a blurb in the *L.A. Times* business section, noting that he was planning to run for political office, caught my eye. In fact, it grabbed me, bringing forth a rush of long-forgotten thoughts about my girlish love and how intensely it had affected me.

Queer stirrings led me to think, "Wouldn't it be a trip to meet him? I wonder what he looks like. I wonder if he's old and gray, or still exactly the same."

I decided to put in a story lead about his run for office to my editor in Florida and give it a shot.

As I flicked on my computer, it occurred to me what a charmed life and amazing job I had. Providing I got a nod from Florida, I could make a long-ago Hollywood dream of mine come true and call it work.

Much to my delighted amazement, Florida did nod, and my story lead was approved. The *Enquirer* wanted an interview with this man about his new career in politics, and I had the assignment.

I got ruffled and fluttery just thinking about it. I was going to meet and actually sit down face-to-face with the man who had so stirred my little girl heart long ago.

It dawned on me how, at the time, I just *knew* he'd fall in love with me if ever we met, and how I had wistfully dreamed he'd wait until I grew up so we could get married.

It seemed poignant and touching as I thought back upon myself as a child and remembered these precious things.

In a way, I really didn't want to meet him. Like most journalists, I had had the experience of meeting some or other of The Great who held a certain lifelong image in my mind, only to be sorely shocked and disappointed at the hollow reality.

What if this happened when I met "him." Well, now I was *going* to meet him, but only if I managed to get in touch and he was agreeable.

The news blurb said he lived up the coast, so I started with that area's directory assistance. Bingo first try, he had an office under his own name.

I rang, told a very pleasant secretary about my request, and marveled at how civilized and warm she was, not at all like the bristly Tinseltown assistants, but just as I thought "he" would be. She said he'd be back in a few hours and would probably call me back himself.

It was real, he was real, it was really happening. It was today, not childhood. He was going to call me on the telephone. The real him, not a childhood TV dream.

Forget the bank, forget the post office, forget the dry cleaners and all my other intended lunch hour errands. I sat transfixed at my desk, staring expectantly at the phone.

"Barbara, I understand you called and that you'd like to do an interview with me. How flattering." The voice was a voice I knew well, a dream voice, a love voice. It was his voice and he was calling me, in my house, on my phone, and speaking softly in my ear. He was real, not just a child's wish.

Trying hard to assume a businesslike attitude, I didn't succeed too well.

Somehow managing to explain my request, I sat open-mouthed as he readily agreed. "Wonderful." I could feel his warmth down the phone line. "It's good timing. Let people know I'm still here and what I'd like to do."

He suggested we meet a few days hence, and somehow it seemed familiar to me as he said, "Why don't you come to my home so we can relax in privacy and take our time? Besides, I'd love you to see this place. It's really special. It's kind of my dream place. We'll talk and I can show you around my little world."

Why this sense of *deja vu*? Why wasn't I even surprised that he had responded so personally? Silly maybe, but I always knew it would be that way.

What should I wear, what should I say, how should I act? I was like a schoolgirl, exactly like the schoolgirl I had been. I was sleepless the night before, tossing and turning in fitful dreams I had had before, many years ago, back at home. I dreamed exactly what I'd yearningly dreamed as a kid and woke up tingling.

The 75-mile trip up the coast to Santa Barbara seemed to take forever. He had told me exactly how to get to his home, exactly which freeway off ramp to take, exactly how the road wound around, exactly where to turn.

Suddenly at the end of the last graceful curve, there it was, a palatial Spanish hacienda on manicured grounds. The big gate was open in welcome, and on the wall, an elegant sign announced the place's melodic Spanish name. I pulled my car through the entry and onto the long blacktopped drive, which cut a smooth dark swath through flat verdant lawns that stretched like an endless putting green around the main house, the stables, the garages, and several guest houses, fanning down to hug the hillside upon which the main house sat.

It was like driving onto the grounds of a country club. I hadn't realized his incredible wealth, but now it was obvious.

I parked my Corvette in front on a turnaround and got out, smoothing the skirt of my sophisticated black suit, feeling glad I had begun investing in good clothes. The suit's vest was rather low-cut, giving me a needed boost in womanly confidence.

I was about to live a dream, my one Hollywood-inspired dream. I was about to meet him.

The house itself was a bricky peachy color and magnificent, with huge carved doors and gigantic clay pots on either side, filled with perfect flowers of every imaginable color. In fact, everything was perfect. It was a study in perfection, all of it. It wasn't cowboyish as I'd half-expected. It was regal, relaxing, rich.

I stood under the entry canopy, rang the bell, and waited nervously. A housekeeper in matronly mufti showed me in, with "Miss Sternig? He's expecting you. Please follow me and make yourself comfortable here. He'll be right down."

"Here" turned out to be a spacious sun room full of huge tropical plants in interesting pots; flowers everywhere; a glass-topped wicker desk by the outside wall of windows, so you could sit there, write your letters, and gaze out over the bucolic gardens; giant wicker seating plumped with beautiful floral cushions; romantic garden statuary here and there; a little trickling fountain; skylights overhead; shafts of sunshine falling across the brick floor. I arranged myself onto the huge sink-into sofa and hoped I could get up again, especially under the duress of meeting him, which would probably overwhelm me.

The moments were unimaginably long, waiting in these private quarters to lay eyes on someone of mystique, someone who had unknowingly been so deeply and memorably a part of me.

God, I didn't want to be disappointed. Would he be awful?

Then his energy and his presence filled the room. He ambled in and stepped the one step down into the sunroom, smiling the quirky smile I knew as well as any lover's. He was extremely tall, six-foot-six, dressed in slacks and jacket, shirt open, hair gray instead of light brown, huge saddle shoes instead of boots. He cut a natty, imposing, and perfectly familiar figure, walking in with both hands extended toward me.

"Barbara. You found it. And you're right on time." His eyes caught mine, crinkling up at the edges just the way I remembered from every TV show and every newspaper or magazine picture I had cut out those many years ago.

It was extraordinary. He acted as if he knew me well, apologized for making me do the driving, suggested we share some wine while we talked, and led me to the kitchen. He chose a fine bottle of white, opened it, poured into a delicate bubble glass, and had me sample it. Lovely, I said. The housekeeper arranged bottle, glasses and napkins on a tray along with some snacks for us to nibble, and said, "I'll be leaving now sir, but I'll see you in the morning."

"Fine, Margaret. Have a good evening."

It seems I was to be home alone with him.

He picked up the tray and we walked through, stepping down into an enormous, quietly elegant living room, at least 40 feet long, expanses of pale carpeting throughout, good wood everywhere, a few large pieces of quietly expensive furniture, bookshelves with leather-bound volumes, a carved game table with green felt on top and four magnificent chairs, very big—and a huge picture window at the end, looking out over another part of the grounds. The two sofas facing each other sat in front of a large fireplace adorned with a pair of bronze sculptures, and he set the tray down on the burnished coffee table in the middle. We both sat down on the same sofa at the same moment, and heaved the same sigh. We looked at each other and our faces broke into smiles.

"Well, I've been looking forward to this ever since we spoke," he said inexplicably. But why? I wondered. Why?

"Can't explain it," he seemed to answer. "Just had a feeling when I heard your voice. You're just the way I thought you'd be."

"So are you," I heard myself answering.

"I hope you don't have to rush off when we're finished. I want to show you around the place, and then I thought we could go to dinner."

This was all happening as it had in my dreams so long ago. He had been instantly attracted to me, just as I always knew he would be if ever we met. I'd hardly said hello and we were already going to dinner.

Sitting comfortably with him in this restful mansion, sipping wine before the fireplace, we began our long interview.

We talked about his political intentions and what had led to them. We talked about his life before, during his famous shows, and how he had always been thinking of business. We talked about type casting and the studio chieftain who had been his special mentor.

Then we talked about why he'd moved so far from Hollywood during his first series, the one he'd done as a young man when I was a grade school girl. He even described the house he'd lived in then, when I'd been a child in Chicago, and told me many personal details, many anecdotes. Of course, he told me all about his political aspirations. The interview was perfect.

When it was finished, we sat chatting. I suddenly heard myself saying, "May I tell you a secret?"

"I'd love it," he said softly.

"When you did that show, I was in love with you. I suppose every little girl in America was, but I was one of them. I loved you so much it *hurt*."

His attention was rapt.

"I can still remember an article about you in a magazine, and a picture of you with your Model T Ford, and how heartbroken I was when you said in the interview you were 'going kinda steady with a girl named....' When we were in the kitchen before, I saw a little sign with her name on it."

"I ended up marrying her eventually," he said quietly. "She waited for me for so long, I finally thought I just oughta. We've got two great kids, and it's been a good life, but not without its problems. You may have wondered—we've been separated for some time now. She lives in the desert and I live here."

He paused a moment, letting me take all this in, and then he lightened things up.

"And that old car—how can you be sitting here knowing about that? I was in college when I had it."

We'd both lost all track of time. My tape had run out long ago and now a soft blue dusk was descending across the lawns outside, the warmth of the day blending into a coastal chill. He stood up and lit the fire, then sat down very close to me in the flickering firelight, looked deeply into my eyes, and kissed me softly.

****

He and I had a serious love affair for more than a year.

During that time, he showered me with love, shared his dreams and visions and projects with me, told me stories I shall never forget, and trusted me implicitly with sensitive information the *Enquirer* would have had a heyday with. He was tender, caring, protective, and very involved. He was somebody important in my life.

It always amazed me that such a huge person could be so refined when it came to the art of love. He had "finer feelings," something rare, and I learned that he put others before himself, cared about mankind, cared about giving back, and had an extremely cute sense of humor.

I saw him to be every bit the hero he had portrayed.

But this idyll was not to be. After suffering a sudden heart attack, he looked his life in the face. Finally on the mend, he agonized emotionally with me. His estranged wife was now begging for a reconciliation, and who could blame her.

He was not only confronting his mortality, he was also dealing with his own values and brutally assessing both. After weeks of turmoil for us both, he came to a decision. There would be no divorce. He'd always been conflicted about the change it would create in the image he and the world had of himself.

"I really think we could have made it," he told me sadly when we said goodbye. "We're two of a kind. I can't explain it, but from the moment I heard your voice, there was a kind of destiny."

****

I saw him again occasionally, always secretly, always with great passion, over the next few years. It was a bittersweet way of protracting the inevitable. Things were not the same any more. The last time he rang me, some four years after we met, I was engaged to someone else and asked him not to call again.

10

Mea Culp-a

efore Bill Cosby became *really*
famous like he is today, he was famous as the avuncular black guy who
clowned around with four-year-olds in pud-
ding commercials. Before that, he was famous
as the affable, cigar-chomping black guy doing rambling comedy bits on *Johnny Carson*.
But even before that, he was famous as the first
black guy in a television series to play a character
who was the full equal of his white partner.

The series was a detective show called *I Spy,* and those who
were around during the Kennedy era will remember it for its wry
humor and cool-guy attitude.

On the show, Cosby's urbane and sardonic costar was an actor
named Robert Culp, whose career never soared afterwards the way
Cosby's did. But Culp was certainly competent at his craft, and still
pops up now and then in series television, or in film.

I seriously cannot remember why the *Enquirer* wanted me to
find Culp and interview him. I can only assume it must have been
something intensely urgent and personal, because after I exhausted
all the usual channels, such as agents, publicists and managers, I was
told to find a home address, go to the house, and doorstep him. Now.

I hated doorstepping.

I hated going up to a star's doorstep—uninvited, unannounced,
and most of all, unwanted—to knock on the door. The general pre-
sumption was that if the star actually answered the door, he would be

so surprised that he would accidentally answer the questions. Or perhaps have you in for tea.

At least this was the Florida home office's ivory tower theory about doorstepping. In reality, anyone with a brain would call the cops if you doorstepped him. I'd hate it if someone did it to me.

In this more dangerous age of stalkers and a world gone nuts, I don't think the *Enquirer* or any of the tabloids subscribe much to doorstepping any more. But it was an *Enquirer* fad in the earlier days, and certain editors asked their reporters to do a lot of it.

I was working on the team of such an editor.

Unfortunately, I had Robert Culp's home address in my contact book. His place was in the hills of Beverly, on a narrow artery off one of the stylish canyon roads.

Like a prisoner being sent out to break rocks, I plodded to my car, stoop-shouldered and demoralized.

I hated doorstepping.

Sometimes I simply didn't do it and told the editor I had. Why was I being so conscientious this time? My girl's school training, I guess.

As I marched toward Culp's door, I thought back to the time I doorstepped James Garner....

****

The affable and pleasing Garner was one of my favorite actors. He'd been the droll cowboy Bret Maverick in the sixties TV hit series *Maverick*, the penultimate fun hero, ten gallon hat pushed back above his forehead, checking out his poker hand and smoking a big cigar, foiling his enemies with fancy footwork rather than heavy gunwork. The role fit Garner like a glove.

In recent times, he was a big hit all over again on TV as Jim Rockford, private detective, and the *Enquirer* liked him.

At the time, he was split from his wife Lois, and had been spotted dating Lauren Bacall. It was my story and the paper wanted it for the front page, but I was getting nowhere.

I had only one source, so to back up my story, I'd left a trail of messages for Garner and Bacall. But they either hadn't received them or chose not to respond. My editor prodded, "If you can't reach him and can't reach Bacall and can't find an insider, Babs, it's the only thing left. I want you to doorstep him."

I'd waited to go to Garner's rented Toluca Lake bachelor house until I was sure he'd be off at the studio, filming *The Rockford Files*. I'd even called the show's production office to make sure he had an early call that day. I was positive he wouldn't be home.

The house was near mine, so this wouldn't take long at all. I'd do the dirty deed as ordered, then go back to my office at home and tell my editor no one answered, Garner wasn't there. Boom boom, no lies, no embarrassing moments, on to the next.

Garner's hideaway was a rambling white ranch house on an attractive corner, right across from Bob Hope's walled Toluca Lake spread. His lawn reached right to the sidewalk, no fence, no gate, completely open, just like all the other suburban plots in the neighborhood at that time. It seemed so normal, so sunny, so unpretentious for a big star like Garner, and I wondered if I could possibly be right that he was living there. Still, he was separated and probably wanted to scale down. Heck, maybe Bob Hope owned the house and was renting it to him, or letting him stay in it.

I parked at the corner, came up the curved walk, rang the bell two times, and waited for a few moments, just to be professional. When there was no answer, just as planned, I hot-footed it back down the front path. Mission accomplished. I wouldn't have to lie to my editor. I'd gone to Garner's house, there was no one home. I was out of there.

Suddenly, when I was almost at the bottom of the path and into the free zone, I heard a familiar-sounding voice call out, "Can I help you, Miss?"

I froze, turned slowly around, and there he was. James Garner. In a blue bathrobe. Calling me. With sleep creases still on his face.

I couldn't believe my eyes.

He was gorgeous ... Jim Rockford ... a slightly older Bret Maverick. Sqaure jaw, kind, bright eyes, thick tousled black hair.

"Uh, I, uh, good morning, Mr. Garner," I stumbled, trying hard to get to my best salesman cheer. I walked back up the path down which I'd almost escaped and arrived again at the dreaded doorstep.

"My name is Barbara Sternig," I offered with a weak smile, extending my hand. "I see I must have gotten you out of bed. I am *so* sorry."

"Well, we're here now. What can I do for you?"

What a nice man.

I choked out, "Mr. Garner, the truth is, I'm a reporter from the *National Enquirer,* I'm working on a story about you, I've been getting nowhere through channels, and my editor insisted that I come to your front door to ask you about it. Your production office said you'd be on location today, so I never thought I'd catch you. That is, I planned not to find you. I mean, my God, I woke you up, but I didn't think you'd be here. That is...."

"Waaaaaaait a minute. Slow down here, young lady. So you're a reporter and your editor sent you to catch me at home, is that it?"

"Yes, that's it. I feel awful that I woke you up on your morning off."

"Don't worry about it. I actually was scheduled to go in at six AM today, but the shots were changed so I got to sleep in unexpectedly. So what was it you were going to ask me?"

He was being a doll. I figured if I blurted it out really fast, it might not be so bad, so I jabbered, "Well, I know you and Lois are split up at the moment, and I understand you're dating Lauren Bacall."

"Well, Barbara Sternig, you are right. I *am* dating Lauren Bacall."

I looked at this rugged, Marlboro Cowboy-handsome man, sleep creases still on the face, standing there in his bare feet talking forthrightly to some idiot girl reporter who just busted in on him. I wanted to ask him if I could get in his blue bathrobe with him.

"You are?" I asked instead. "So is it serious?"

Garner laughed. "It's serious friendship. We've known each other for years. She's keeping me company during my separation. She's a great lady and I love her. You can print that."

"Thanks a lot," I said. "You're such a gent. Will you forgive my intrusion?"

"Yes, I'll forgive you, but why doesn't a nice girl like you get rid of a lousy job like that? This isn't for you."

As I stood there in the warm morning sunshine chatting with James Garner in his bathrobe, I wasn't so sure. The job actually was pretty damn nice.

But Garner was the exception, a tolerant guy.

****

Now it was time for me to try the same thing on Robert Culp and I wasn't feeling too sanguine.

A few deep breaths, and trying to be unobtrusive, I covered the short distance from where I'd parked, to his house.

As always, I'd dressed professionally, so I walked gingerly in my high heels along the steep and narrow hillside lane. The house was right against the street, with the driveway alongside the structure. Next to the garage there appeared to be the kitchen door, and I knocked on this.

I could hear footsteps clomping down the hall on the other side of the door and wondered if it was Bob Culp himself. Culp. **G**ulp. The door opened.

"Yes, can I help you?"

It was the Mexican maid.

"I'm here to see Mr. Culp."

"Meester Culp no here right now."

"Will he be back soon?"

"Yes. Soon. You like to wait?"

Hmmm. Would I like to wait? Within the framework of door-stepping, if the victim were not present, was it kosher to actually cross the threshold and come inside?

Angel on one shoulder, devil on the other, I considered my answer.

What the heck, I could always keep on thinking inside the house, and then if it felt unbearable, I could always beat a hasty retreat.

"Yes, I'll wait."

"Come in, señora."

She walked me to a long bench in the kitchen, next to the door, and I sat down.

This was very nerve-wracking. Culp was going to go nuts when he walked in his door and found me sitting in his kitchen. Who wouldn't?

But something glued me to that bench. For some reason, I just had to have this outrageous experience, just had to take it to the limit. I was *Enquirer*, no doubt about it. I could hardly wait to see what would happen. At the same time, I was a nervous wreck.

When Robert Culp came home about fifteen minutes later, the maid led him to me. I could hear her telling him as they came nearer, "La señora has come here to see you, Meester Culp."

He was suddenly standing in the doorway, a half-puzzled, half-threatening look on his face. "Who are you?" he asked brusquely.

"Oh, Mr. Culp—your maid brought me in to wait for you. I hope it's all right."

"It depends if it's all right. Who *are* you?"

"Well, actually, I'm a journalist, Barbara Sternig? I'm a reporter with the *National Enquirer*?" I said, turning my sentences up at the end, in hopes of verbally ingratiating myself somehow, like a wolf cub looking up at the chief wolf.

"I wondered if I could just ask you a couple of questions?"

"*National Enquirer*? And you just walked into my house?"

"Well, I asked for you and your maid said you'd be right back and told me to wait for you."

"My maid told you...." Culp stopped, mouth slightly agape, eyes narrowing, and he gave his head a disbelieving little shake, as if trying to clear his ears.

"I would like to suggest that you leave my house now, or else I am going to lose my temper and I am not sure what I am going to do, but it is not going to be a good thing, not for you and not for me."

He spoke deliberately, in a rising crescendo, and it was obvious a volcano was about to be unleashed if I didn't disappear and fast. All the time he spoke, I was edging toward the door, as quiet as a mouse. I thought it best to do as he said.

Doorstepping rarely worked.

****

It was Christmas about six years later. Every holiday season, Jean and Casey Kasem (he of Pop Radio's *Top Forty Countdown*) gave a huge star-studded party at their sumptuous Holmby Hills mansion, and it was always one of the most sparkling parties of the year, attended by loads of celebrities. Dumb-like-a-fox blonde bombshell actress Jean was a friend of mine and she invited me.

I had a brand new boyfriend who'd been wooing me during the holidays. He wasn't involved in Hollywood at all, but he was highly starstruck and jumped at the chance to rub shoulders with the elite show biz crowd at Jean and Casey's.

As we walked in, Jean and Casey greeted us warmly, and as we wandered around spotting celebrities, my boyfriend's face lit up as brightly as the Kasems' towering Christmas tree. We got a drink and walked toward the mansion's huge library, taking note of each famous guest. My guy was very wide-eyed.

Suddenly, he squeezed my arm and said, "Hey look, there's Robert Culp. I remember him from *I Spy*."

Sure enough, it was Bob Culp all right, looming tall, standing alone, not looking particularly happy. Much like the last time I'd seen him.

"Should we go say hello?' I asked. "Why sure," said my beaming beau.

I obviously thought of the kitchen caper, but silently dismissed it. It had been several years ago, and I figured I'd be so out of context here, a guest of Jean and Casey's just like Culp himself, that the actor wouldn't put it together, not in a million years.

But just to be sure, as we approached him, I introduced my date instead of myself. "Hi Bob, how lovely to see you. My friend here spotted you in the crowd, so we wanted to say hi." I said, holding out my right hand to Culp and pulling my boyfriend towards us with my left.

I introduced the two men and added "and I'm Barbara" as an afterthought as they shook hands. My gregarious boyfriend flashed his best charisma smile and immediately engaged Culp in admiring conversation, leaving me in the background, right where I wanted to be.

As we spoke, my boyfriend asked all the questions I wanted to ask. His interest had no journalistic agenda and conveyed his own congenial kind of layman's awe, and Culp, flattered, responded in an unguarded way. I just listened. He revealed that only days before, he'd been booked for a guest appearance on the *Bill Cosby Show*, in a friendly nod to their *I Spy* connection. Superstar Cosby still liked his old TV sidekick.

It sounded like a story to me.

Later in the evening, as my boyfriend flitted around the celebrity-laden party like a kid in a candy shop, I ended up next to Bob Culp again. Casually, I said, "You know Bob, it's interesting that you'll be working with Cosby again. I'm a journalist and I'd love to do a story about it. Would you be up for that?"

"Who'd it be for?" he probed off-handedly.

This was the moment of truth. When I said the word *"Enquirer"* would he put it all together and recognize me?

"A major publication, for sure," I replied. "Maybe the *Enquirer* because of all their readership. Whoever, I'd be happy to give you a readback and copy approval, just so you'd be perfectly comfortable." I looked up at him, scanning his face for any flicker of recognition. He looked at me with no particular emotion one way or the other. If anything, he seemed bored to tears.

"Yeah, I'd consider that. Call my office and we can set it up."

He proceeded to give me his office phone number, which I wrote down on a cocktail napkin, and, feeling like the cat that ate the canary, I rejoined the party.

A few days later, it was all set up, and I met Culp at La Serre, an airy French eatery in Sherman Oaks, cool and calm inside with lots of plants, skylights, brick floors, white trellises, private gazebo tables, obsequious waiters.

We arrived at the same time and walked in shaking hands and chatting. Much to my relief, still not a hint of recognition crossed his face. We spent twenty minutes or so on small talk, then be began describing what he'd been up to since his days with Cosby in the sixties.

Getting into the interview, he was good-natured about the decid-edly disparate success levels the two of them had achieved, express-ing a kind of resignation about his acting career, and he gave me cute anecdotes about the shooting of the *Cosby* episode. It was good copy. Our readers would love it.

We lingered over elegant *fruit de mer* salads loaded with squiggle-legged calamari and sweet hunks of fresh crab meat, served in great big sea shells, we drank a good bottle of chilled white wine, and we talked about the many other interests he had developed over the years. Culp still enjoyed acting best of all and would rather have been do-ing more of it. The conversation naturally turned to how strange life can be.

Finally, Bob Culp said, "Yeah, you never know how things can change. I guess the *Enquirer* has changed a lot too. This has been a very enjoyable afternoon, we've had a good interview, and you're a very warm and professional lady.

"But with no offense to you, they used to have some really sleazoid people on that paper. Would you believe that a few years ago, some woman who was supposedly working for them actually had the audacity to come into my house and sit in my kitchen waiting for me until I got home? Obviously you wouldn't do things like that, but she had the gall to come into my *home*, for Chrissakes, and ex-pect me to talk to her in my Goddam kitchen."

I could feel a hot pink hue rising from my chest to my forehead.

I grabbed my water glass and took a long swallow of its cooling contents. "You know Bob, a lot of people used to say they worked for the *Enquirer,* but the paper had never heard of them. Do you remember her name? I could probably tell you if she was legit."

"No, I don't remember the name. She was nicely dressed, well groomed, I remember that—but just unbelievable. She came into my *home*, for Chrissakes.

"That's amazing," I marveled.

11

Pat Sajak Gets Married

fter twelve or thirteen years at the *Enquirer,* I had a chance reunion with a man who'd been my first real sweetheart when we were both in our early twenties.

My job had been so demanding for so many years, that it suddenly struck me how lovely it would be to settle down at last, particularly with someone not in the business. Robert had always loved me and with that comforting thought, I immediately got engaged and soon found myself in the middle of an unfortunately mismatched marriage.

My husband of less than a year didn't cope well with my *Enquirer* lifestyle. He was an old-fashioned midwestern guy who'd always thought his wife should stay home.

I thought that was quaint and protective until I was the wife in question. When I was called to Lantana to work in the home office, or when I was sent out of town on a moment's notice, he thought I was off with another man. It's the only reason his ex-wife back in Wisconsin had ever gone anywhere without him. In his mind, there was no legitimate reason a woman would leave her husband's side and be away from home.

With my job, this was a problem.

My poor husband also knew I had proceeded with our marriage despite having some serious eleventh-hour doubts, and this didn't help his insecurities.

Unfortunately, neither one of us had brutally assessed, until we were already hitched, how much I still liked my free-wheeling career, and how many worlds apart we were.

To compound the problem, he was an emotional Italian and handled his anxiety with towering rages, which not only terrified me and my dog, but soon eroded what warm feelings and Pollyanna hopes for the future I still harbored.

The pressure was intense. The marriage was doomed.

Our separation happened in early December of 1989, and I kept it to myself during the holidays, not wanting to ruin Christmas for my family in Colorado with such unfortunate news, and too embarrassed to admit to my friends in L.A. what a gigantic boo-boo I'd made.

Not a fun Christmas. I wore dark glasses to church in the morning to mask misery-reddened eyes, and then spent the day which I'd always passed in the warm embrace of my large family, entirely by myself. What I'd hoped would be my first wonderful, safely married Christmas was instead the worst day of my life.

I was delighted when I got a New Year's assignment on the road.

It seems just as I was breaking up, *Wheel of Fortune* host Pat Sajak was getting spliced, marrying his twenty-four-year-old model/girlfriend Lesly Brown in her hometown of Annapolis, Maryland. Even though he was divorced, we were hearing it was going to be a big Catholic do.

Not that I really wanted to think about weddings, and not that a road trip would cure my woes, but at least it would be a temporary distraction.

I got on the airplane a few days after Christmas and exhaled a huge sigh of relief to be leaving Los Angeles for a while.

As a further plus, weddings were always fun to cover, and Sajak's had possibilities of being especially so.

I almost felt like I knew him. Before becoming host of *Wheel*, he'd been the amusing weatherman on channel 4, our local NBC affiliate, so he was a familiar face on L.A. television long before everybody else met him.

Plus, while Pat was on KNBC, I had dated a TV newsman from the station, had met Pat at a few parties, and had heard his career tale. Later, I'd covered his divorce, his trial marriage with a local newsgirl, all the antics of his letter-turner pal Vanna White, and his rise to *Enquirer* front page status as host of the popular game show.

I remembered that Sajak had started out on TV in Buffalo, New York, in the seventies, and then in the eighties managed to land the prized NBC weatherman slot in Los Angeles. This was the big time, and it turned out to be his big break.

Once viewers got used to his sardonic, even sarcastic, persona, they loved him, and eventually he got noticed by the King brothers of King World Syndicate, which owned *Wheel of Fortune*. The brothers gave Sajak his ultimate dream job: Game Show Host.

The deal was, Pat and wife Sherrill, whom he'd brought with him from Buffalo, were happy at first, as Pat started his new Hollywood weather gig. They lived in suburban, non-Hollywoodish Glendale, in a big old frame house with a big wooden front porch. It was on the other side of a freeway off ramp abutment, on a street in an average neighborhood, surrounded by much smaller houses.

The source who told me where it was said, "It's on a somewhat tacky cul-de-sac in a not-too-elegant neighborhood of an away-from-the-limelight town."

As it turned out, for Pat, there were bigger fish to fry.

It wasn't long after he arrived in Hollywood that he began to champ at the domestic bit. By the time he got the job as *Wheel* host, he had outgrown not only his house, but also his past life and his past wife.

Pat divorced Sherrill. They had stuck together about ten years and Pat had even adopted her son, who was now twenty.

I had the dubious pleasure of knocking on Mrs. Sajak's door when word got out that Mr. *Wheel* didn't live there any more, and I covered the whole ugly splitup. Mrs. Sajak was heartbroken and hoped until the end that Pat would come home again. Of course he never did.

Not a very original plotline, but it still happens in Tinseltown all the time.

Pat got a new cool haircut, moved to Rhinestone Drive in the hills above San Fernando Valley, and started dating Lonnie Lardner, a local television news reporter who was the pretty niece of cowboy author Ring Lardner.

I ended up having the dubious pleasure of knocking on Ms. Lardner's door too, when word got out that Mr. *Wheel* and she were moving into the Rhinestone house together.

Should I say it again? Doorstepping rarely works. But in this case I caught Lonnie off guard, posing as a messenger sent by Pat to pick something up from her. She was a pretty wily journalist herself, but her first ingenuous reaction spilled the beans, and we had our confirmation of the story.

Indeed other sources also confirmed it. Pat and Lonnie were actually well known in L.A. news reporting circles as an item.

And as a dumb-luck capper, Lonnie appeared as a featured speaker at a Hollywood Womens Press Club luncheon I happened to attend, and in the Q&A after, admitted blushingly and a little proudly, that Pat was her honey.

All this was fine, but Pat wasn't even divorced from Sherrill yet, and there was a lot more to come.

By the time he became a free man, parlayed his *Wheel* fame into a shot at his own late night talk show, told the world he wanted to be the next Johnny Carson, lost his own late night talk show due to lousy ratings, recovered, and then got even more famous on *Wheel*, Pat grew tired of working girl Lonnie. She was local. She was businesslike. And while she was pretty, she was far from glamorous, and she was in her thirties.

It seemed Pat had eyes for a little more oomph. It seemed Pat was going younger. It seemed Pat was "going Hollywood."

What happened next seemed to confirm it. Forty-two-year-old Pat lost his head over a twenty-four-year-old lingerie model named Lesly Brown, another shapely brunette like Sherrill and Lonnie, only more so, whose biggest claim to fame was a poster on which she posed in skimpy shorts and crop top, all belly button and pouty lips.

Her father was a wealthy dentist, her mother a pampered matron in Annapolis, Maryland.

This was the lush and stately eastern town also famous for its early American museums, its horse-drawn carriages, its lovely and historic port, the sometimes infamous United States Naval Academy, and for my favorite—its ancient State House.

I knew I had to set foot inside that modest old domed building, completed in 1694. It's where General George Washington resigned from the Continental Army to run for President, it's where the treaty of Paris ending the American Revolution was ratified, and it once actually served as the U.S. capitol, for about six months during the 1780s.

Annapolis is long on history.

Now Pat Sajak would become part of it.

A few days before New Years Eve 1989, I flew into chilly Baltimore, got my rental car, and somehow found my way in the wintry dark, across the confusing labyrinth of freeways to Annapolis, where my first order of business the next morning was a run out to the posh suburban home of Dr. Michael Brown and his family.

The address was right there in the phonebook, but of course, I wasn't sure whether this was the right Dr. Michael Brown. As I drove along the peaceful roads, I was amazed at the beauty of the wooded landscape with its gracious well-spaced brick homes set amidst huge stands of oak and elm, the winter-bare trees probably dating back to colonial times. The spacious lawns, even in their brown December hues, looked beautiful.

I found the house with little difficulty. It was set back on a secluded, wooded street in a brick-gated neighborhood, and it was a lovely place, like something out of *My Three Sons*. The large white two-story frame home featured immaculate shutters, bright brass fittings, and a long brick walk coming up to the sheltered front door.

What made me blink in wonder as I drove slowly past it was the sight of several huge white trucks parked in front and back, with the name of a marquis company emblazoned across the sides. A team of workers had already laid the huge tent out across the back yard and were busily preparing to erect it. I could see it over the hedges.

Apparently, I had the right Dr. Michael Brown.

I drove up and down the cloistered street a few times, then parked, waiting for one of the guys to come back to the truck. Then I got out of my car, and posing as a neighbor on a walk, curiously asked him what was happening.

"Oh, big wedding on Sunday. It's going to be a tented affair."

"Wow, is it one of the Brown girls?"

"Yeah, that's the name. Bride's dad is a dentist?"

"That's right," I confirmed. "Gosh, this looks fantastic! Is she having the wedding right in the tent?"

"No, I don't think so. Reception. Somebody said the wedding's at the old church in town, and then they come here for the party."

"Well, looks like fun. Don't get too cold now," I said, walking on with my hands in my pockets.

When he returned to the tent, I jumped back in my car, and making good mental notes of all I saw, I headed back to town to find the "old church."

There must be loads of "old churches" in a town like Annapolis, with its history dating back to the 1600s. We'd heard it was going to be a Catholic ceremony, so that narrowed the field a bit. But where to start?

I decided on a quaint little maritime museum in a rough-hewn colonial building in the heart of town, right across from the port where winter boats bobbled in the chilly water.

Museum people always know stuff.

Engaging the museum lady in conversation, I gathered from her that the nearest Catholic church was St. Mary's, built in the early 1800s and still very much an active parish. It was old, it was Catholic, it was probably the right church.

The woman told me it was very close by, just up the street in fact, in the heart of town, in the real village of Annapolis.

I walked a block or two, and soon saw a beautiful old spire and bell tower atop a brick church that fairly exuded tradition.

I stepped inside the vestibule and stood before the glass-encased events board, noticing out of the corner of my eye a group of young women clustered around a lady holding a clipboard.

Scanning the events board, I observed that seven PM on Sunday, New Years Eve, was blocked out for a wedding. Could it be "my" wedding?

I had one ear cocked to hear what the woman with the clipboard seemed to be saying as she doled out information to her group. She seemed in charge of something and I thought she might be a church secretary or assistant. Maybe she'd know about the seven PM wedding.

Waiting for an opening to ask my questions, I heard her say, "So you bridesmaids will each be paired with one of Pat's gentlemen, and Saturday night at the rehearsal, we'll decide who goes with whom."

I froze, instantly shifting gears and trying to blend into the group.

This woman had to be the Sajak wedding director! My timing was incredible. I had stepped into the right church just as she began a meeting with some of the wedding party.

They walked toward a room at the side, and I casually walked with them. A wealth of confirmation, a wealth of information I had already gleaned from her one little unguarded sentence. I gazed absently over the woman's shoulder onto her clipboard. On the top line it said, "Brown-Sajak Wedding, 7 PM December 31." I was memorizing every name on the list, when suddenly she turned to me and said, "Can I help you?"

"Oh yes," I responded a little stupidly. "I was wondering what the weekend mass schedule is. We're visitors and you looked like you might be from the rectory."

"Well, I have no idea. I don't work here. This is a special event. You'll have to ask someone in the office."

"Oh. Okay. Well, thanks."

As I walked away, she resumed talking to the girls and I craned my ears to catch every word she spoke. She mentioned a couple of the ushers' names and referred again to Saturday night's rehearsal. I stood at the events board pretending to read it until the wedding director, a Miss Jones, and her little group walked back out the front door of the church. I quickly took out my notebook and wrote down every name I'd seen on the clipboard.

The wedding was definitely seven PM on Sunday, New Year's Eve.

Now all I had to do was figure out a way to get me and my cohorts in.

My attention focused on the board I'd been blankly staring at while eavesdropping on Miss Jones, and I noticed that the last Mass held on Sundays was at five-thirty PM.

Right there in the church vestibule, that little devil came in for a crash landing on my shoulder.

Every Catholic church has confessionals along its outside walls, small cubicles where the penitent faithful kneel in the dark while priests on the other side of a cloth window hear and forgive their sins. If there *was* a five-thirty Mass on this particular Sunday, which was also New Years Eve, I would most certainly attend, and then, if it was humanly possible, I would slip into an empty confessional during Mass and I would simply wait.

I would wait in the confessional for Pat Sajak's seven PM wedding to start.

If nobody caught me, I'd be secretly, silently there. If I were the only one to think this deviously, it would work.

I stepped inside the quiet church and walked reverently up the aisle toward the front, toward the confessionals. Genuflecting, I slid into a pew and knelt, uttering a prayer for God's forgiveness. "Please God, this is nothing personal. In nothing do I mean disrespect. You've put me here to do a good job. Please help me accomplish my goal."

As I prayed, I glanced at the confessional cubicles. It was my supreme good luck that instead of full wooden doors on the penitent's booths, St. Mary's had doors with windows in them. The windows were about fifteen inches high, and went the width of the doors, with closely gathered curtains stretched across them on the inside of the booths. If I stepped into a confessional booth, I could easily pull the curtain back a fraction of an inch and see everything outside.

I couldn't wait to tell my editor of my inspiration, tinged as it was with irreverence. I was bubbling, though a few of the bubbles were undoubtedly caused by a gurgling guilt that accompanied my drive to get my story.

Every assignment sparked new heights of bold inventiveness, but for a Catholic boarding-school girl like me, hiding in a confessional during Mass to spy on a wedding had to top anything I had schemed up before. It took my mischief to a higher level, so to speak.

I prayed another little prayer that God would understand and not take my antics as a serious affront. I certainly did not mean it that way. My plan was pure journalistic pragmatism with no intent to insult or offend God or to demean the religion of my youth. Besides, I thought, it's not like I was going to talk to a priest. I was merely going to secret myself in the empty confessional and look.

"All in all," I thought, "things on this assignment are going very well, very well indeed."

****

Back at my hotel, I rang my editor Larry Haley in Florida to give him the word on my morning's endeavors. He was over the moon at my progress. I intimated I was working on a way to hide in the church to observe the wedding, but didn't get too specific in case it didn't pan out.

"Hey Babs, I've sent a tryout up to help you out. She's been in TV but she's really caught on to how we work, so she'll be another body to help you cover the bases. She should be arriving about now. Your photographer will get there tomorrow, and he's bringing his wife because they work as a duo. They'll all be staying at the Holiday Inn where you are."

The team was shaping up. The chips had a good chance of falling in the right places.

After hanging up, I checked my messages back home.

My husband, who had fled L.A. for Ft. Myers, Florida when we separated, was trying to reach me. His taped message exuded a misery of soul that gave me a clutched feeling I couldn't deal with right then. I'd have to call him back later.

Right now, I had work to do. Larry's eager young tryout reporter, Cathy Griffin, had just checked in and my phone rang with her call practically the instant I hung up from Larry. She was raring to go.

I gave her my room number and when she got there, I opened the door to find before me a short, pretty, blond, roly poly girl with a soft southern accent. She carried a big wire notebook.

"I left Lantana in such a rush, with only an hour and a half to make my flight. I don't even have a coat because I thought I'd only be working in Florida for these couple of weeks."

Sounded familiar. "Life at the *N.E.*," I smiled knowingly. "You can get a coat at the mall, don't worry. Larry will okay the expense."

I filled Cathy in on everything I'd learned during my very productive morning, and she furiously scribbled down notes of addresses, directions, times and names I'd learned.

I told her about that giant marquis in the back yard of the Brown family home, and she piped up, "I can try to sneak into the tent as a caterer. How 'bout it? I've done it before at Delta Burke's wedding last summer, and it worked like a charm. I served hors d'oeuvres through the whole thing, got the whole story, and nobody even blinked."

I liked this girl. She thought sideways, *Enquirer* style.

I told her, "There's an open field behind the house and it might be possible in the dark to come through that way, avoiding any security out front. It'd be muddy, cold and uncomfortable, but it might be the only way."

Cathy chimed, "Believe it or not, I brought my white tuxedo shirt, black slacks and dickie bow from Delta's wedding with me, just in case. What do you say?"

"Perfect. If you can find the caterers first, you might even be able to get hired on as a server. I'll leave that whole scene to you, okay?"

Then I gave my new cohort *la pièce de la résistance*. "Now listen, I think I've got a way to be inside the church for the whole wedding. I'm sneaking into a confessional before it starts. I've scoped the church, it looks like there's a five-thirty Mass, and so that's when I'll slip in. If it works, I'll just stay there for the whole wedding."

Cathy gave a disbelieving gulp, then we both started laughing our heads off.

"God'll get you for that one, Barbara," she said, "but I love it!"

Our plan was shaping up. Since the photographer was bringing his wife, they could be our couple attempting the front door at the church, Cathy would do her caterer bit to sneak into the reception, I'd go for the confessional, and then, win or lose on that, I'd quickly change into cocktail attire and the fluffy fur coat I'd brought, and try to get in the front door at the tent reception.

Before zero hour, I'd buy a big gift and have it wrapped in sumptuous wedding paper with lots of beautiful bows. Never show up empty-handed at a wedding.

This was my own personal wedding crasher's technique, formulated over many years and many celebrity weddings. The fur coat and the big gift got me inside the private receptions of many a celeb bride or groom, including Cindy Williams, Gregory Harrison, Kenny Rogers, and Whoopi Goldberg, to name a few.

Yup, fur coat, big gift, look the part, walk right in as if you belong, then mingle like mad. That's the way I normally did it. Stop for no one. Your name's not on the list, say you just received your invitation, delivered by hand, yesterday. Say you're a neighbor. Say you're Cousin Darla from Jersey. Stand your ground and let them make all the moves. They might banish you and send you packing, they might call for someone in the know to scope you, but most of the time, rather than chance embarrassment to the bride and groom by turning away someone who looks so legit, they'll act on their own and let you in.

Then, you simply drift through the reception chatting amiably and drinking champagne as if you'd actually been invited. It can be fun. It's definitely a challenge.

It was my time-honored *Enquirer* technique.

As for Pat Sajak's nuptials, barring extraordinary security measures, we had a good shot.

Come on, even though Sajak was mighty popular, he wasn't exactly Michael J. Fox or Sly Stallone. How much security would he go for?

Only later did we learn that Sajak had quietly arranged for a cadre of burly off-duty Maryland State Police to guard him and his party and to keep the unwashed, the unwanted and the unwelcome away from his wedding.

But at that moment, Cathy and I figured that with luck we could crack it. At the very least, we would give it a helluva go.

****

As fine as we were feeling, my estranged husband was a mess. After Cathy left to buy a coat and head to the Brown home, I returned his call, only to end up in an emotionally wrenching festival of telephonic pain.

No clean breaks for us. Instead, we decided to prolong our misery and have him hop a plane the next night to come up and join me for New Years weekend in Annapolis. A band-aid attempt to feel better, this self-indulgent solution would give us a chance to reopen all the hurt, and then to say our heart-rending goodbyes all over again.

Just for fun.

"There's one thing," I said tentatively, "I haven't told a living soul we're separated, and I really don't want my office to know about our personal problems, so let's just pretend we're fine, okay?

"And also, please, no yelling. I'm not trying to be awkward, but you've just *got* to understand how under the gun I am to cover the wedding, and you *mustn't* take it personally."

"No, no, I know you have to work," said Robert. "I understand. But at least we can be together for dinners and in the room—and I promise, I'll be fine. You just do what you have to do."

And who knows what *that* might be, I thought silently.

Then, to Robert, "I'm sure we'll have some time, and maybe that's what we need to help us get through this thing. Hey, maybe you can even help me on the story. You'd be great at stakeouts or getaway cars, or stuff like that, yeah?"

My husband was a great driver, and had engineered a few escapes of his own in his day. "That'd be up my alley," he smiled.

"And when I'm masquerading as a guest, you can pose as my husband," I added, laughing.

Silence on the other end of the line. Oops. Robert did not find my little joke in the least amusing.

I hung up hoping his fragile emotions could handle actually being on assignment with a single-minded, pig-headed, won't-take-no-for-an-answer, gotta getta story, rampaging *Enquirer* reporter who was determined to get the job done.

****

That night, Cathy and I reconnoitered over dinner at a local seafood eatery where we hoped some of the locals would have Sajak spottings to report to us.

She now sported a black wool carcoat she'd gotten on sale at the mall, and eagerly showed me her other acquisition, a very interesting soft black turban, the kind Lana Turner might have worn in the forties.

"We might need it as a disguise," she confided.

Cathy was fun.

She also proudly told me she'd gleaned the name of the caterers who'd been toiling round the clock on the wedding food, and had scoped their trucks at the Brown home.

"I might be able to sneak inside one of their trucks on D-Day and drive onto the premises that way. One of the caterers took a liking to me and even told me the menu. I told him I'd worked as a waiter and could use a night's work if he could get me the job. He's going to check."

Cathy had also gotten a good gander at the tent, and had figured out a route right up to it from across the field in back. After dark, she'd actually given it a test run just to make sure it was possible.

"I got right up to the edge of the tent and nobody could see me. The earth is very spongy but if it gets colder, it should freeze solid.

And if everything's the same with that tent on Sunday night," she told me, "I can get in. I tried it. The tent side is loose. I can lift it and crawl in."

"Let's hope they don't post guards along the outside of the tent that night," I said, "and let's hope it's not sub-zero."

As we ordered a big seafood dinner, I chatted up our waiter. "Heard about the big celebrity wedding on Sunday? We came out from Hollywood to go."

"Really?" His eyes lit. "Whose wedding is it?" he queried conspiratorially.

"You've gotta promise not to tell," I whispered.

"Oh, I promise. Seriously, I promise."

"Well, it's Pat Sajak. He's marrying a local girl, dentist's daughter."

"You're not going to believe this, but I just read about it in our local little paper that came out this afternoon. It's Lesly Brown, isn't it?"

"Yes, that's it! Bingo!"

" My sister went to high school with her. It didn't say when, but it said she was marrying Sajak. How cool! You're going?"

After all my shenanigans, it was on the newsstands. I hoped other national press would not pick it up. I spilled that we were journalists on assignment and made my pitch.

"So," I asked, "do you think you might hear anything about it?"

"Yeah, in fact, I could ask my sister. And who knows, Lesly's parents come in here every now and then, so maybe I'll even see them."

By the end of our meal, he was on our side, promising that he'd keep his eyes peeled for Pat and company. I slipped him a $25 tip just to keep him on our side, and told him we'd be back the next night for a beer and to check in with him.

All in all it was a good day's work.

****

Next morning, Cathy and I met up for breakfast in the coffee shop, only to be joined in mid-egg by photographer Brian Anderson and his cute wife Lisa, who'd just blown in from L.A. on the red-eye.

We held an impromptu meeting to fill them in on everything we had so far, and to figure out how best to use our time and manpower.

Brian said, "I just want to throw out to you that Lisa often works with me, and we've gotten into quite a few weddings coming in as a couple instead of a solo."

"Larry told me," I said.

"Yeah," said British Brian, "we've found they're usually less likely to stop a couple."

"You'll go for it. It's already part of the plan. You'll try to get in at church," I said. They were an attractive couple, they'd brought the right clothes, they had experience with these things, and hopefully they could make it work .

"If you make it in, then just go right on to the reception as well."

"Great stuff," said Brian, as Lisa quietly smiled at his side.

"But you know," I reminded, "if you get nailed at the church, you're toast for any further upfront approach. Then they'll know you by sight. But for now, let's make that the plan: you two will do the church; Cathy's in with the caterers and will hopefully get inside at the reception; and I'm going to get inside the church earlier in the evening and hide."

"Choir loft?" Brian asked.

"No, confessional."

He hooted appreciatively.

"So that's the game plan," I said. "One way or the other, we're covering this thing."

After one last cup of strong coffee, Cathy left to go back to her caterers, the Andersons went up to grab a couple hours of shuteye before we'd reconnoiter again over lunch, and I myself headed back over the river and through the woods to the Browns' suburban spread.

As I pulled slowly into the posh subdivision and turned my car onto the Browns' street, I noticed, some distance ahead of me, a small brown Mercedes pulling over and parking right in front of the wedding house.

I slowed to a crawl to get a glimpse of the driver, and as the car door swung out, I was stunned to see a rosy-cheeked Pat Sajak step out, lean back down across the seat to lift a large box out of the car, and then walk at a brisk pace up the front path, in his distinctive little steps.

Hoping my red rental car wouldn't be noted, I stopped up the street and just watched as he rang the doorbell, hugged the handsome woman who answered, and then disappeared with her into the house.

So Sajak was in town! It was only Friday and he was here. And I'd seen him for myself. Again, my timing was incredible.

Pulling up the side street, I could see the tent was now completely erected at the back of the house, and was seemingly connected with the main house via a tent tunnel.

I parked under a big tree along the street, where I had a clear view of the brown Mercedes, and I waited for an hour or so to see what would happen next.

A florist truck pulled up and there was a flurry of activity unloading cascades of white flowers. Sajak popped into view a couple of times as the flowers were brought in, and I wrote down the florist's name off the side of the truck. We'd contact them later.

Late that afternoon, Robert flew in from Florida and joined our group.

He was tall, handsome and congenial, and fit in easily, apparently putting his inner anguish on hold for now. To the others, we appeared as a happy newlywed couple. I didn't want the gossip mill churning any bad news about me just yet.

Funny enough, our little masquerade made us both feel much better for those days.

He became part of the team, plotting with us and volunteering to drive getaway on the night of the wedding, to go with me to the reception, and to stand by on a hotel phone on wedding night between car runs, as a sort of message board for everyone. It was still before cell phones.

Saturday night, after a day of spying, gift-buying, calling, contacting and coordinating, we all went out on expedition to the wedding rehearsal, showing up at St. Mary's Catholic Church in three cars, and covering all entrances and exits. Just to be safe, we got there at six PM.

Just before seven, two limousines pulled into the churchyard and we saw lights snap on inside the church.

Brian was poised in his vehicle with a long lens trained on the church's back door, but the darkness made for fuzzy pictures. We could see figures climbing out of the limos, but couldn't be positive who they were.

"I'm going to try and get in," I said, pulling my hair back into a ponytail and wiping my makeup off. I clambered out of the front seat as my husband rode shotgun at the wheel of our rental car.

Up the steps of the church I went, pulling on the heavy front door until it budged toward me.

As the door swung out, a large man in a dark overcoat stepped out of the vestibule and into my face. "You can't come in here," he warned.

"But I've come to make a visitation," I protested.

"I'm sorry miss, this is a private function."

"But the pastor instructed me to make a visit."

"Madam, you cannot come in here," he insisted, blocking my path as I tried to peer inside. "You'll have to leave. You'll have to come back tomorrow."

The man pulled the heavy church door shut, leaving me standing at the entrance. I walked back down the steps and around the corner to where my husband had parked the car, and got back in. "Private do," I explained. "Big thug at the door. Sounds hopeful to me."

I could tell he was beginning to understand a tiny bit of what I did on the road.

"Do you mind driving?" I asked.

"Mind? Not at all. I'd like to."

I got out and walked in the darkness around to Brian and Lisa's car.

"Get anything?"

"It's pretty dark, but I'm using 1000 ASA film, the fastest there is. Something might show up."

While we all kept our posts, I reapplied my makeup and fluffed up my hair for later, because we'd definitely follow the rehearsal group to their dinner.

After an hour or so, the back door of the church cracked open and a group of about ten people piled back into the limos. They pulled slowly out of the churchyard and swung onto the main street of Annapolis and, CIA fashion, all three *Enquirer* cars got into the traffic lanes behind them.

Keeping our distance, we followed the stately-moving limo party up the main street of Annapolis, careful not to lose them at traffic lights. They rolled along through the town center, only five blocks, until they turned and pulled into the entry of the elegant Annapolis Radisson Hotel.

And there, under the bright lights of the hotel's high covered entryway, we saw a doorman jump down, open the limo doors, and solicitously help Sajak and Lesly out, followed by their laughing wedding party all piling out of the stretch cars one by one and sweeping into the hotel.

To our excited delight, from the car right behind these limos came an added bonus—as out stepped Pat's *Wheel of Fortune* costar, the world's most famous letter-turner, Vanna White, along with her fiancé, L.A. restaurateur/playboy George Santo Pietro. Our bloodhounding was right on.

Not wanting to get stuck in valet parking, our group all found open spaces on the street and then walked separately into the hotel.

Robert held my arm protectively as we walked up to the hotel entrance, and to the doorman, I said, "We're with the wedding rehearsal party. Which way?"

"Straight through the lobby, folks, across the bar area and right on into the Corinthian restaurant," he told us.

Confidently Robert and I strode into the Weather Rail Bar, half way between the hotel's front entrance and the entrance to the Corinthian .

"Let's stop here," I said to him in a whispered aside as he kept marching toward the restaurant. "We can see everything from here."

He obeyed and smoothly slid onto a barstool beside me.

Facing him and smiling, I said, "Gotta educate you in *Enquirer* techniques. See, they'd stop us at the door to the private party, but this is a public bar and anyone can sit here. What're ya drinkin'?"

"Bloody Mary. Double!"

We hadn't had any dinner, and we both needed nourishment of one sort or another. As we sipped the rich drinks and chewed on our celery stalks, Cathy Griffin walked by.

"Cathy!" I stage-whispered. "C'mon. Sit down. Have a Bloody Mary." I felt for Cathy, traveling solo while the Andersons and now Robert and I were working as couples. I knew what solo felt like from scores of assignments, and I wanted her to know she was part of everything too.

Cautiously, she sat. "Do you think it's okay if we're seen together?"

"Don't worry about it. They're all busy in there and not paying any attention at all to the bar out here. At least not right now."

It was true. We could see through the windows of the Corinthian Restaurant, with its low lighting and its music tinkling in the background. Everyone was busy mingling, talking, visiting, drinking. In the Weather Rail, there were a few couples at the little cocktail tables, and just us at the bar.

The Andersons had drifted past and sat down in big cushy chairs in a lobby just outside the restaurant. I could see Brian's cameras bulging in a bag he put down on the floor, and that is where they stayed.

Our Bloodies arrived, and we toasted success.

The bartender turned out to be a gregarious chap named Dan and when I started murmuring excitedly to him that we'd seen Sajak and Vanna come in, he spilled the news that Vanna and George were actually staying in the hotel, as was Sajak himself.

Since he seemed tuned in on the celebrity scene, I finally clued him about who we were and why we were there.

Dan immediately jumped on the fun train and from then on was our insider, especially after I told him I could pay him for any help he gave us, starting with the $50 bill I plunked down on the bar. Sources always talk better after money says the opening words.

He soon introduced me to a couple of his buddies who were working the rehearsal dinner as servers, and who later gave me the full lowdown on the party. As we sat there, the chef came out for a word and ended up telling me he'd planned the menu with Lesly during a special trip she'd made to Annapolis from L.A. about a month earlier.

He revealed that Pat had given her an unlimited budget for her trip and for their rehearsal dinner, which was Pat's treat, and she'd chosen the most expensive entree he'd suggested.

Meanwhile, we all sat there, dining not on expensive entrees, but on those crunchy Japanese bar snacks and the celery stalks from two or three Bloody Marys. The combination of empty stomachs, released tension, and delicious drinks got us pleasantly plotched as we watched the Sajak group inside gorge themselves on filet mignon with sauce Bernaise, broccoli crowns with slivered almonds, medley of wild mushroom, baked potato, plus Caesar salad.

As we considered ordering a pizza rather than leave our post, we suddenly saw Vanna White and her beau sweep out of the party in a cloud of expensive perfume and laughter, and move obliviously past us.

"Come on," I said, grabbing Robert's hand. "We're following them. Cathy, you stay here to cover, and afterwards, when it's all done, we'll meet up in my room at our hotel and compare notes. Tell the Andersons we've gone. We'll bring you some food."

As we rushed out the front entrance of the hotel, we turned our heads away from Vanna and George, who stood with arms entwined, cooing like a couple of little lovebirds under the big hotel portico as they waited for their car.

They ended up in the town center at a cute little Italian joint called Maria's and we were in the door right after them, getting a table in the corner. As they leaned toward each other lovingly over a bottle of red wine, Robert and I leaned into a big pizza with everything and ordered another one to go.

I was hoping for a bonus—like George popping the question before our very eyes, but despite their coziness, they just nuzzled and sipped.

As it turned out, Vanna was yet to endure a year of doubts about her choice of playboy George—until finally, her biological clock got the better of her. On the spur of the moment exactly one year later, New Year's Eve, 1990, she and George wed in Aspen, with the *Enquirer* paying top dollar to cover the event, I might add.

For now, however, he was just her boyfriend, her escort, her Hollywood companion, and our excuse to have something to eat.

When they left Maria's, we didn't follow.

Back at the hotel munching their pizza, our little team felt confident, but of course, the real assignment was still before us. We still had to crack the wedding.

****

During our final meeting the next afternoon, everyone was tensed and ready. The plan was, Cathy would go out to the tent at four o'clock, dressed in caterer's kit to breach the perimeter and sneak in under a flap. Secreted on her person, inside the folds of her shirt, she had a Sure-Shot camera. If all went well, she'd be inside for all the final preparations and for the party itself. At the end she could chance a picture, or maybe not.

Robert and I would go to five-thirty Mass at St. Mary's, during which I'd slip into a confessional. He'd then leave and go back to the hotel and wait until I called him to pick me up, either before, during, or after the wedding, depending on my luck. I'd have a Sure-Shot camera in my bag.

Brian and Lisa would arrive at church dressed to the nines before seven o'clock and would try to hustle their way into the wedding, front-door style. That failing, they'd go back to the hotel, then make a run at the reception. Brian's picture-taking would be left to his own expert discretion.

After the confessional, Robert would pick me up, I'd change into cocktail attire and fur coat, grab my big gift, we'd get in the huge Lincoln Town Car we had rented that afternoon and pull up very elegantly in front of the Brown house to try to get in. Both Robert and I would have Sure-Shot cameras hidden on our persons, but no ID in any pockets.

We all agreed. If anyone got arrested, leave word on my room phone. If anyone needed a ride for any reason, leave word on my room phone. We'd all check my messages to find out what was happening to the others.

The clock ticked down.

Cathy left for the Browns in her caterer's outfit, with no ID on her person and her camera tucked inside.

Robert and I left for St. Mary's, with me decked out as a church lady.

The Andersons started dressing in their wedding finery.

Robert and I arrived at the still-nearly-empty church early for five-thirty Mass, in plenty of time to claim our aisle seats directly adjacent to the dark wood confessionals along the left side. Before sitting down in the pew, I unobtrusively pulled the confessional door to make sure it wasn't locked. It opened easily.

My heart pounded as the church filled, the service began, and I thought ahead to the task before me. The comforting Mass ritual seemed so quiet and familiar, but this wasn't like any Mass I'd ever gone to before.

Robert, who wasn't even Catholic, stood tall next to me, and patted my hand when he realized how nervous I was feeling. Then, during the gospel, when everyone was busy standing up for the reading and looking through their missalettes to find the right page, I slipped wordlessly out of my seat, took two steps across the aisle, pulled the confessional door open, and stepped in.

I exhaled a sigh of relief, and let my eyes get accustomed to the darkness of the cubicle. I pulled the left side of the gathered curtain ever so slightly back and got a clear view of the altar, then pulled the right side of the curtain ever so slightly back and got a clear view of the rear of the church.

But how would I see all the happenings in the middle? That's where the wedding procession would mainly take place.

A brainstorm hit, and I reached inside my pocketbook, fishing for a fine-tipped ball point pen I always carried with me. Extracting it in the dim light, I pulled the cap off and meticulously poked a hole through the threads of the curtain at eye level, creating a tiny undetectable peep hole just about in the middle of the fabric.

It worked.

By squinting, I could see perfectly out of the hole. Now I could see the back, middle and front of the church.

I didn't dare kneel, for fear that my weight on the kneeler would activate a light above the confessional door outside, to show others that the booth was occupied. That's how it worked in my church at home, and I didn't want to take a chance. So I simply stood, looking out my peep hole.

It suddenly occurred to me I could make it even better. I took my pen out again and began poking a whole line of tiny holes, one by one, into the curtain, at eye level along its entire width.

Now I wouldn't have to pull the curtain aside at all, but could just peer through my line of peepholes and see what was going on at any given angle in the church.

I looked out the middle hole and saw Robert gazing at the curtain as it moved ever so imperceptibly with each little stab of my pen. No one else seemed to have noticed my escape from the congregation, but of course Robert was a cohort, and I'm sure he was fascinated to know what in the world I was doing in there. He turned his gaze back at the altar and played it cool.

Soon, the Mass ended and I peeked out my special view panel, watching the congregation receive their final blessing. I sincerely asked God at the same time to grant me one too.

Now the congregation was breaking up, and I saw Robert step out of our pew, coolly ignoring what he knew was behind the confessional door, giving neither glance nor signal, but just leaving. I felt relief, but also a little shudder of loneliness and uncertainty as he left. All the people filed out, going in peace to love and serve the Lord.

Pulling Cathy's black turban out of my purse, I stuffed my hair inside it, and got ready to serve the *Enquirer*.

I'd worn no makeup and had traded my own outerwear for Cathy's large black carcoat, an unfitted garment which made it hard to tell what shape I was. I wanted to look as nondescript, or even strange, as possible, and I'm sure the turban helped achieve this purpose.

It was bloody hot in that confessional in my wool coat and thick turban. Coming from California, I'm always shocked at how hot easterners keep their winter houses, winter restaurants, and apparently, winter churches too. But I had to keep my costume intact, just in case I was inadvertently discovered. I had to be ready for ... for ... for what? For whatever happened.

Was it all *going* to happen? Were we right on? Were we horribly deluded?

After a few minutes, everyone was gone. I heard the large outside doors swing shut with a thud that echoed through the church.

Then the bright overhead lights suddenly snapped off, and I stood alone in the confessional afraid even to breathe too loudly. The church went very, very quiet and very, very dark. The altar was dark. The pews were dark. The choir loft was dark. Only a rack of votive candles blazed before a statue near the sacristy.

I stood in the stifling confessional, shuffling from foot to foot. I peeked out through my tiny pen-pricks.

Save for the candle glow, the church was inky. I didn't move.

I stood there for at least ten minutes, determined to stay until something ... or nothing ... happened. I wouldn't desert my confessional until I felt the moment.

Silently I reasoned with myself, "No matter what, I have to wait until seven o'clock. The Mass must have lasted forty minutes, plus ten minutes of standing here, it must be about six-thirty now. How are they going to decorate this church and seat a hundred and fifty guests and line up the wedding party in half an hour? Can that be done? Something's not right. There's nobody here. Something's horribly wrong. Maybe we're wrong. Maybe the wedding *is* at the tent."

I suddenly cursed myself for not sending Brian and his wife to the tent, instead of having them come here to St. Mary's, where I was already safely inside. "How could I be so stupid? How could my intuition be so misguided? I should have covered both bases at seven o'clock."

I stood, beads of sweat forming on my face and then beginning to trickle down the center of my chest. I was boiling. I started breathing hard, feeling trapped, feeling faint, wondering if I should bolt, get some cold air in me, and regroup my team.

Then the lights went on.

Every light in the church suddenly blazed on at once.

A team of four or five women merrily entered, their voices echoing off the stone walls as they barked orders to each other and bustled quickly back and forth.

I snapped to, peering back and forth, back and forth through my little panel of peep holes, from back of church to front. I saw them briskly carry in huge white standing baskets filled with lush flowers, which they placed all around the altar.

One woman unrolled the white carpet from the back of the church to the altar.

In the choir loft an organist began practicing Grieg's "Wedding Day at Troldhaugen" over and over again, stopping and starting, stopping and starting, until she got it right.

It was one of my favorite pieces, and feeling elated now, I couldn't help humming along in my mind ... Duddle-a da da da da da da da da dahh TUM TUM TUM .... I didn't dare get too happy and start singing out loud for fear of discovery, but I surely felt like it.

The women chattered back and forth about every detail. "These white roses, tulips, carnations and stephanotis are just like her bouquet."

"I hear her dress is gorgeous, totally covered in bead work."

"They're not starting 'til seven-thirty."

"Straighten that runner, dear."

199

"Here, put the reserved ribbons on the first three rows."

"You should see their tent, dear, out at the Browns'. We were out there with Miss Jones this afternoon. It's huge!"

On and on they chuntered, as I watched and listened, and I felt one more time like the cat who swallowed the canary. I was on the damn bird's perch. And I was the cat, for crying out loud.

Duddle-a da da da da da da da da dahh TUM TUM TUM.

My scheme was going to work. I was IN. I was about to watch Pat Sajak get married from inside a confessional.

The minutes passed. The ladies toiled fast, arranging every last detail inside the church. I was a little surprised Sajak and Lesly hadn't gone a bit more all-out with their church decorations, but they must have figured the tent was where it'd really happen, so why bother.

The ladies were almost done.

I heard one of them say a few guests were arriving outside, and I wondered if it was my Brian and Lisa. Even if they didn't get in, no problem. I was watching everything from inside my confessional, through a bunch of tiny little holes in the curtain, and it was going to work!

That's when I found out about the off-duty Maryland State Troopers.

"You know, they've got security up the gazoo. They hired all these off-duty state troopers to act as bodyguards, fifteen or twenty of them. The guys had to be at least six-feet-two to get hired for the job. They've got a list of every guest and you've got to have your name on it, or you don't get in. The off-duty troopers kick you out."

My heart sank a little, but on the other hand, I was already in.

"Pat Sajak is paranoid, I guess, about the tabloids. They're always writing about him and Vanna White. I heard him say those tabloids ain't gettin' in his wedding. He's not even letting the guests bring a camera, in case they sold it to the tabloids."

Hello. Roll call.

"They do all kinds of crazy stuff at those tabloids. They might even hide right in this church, in a confessional or something."

The ladies were cracking each other up, but I stood frozen in my tracks, frozen in my confessional. I was electrified. I was erect and stiff. I stopped breathing.

"Say, you don't think we should *check* the confessionals, do you, just in case the *National Enquirer's* in there?"

Their hysterical laughter continued. But then, the laughter slowed to a titter. I could tell something had begun to dawn on them. Then they stopped laughing.

"No, no, no, no," I mentally intoned, hoping the strength of my desire to remain hidden would transmit my telepathic command to these church ladies. "No, no, *don't check the confessionals. DON'T CHECK THE CONFESSIONALS.*"

"You know, the *National Enquirer* could be in one of these confessionals."

The vibration I felt was now nervous and tentative, and all at once one lady jumped in and ordered, "We'd better check, just in case."

Then it began. They started banging open the doors of the confessionals on the other side of the church.

I crouched above the kneeler, still loathe to put my weight on it, for fear I'd illuminate an "occupied" light outside. Heart pounding, braced for discovery, I hovered over the kneeler, head down, turban pulled low, black car coat swathing me like a cloak, hands clutched together as if in saintly meditation, waiting, waiting to get nailed, waiting to finally rest my knees on the kneeler. Would they make the rounds of the whole church?

Bang! (footsteps) Bang! (footsteps) Bang! (footsteps) as the church lady clomped from confessional to confessional, opening each door, looking inside, then slamming it shut behind her and moving on to the next.

My face was scrunched into an expectant mask as her clomping shoes came closer and closer, then reached my door, then stopped, then the doorknob turned.

Suddenly, just as she opened the door, I knelt down on the kneeler, and what seemed an impossibly bright and accusatory light streamed into the little cubicle upon me as I crouched, quivering.

"My GOD, there IS someone in here!!" she shrieked.

I looked up with a blankly frightened expression. "Where's the priest? I've been waiting in here for a long long time." I squinted my eyes, hoping I looked a little lost.

"Madam, you can't be in here."

"But I need to say my confession. I've been waiting for the priest for a long time."

"But you can't ... madam, you have to...."

I heard myself pleading, "Please, couldn't you get him for me?"

What was I thinking? I was caught. The jig was up. I was fried. There was no way they'd let me stay now that I was discovered, but something still wouldn't allow me to let it go. I had to push it to the limit. I was *Enquirer*.

Somewhat to my horror, the woman said, "All right, wait here."

In a very few moments, as I knelt crazily in the confessional, my Catholic conscience engulfing me in feelings of extreme unease, the little cloth window in the priest's cubicle opened and he said, "Yes, my child?"

It had been so many years since I'd practiced the sacrament of confession that I couldn't even remember what you're supposed to say.

Stammering, I said, "Well, father, uh ... Bless me Father, for I have sinned."

That was it. It was coming back to me.

"Uh, it's been a long long time since my last confession."

Cringing inside, I shut my eyes tight and raised my head heavenward. Silently: "God, I don't mean any of this. This doesn't count. This is just part of my crazy job. This is not a real confession, this is just an act. Please God, in advance, please forgive me for this."

After my awkward pause, came the disembodied voice from the other side of the curtain. "Do you have anything specific you want to mention?"

I suddenly felt like the little six-year-old sitting in the dark confessional trying hard to come up with a good enough sin. My mind raced.

But wait a minute. What about my present offense? Line of duty perhaps, but it surely qualified. With excruciating candor I said, "I've lied. I've lied and I've tricked people."

The priest seemed non-plussed as he listened to someone who he'd been told looked, and who now indeed sounded, nothing short of deranged.

"Are you sorry for these and all your sins?"

"Oh yes, Father."

"Anything else?"

I could tell he was rushing, because the wedding was about to begin, so I didn't belabor the point further.

"Well Father, that's the main thing."

"For your penance, say three Hail Marys, and now, your Act of Contrition."

My Act of Contrition?

Silence.

I couldn't remember how the Act of Contrition went.

I thought, "If the priest could just jump-start me, I'm sure it would come back to me."

"Um, um, um....."

On the other side, he intoned, "Oh my God, I am heartily sorry for ...."

"... for having offended thee...." I added, then faltering again. On and on to the end I stumbled, as the good father on the other side gave liberal prompting, just to get me through it, and get me the heck out of the church before Pat Sajak's wedding started.

After confession, you're supposed to kneel outside and say your penance. So I groveled into a pew and knelt down, head bent low, eyes closed, hips slunk back against the seat, hands clasped before me.

The ladies kept scurrying around me, and finally one touched me on the shoulder and said, "I'm sorry, but you'll have to leave the church now."

Calling up every bit of air-headed determination I could conjure, I pleadingly replied, "I'm not done praying yet. I have to finish my penance or it's no good."

Of course, in the end, all of this served no purpose whatever. Nothing was going to happen in that church until I left. I rose and started to walk out, back toward the front door and the street. Maybe at least I could check out the arriving guests.

One of the women grabbed my arm firmly and led me to a side door. She had lost her patience and just wanted me gone.

Roughly, she stated, "You have to go out the side door and you have to go now. You cannot be in here any longer. There is a wedding about to begin."

She opened the door and shoved me summarily outside into the fresh cold air, which I gratefully gulped. Walking away, I ripped off my turban and flung open my heavy black coat. It had started raining, and I let the beautifully cold drops plop on my face and body, grateful for the refreshment.

Not wanting to show my unmasked face in front of the church, I ran across the street to a pay phone under a big tree and dialed Robert back in the room.

"Come and get me. I'm nailed. They found me and kicked me out. We go to Plan B."

In a matter of minutes, he pulled up at the curb, and I breathlessly jumped in. As we reached the corner, I saw a swarm of umbrellas going up the steps of St. Mary's, gathering into a bottleneck at the door, and forming a line back down onto the sidewalk. "Do you suppose that line is because some crazy lady in a turban wouldn't leave the church until she said her confession?" Robert laughed.

"Hey, let's just go past, just in case," I suggested.

Robert swung the car to the right and we drove slowly past, peering into the group, and then around the block and to the rear. I took note that Brian and Lisa were parked across from the church, long lenses trained on the door.

"Looks like the Andersons didn't get in," I observed. "There they are in their car. DON'T WAVE! Or maybe they haven't made their move yet."

As we zoomed back to the hotel, the rain began to pour down even harder, and I regaled Robert with the full story of my escapade in the church, an escapade which was destined to become part of general *Enquirer* reporter lore for some years to come.

"Okay, time for the second show," I told my amused partner in the room, as I stripped off the drab outfit I was wearing and began transforming myself from bag lady into glamorous Hollywood wedding guest. The dress, the makeup, the hair, the good jewelry, and of course, the fluffy fur coat hanging at the ready.

The works.

Robert had brought along the tuxedo he'd worn in our own wedding, and quickly donned it, along with a red dickie bow and cummerbund I'd bought for him. We looked splendid, fit for a party in any tent anywhere.

Sitting there in the room, we watched the clock, estimating when the church service would end and when the reception would be truly underway. We were striving for a late arrival, to maximize our chances.

As we waited, there was a knock on the door, and in stepped a bedraggled Brian and Lisa.

"They've got guards everywhere, huge tall ones at that. We didn't make it into the church, because the wedding director was standing there with her guest list checking every guest's name and invitation at the door. We tried to breeze by her, but she's tough. No go."

Lisa added, "Well, then we sat and tried for some arrival pictures. I think we got a good one of Lesly arriving, don't you, Brian?"

"Donno. We'll see when they're developed.

"Anyhow, now the wedding lady knows what we look like, so we rushed out to the house even before the wedding ended, to try to get into the tent before people arrived out there. But it was the same thing—heavy security. They've got a table set up, big bodyguards standing around, and a guy with a clipboard checking everyone out and checking everyone's name off the list. We were like sheep to the slaughter. We tried, but we didn't get in there either."

Brian added, "We can go back in another car and I could park on a side street to try for some shots, but it's a bloody mess out there, pouring with rain."

We could hear the growing storm beating against our window as we sat.

"You can try. Why not?" I said, really feeling their frustration. "Meantime, Robert and I will try the tent too, in a little while. I'm hoping that Cathy's caterer trick worked and she's inside the tent right now."

"We saw you go by in the Town Car outside the church," Brian said. "Did your confessional thing work?"

"Well, not entirely. I was inside the church while they did all the preparations, so we've got that part. But finally, they found me in the confessional at the last minute. I really thought I was in, but I got the hook just before it started."

Brian and Lisa hooted, as if it were a sporting event and our team had just made a few points.

"Believe it or not, I even said my confession! I wouldn't leave, so they went and got me a damn priest!"

We all laughed and laughed, and I wondered aloud if God would forgive my shocking behavior. "Do you think He'll understand?" I asked the group between gasps.

"I should think so," giggled Lisa. "He made Pat Sajak famous in the first place, didn't he? And he made you a reporter. It's a dog-eat-dog world."

"It's really raining out there," said Brian. "*Pissing* down. That tent is leaking like a sieve, from what we could see at the entrance."

"Well, we're next. We're going. We're giving it our best. Nothing to lose now, is there? It's about the only run we have left. Why don't you two go to the Radisson and wait there for us. We'll join you when we can."

It was nine-thirty. To departing good wishes from the Andersons, Robert and I walked down to the garage, climbed into the Town Car and drove through the rain to the party.

Into the subdivision we rolled, turning left onto the Browns' street, windshield wipers flapping madly, rain beating down all around us. We could see the huge white tent rising behind the house, like a well-lit soggy bubble, illuminated from within.

We'd timed our arrival well. Most of the guests were already inside, and just as we pulled up, the rain and wind intensified practically to gale level.

There was no lineup, and the valet parkers leapt to our doors, holding a big umbrella over me as I got out. It was almost useless trying to keep my fur and my hairdo from being drenched in the downpour while they pitted umbrella against wind, striving to keep the bumpershoot from going inside out.

Robert raced around to my side and joined me under the black nylon dome as I lifted my elegant gift from the back seat. Then we raced together up the same path where I'd seen Pat Sajak arriving just the other day.

Robert and I stepped inside, brazen gate-crashers from the *National Enquirer*, huffing and puffing and exclaiming, shaking the rain from our clothing and our hair, turning the rain-soaked umbrella upside down, making a very wet, very dramatic entrance.

I turned, saying, "Can you BELIEVE this rain? I've never *seen* it this bad."

The guards at the door were all smiling and solicitous as they welcomed us in from the storm, and helpfully took the dripping umbrella from Robert. Four very large men in black suits stood around in the foyer, which was actually part of the real house, not the tent. One had a clipboard.

"Terrible night, isn't it?" said the man with the clipboard. "Are you all right? May we take your coats?"

"Oh thank you," I said, handing my wedding gift to Robert as I slipped out of my long fur to reveal my low-cut, slinky cocktail dress. "I feel a little soggy."

One of the huge men took my fur and Robert's overcoat, shook them and hung them on a groaning coat rack piled with expensive looking coats.

"Oh, here," said the clipboard man. "You can put your beautiful gift right over here."

He motioned me to a corner where a pile of gifts was growing. Mine, with its extravagant bows, stood out. "Oh, thanks—that's perfect," I said as I carefully placed it with the others.

"May I have your name, please?" He had finally gotten around to it.

Robert and I had agreed we would be the Rosses from up the street.

"Ross, Mr. and Mrs. Robert Ross," he said, fiddling absently with his tie.

The man looked down on his clipboard, already having welcomed us in, already having taken our umbrella and our coats, and already having accepted our large wedding gift. To this day, I attribute our rain-soaked entrance with creating a lapse in guardedness on his part. The confusion caused by the foul night served to sidetrack him from the real issue concerning him—Did We Belong Here?

"Ross, Ross, I'm not finding it. Do you mean Rosswell? There's a Dr. Rosswell here."

I toyed with saying we were Rosswell, but any such ineptitude at the door would ruin everything. "No, it's Ross," I said.

"Gee, folks, let me see here," he said, flipping to the bottom page to see if it was a late add-on.

"We're neighbors, good friends of the bride's parents," I said. "We live just over there. Actually, Maria just sent our invitation over by hand a couple of days ago, so maybe it didn't get added on in time. Could that be it?"

Thank God I'd found out the first names of Lesly's parents.

"Yes, ma'm, it could be," he said, still intently searching his list.

Our confident and rightful attitude seemed to be working. "We've been in Europe and didn't think we'd be back in time, but then we arrived on Wednesday." Then I shut up.

That seemed to do it for the man with the list.

"Look, let me just write your name in, and you folks can go on into the reception."

I put my arm casually through Robert's and we strode out of the warm foyer and down into the tunnel, with its long plank runway that turned a corner and led through into the tent. Streams of water were running down the sides of the tunnel, drips plopping onto our heads and into our path, giving us a perfect excuse to run quickly inside.

At the end of the tunnel, we pulled back the flap and *Voila!* we were in.

Triumphantly, we stepped into the huge circus tent of a wedding reception. My husband's face was almost bursting at the seams with repressed exuberance, and I just hoped he would remain cool and not blow it for us by any jittery or over-zealous moves.

A skirted table at the entry to the tent was covered with place cards noting the names of guests and their table numbers, so I reached down and grabbed one marked "Taylor Wells." It was a name I'd heard Larry Haley mention as a possible guest from California. If worse came to worst, I had a legit name.

"I think we ought to separate," I said to Robert, "just in case they catch on that we've crashed. We'll be a lot easier to spot if we stay a couple. If you get caught, wait for me in the car, and I'll do the same if I get caught."

He drifted off into the crowd, and so did I. As I melted in, eyes peeled for Cathy, a server went by with a tray of champagne and I grabbed a glass, unable to resist giving myself a toast.

Just then, there was a stir at the tent entrance, and as other guests clumped and hovered to get a view, in breezed Vanna White, sleek in a pale brocade cocktail suit, with her blond hair straight, all smiles, and tightly entwined with a smooth-looking, tuxedoed, hair-slicked-back George Santo Pietro. Just to thrill the crowds, they faced each other, waltzed across the floor, and then George drama-dipped Vanna almost to the floor.

The other guests applauded with delight. Most of them were regular people, not accustomed to seeing celebs in person, and certainly unused to the theatrics of Hollywood's chosen darlings. They liked it.

A frigid breeze blew through the tent from beneath the canvas sides, and I shivered in my skimpy little dress, easing over to a corner. Off a tray I plucked a tiny cocktail wiener wrapped in crust and gratefully took a bite. No telling if dinner was in the offing for me. I was just happy to be safe inside, and so far, unfingered.

In fact, it gave me an incredible sense of accomplishment and purpose. Now I could do my job. If everyone would just let me be, I wouldn't bother anyone, I would quietly gather the information I needed, and then, I'd be gone.

Around the perimeter of the tent hovered huge men in black suits, each with vigilant eyes, all with little earpieces in their ears. It made me plenty nervous.

To blend in better, I started conversing with a respectable looking couple, probably friends of the elder Browns. "Isn't this wonderful?" I marveled effusively.

"Oh yes, we watched them put the tent up and it's amazing how they did all this in just a few days."

"Oh, you're neighbors then?"

"Yes, we've lived here for years, and have watched all the Brown kids grow up. We're so happy for dear Lesly, and marrying someone famous besides. Are you a friend of hers?"

"No, I'm actually a friend of Pat's," I lied, figuring maybe God would retroactively include this one into my already completed confession.

"Oh, isn't that exciting? So you're from *Holly*wood?"

"Yes, that's right," I smiled, not wanting to make too much of it.

"Well, you know, they're being so careful about pictures because of Pat being from Hollywood. All of Mike and Maria's friends were a little disappointed about what it said on the invitation, but I guess you're used to that."

"What do you mean?" I queried.

"Well you know, about that line on the bottom, 'Absolutely no cameras allowed.' "

"Oh THAT," I recovered. "Yes, I know they were worried that the tabloids would get a picture. I know Pat always worries about that."

Hmm, I said to myself, how much more honest can an *Enquirer* reporter *get* in a conversation.

The woman continued, "Well, I really wanted to take snapshots, always do at weddings. After we got the invitation, I asked Maria if that applied to old friends like us, and she said Pat just insisted on it, no exceptions, but she'd get me copies of the pictures later."

It suddenly occurred to me that I'd better get over to Robert immediately and warn him not to get trigger happy with that Sure Shot camera in his pocket until the very, very end, after we'd eye-witnessed the whole party.

The couple graciously asked, "Oh, have you found your seat yet? Maybe we can all sit together."

"Gee, I haven't found it yet, but when I do, shall I find you?" I fudged, making more pleasantries, then quickly moving back into the sea of people to find Robert.

This was quite an initiation for him into *Enquirer* technique. It was a very tricky wedding. On the invitation: "No cameras allowed," no place to sit during the dinner so we'd stick out like a sore thumb, heavy security by off-duty troopers, and just a crazy stroke of luck that we even got in.

We could still get nailed at any moment. The troopers kept looking at me as I wandered around, and I was afraid they'd rattle Robert if they started following him, too.

I needed to find him, reassure him, and tell him to go easy with the camera.

As I headed across the tent floor in Robert's direction, I scanned each table I passed to see if there was even one seat without a name card on it, but Miss Jones had been thorough. Every seat I saw was assigned. In a pinch, we could always sit at Taylor Wells' seat, but when he arrived, that could put the finger on us.

Suddenly, this troubling thought went on hold as a hush fell through the tent, the orchestra gave a heralding strain, and the MC announced, "Ladies and gentlemen, Mr. and Mrs. Pat Sajak." Wild applause, loud music, and there they were, making their entrance from the house, parading into the tent in a grand march, followed by their attendants.

I could see Robert across the room, wide-eyed, his height giving him a head up on the rest of the room. I could see his eyes popping, his face revealing all the nerves he'd suppressed so far. He was getting agitated and I hoped to hell that camera wasn't about to burn a hole in his pocket and blow our cover.

I could see him reaching inside his jacket, and I walked fast, fast, fast, to reach him before he took things into his own hands.

"Robert!" I called out.

I could see the camera coming out of his vest pocket.

"Robert!"

He had it in his hand and was removing the case.

"Robert!" I was at his side, and took his hand, tightly gripping it and the camera it held.

"Isn't it great? They're here!" I kept gripping his hand, squishing his fingers around the camera, hiding it. Everyone was clapping loudly. He looked down, eyes wide.

"Oh look," I said, loud enough for the people next to us to hear, "they've got a photographer after all, even though guests weren't allowed to bring any cameras in." Indeed, some guy in a tux was snapping away. I shoved an elbow unobtrusively into Robert's ribs.

He got the point and the camera was restored to its hiding place inside his jacket. Under my breath, I whispered, "Wait until the very end."

But now we knew they had a photographer inside. Could be their own hire, or more likely, could be they sold the wedding story to a publication who'd be paying them big bucks for the exclusive and would even present them with a magnificent wedding album as part of the deal. We'd done the same thing ourselves for many a wedding exclusive. In fact, our photo department had offered $25,000 to Sajak through his reps, but he had turned it down cold. I figured *People* must have gotten the deal.

In any case, despite Sajak's best-laid plans, the *Enquirer* was in the house, and an uninvited picture *was* going to be taken. Perhaps later on, I could snap my shutter at the same instant the hired guy's flash went off. If I did it right, no one would notice. If I did it wrong, I'd get kicked out, but by that time I'd have the whole story anyway, and we'd get the picture some other way.

Surreptitiously, I told Robert not to take his picture until after I'd taken mine. He was new to this and this way, he'd have a guideline. He'd be my ace up my sleeve. I decided I'd snap when they cut the cake.

We separated again, watching as more drenched people entered the tent and complaints rose about the leaks that were springing everywhere, splashing onto people's heads, or draining right onto the tabletops. The edges of the tent were getting sodden, with puddles forming and threatening to inundate one whole corner.

Finally Pat and his bride took their seats on the dais, and the hundred and fifty or so guests began to sit down. For me and Robert, it was like musical chairs. Pretty soon, only the off-duty state troopers and we were still standing.

One guy started heading toward me, and on the opposite side of the room, I saw another one heading for Robert.

Were we about to get tossed out in the rain? Were they really looking at us, or were we just paranoid? At that instant, Robert and I both lucked out, almost simultaneously scoring empty single seats and quickly settling into them.

If the guards suspected us, they did not choose this moment to act upon it.

Seated, we were safe. A little table talk, a little party—the toasts, the meal, the dancing, the bouquet throwing. We saw it all. Finally, my personal photo opportunity arrived. Pat and Lesly rose and headed for the cake table to cut their ornate cake.

A server approached my table with more champagne, and when I looked up, there was Cathy Griffin in her black slacks, white tuxedo shirt and dickie bow, doing the pouring. I could see her Sure Shot camera bulging in her pocket. She gave me a wink and a high sign.

Everyone got up and gathered around the cake table, including me and Robert.

When the photographer snapped and flashed, so did I. The results were instant and harsh. Sajak reacted swiftly, practically dropping the cake knife on his bride's toes and screaming, "There, there—get that camera. It's her!" His arm went straight out, Hitler style, pointing right at me as he shrieked.

I was immediately surrounded by three enormous troopers in black suits, and I went without a fuss. One of them said to his mate, "That guy over there—get him too. He came in with her."

The hired snapper was bonging off picture after picture, and I saw Robert flash one too. That sealed his fate. Two guys pounced on him, roughly grabbed his arm and started yanking him toward the tent tunnel.

Back near the door where we'd entered, inside the warm foyer, the security guards relieved us both of our cameras, opened them and pulled the rolls of celluloid out with a flourish, exposing anything we might have gotten.

One of those things. They couldn't erase what we had in our heads.

As they angrily quizzed us, we stuck to our original story—we were neighbors named Ross. Very summarily, the security chief who'd written our name onto the list only a couple of hours earlier, roughly grabbed my purse right off my shoulder and emptied its contents onto a table. Both our driver's licenses and our room key were tucked inside my bra, so they found nothing more incriminating than a lipstick, a compact and another roll of film.

"Since you nice folks don't have any ID tonight, " he spat, "you can stop by here tomorrow, say hello to your good friends Dr. and Mrs. Brown, and pick your cameras up."

"Fine," I postured.

"I doubt we'll be seeing you," the guy smirked.

He was right, of course.

Someone got our coats out of the huge collection slung in every corner of the foyer. Then, only a little the worse for our public humiliation, we were gone.

But we had the story. And Cathy was still inside for good measure.

It wasn't even midnight yet.

Robert and I headed in our Town Car for the Radisson, where we met Brian and Lisa and treated ourselves to a couple of bottles of New Year champagne.

****

That's how we and Pat Sajak saw in the 1990s.

The beginning of a new decade. The beginning of Pat's new marriage. The end of mine. I only saw Robert once again after that. The marriage was over, but the crazy confessional caper finally showed him what I did for a living.

About the Author

Barbara Sternig had an idyllic childhood, as one of eight children of a conservative elementary school principal in the leafy Chicago suburb of Glencoe, Illinois. Dad insisted that all of his eight children be well educated and well behaved. In her soft way, Mom agreed.

Nothing in this background predicted Sternig's future.

But after a fifth grade project—the production of a class magazine—Barbara was hooked for life on journalism. She did her first celebrity interview at age 14, grilling her favorite Chicago rock and roll DJ, Wally Phillips, for her high school paper.

After gaining her journalism degree from a quiet mid-western university, the slim brunette began her career writing commercials for Chicago's great rock and roll radio station, WCFL. There she met and mingled with the music greats of her youth and got hooked on the fun of celebrities.

When her disk jockey boyfriend broke her heart, Barbara headed as far away as she could go - which just happened to be Hollywood. Starting out at all-news radio station KFWB, Barbara soon landed up as legwoman/writer/producer for pioneering TV Gossip Queen Rona Barrett. Sternig wrote Barrett's syndicated Hollywood report which aired on some 60 television station nationwide, ghosted Barrett's byline fan magazine column every month, and spent her nights covering every major celebrity function in Tinseltown. She also developed a precious bookful of important connections.

These she brought to the *National Enquirer's* Hollywood bureau, but only after carefully weighing the papers's notorious reputation. Even after taking up their lucrative offer and beginning a try-out, Sternig considered the paper, not herself, on probation. Within days, she had proven her ability to deliver interviews, and proceeded for the next two decades to bring to the paper her own style of getting the job done, ending up in the thick of endless celebrity mischief as a *National Enquirer* senior reporter. She was eventually dubbed "Champagne Babs" by her fellow reporters, because of her penchant for drinking champagne in Hollywood night spots while prying information from her confidential sources.

Her bold antics in pursuit of front page news for the *Enquirer* earned her the respect of her colleagues, many of whom were battle-scarred veterans of London's Fleet Street. She circled the globe several times while chasing the famous and infamous on assignment.

Since leaving the *National Enquirer*, she has continued her two favorite pursuits—writing, as a regular free-lance contributor to celebrity-oriented publications and shows; and world travel, including treks across East Africa on safari, exploration of the Norwegian fjords and Iceland, escapes to remote islands, visits to mysterious sites in Arabia, and a thousand-mile voyage up the Amazon. She had the opportunity to share these and other travel experiences with listeners to L.A.'s talk radio stations KMPC and KLSX-FM, where she often guest-co-hosted a weekly travel and dining show. She teaches a course in celebrity reporting at a local Los Angeles college.

Sternig is divorced and lives in Toluca Lake, California.

INDEX

A

B

C

D

E

F

G

H

J

K

L

M

N

O

P

Q

R

S

ORDER FORM

(for photocopying)

SECRETS OF A TABLOID REPORTER
My Twenty Years on the National Enquirer's Hollywood Beat

Please send me the following:

Number ordered

SECRETS OF A
TABLOID REPORTER.................._____X $14^{95} each_____
CA residents add *8.25%* tax per book _____X   1^{24} each_____
Shipping and handling within USA_____X   4^{00} 1st book_____
add $1^{00} each additional book_____
Total amount of check.........$_____

Please "enquire" for terms and details on quantity purchasing and international mailing charges.

Customer Information (please print):

Name:_____

Mailing Address:_____

City:_____State:_____Zip:_____

Phone:_____/_____Best time to call:_____

Fax:_____Email:_____

Date of Order:_____

Book Ordering Information:

SEND THIS ORDER TO: OR CONTACT US AT:
Front Row Publishing   Phone: (818) 769-1274
P. O. Box 1125   Fax: (818) 769-1274
Studio City, CA 91614-1125   Email:FrontRowPubl@aol.com

Please make check or money order payable to: FRONT ROW PUBLISHING

Have fun and learn more about **SECRETS OF A TABLOID REPORTER.**
For Table of Contents and Chapter Excerpt email FrontRowPubl@aol.com now!